Through the Year with John Newton

THROUGH THE YEAR WITH

John Newton

365 Daily Readings from *John Newton*

Edited by

Stephen J. Poxon

MONARCH
BOOKS

Published by
Lion Hudson Limited
Wilkinson House, Jordan Hill Business Park
Banbury Road, Oxford OX2 8DR, England
www.lionhudson.com

Hardback ISBN 978 0 8572 1967 1
Paperback ISBN 978 0 8572 1946 6
e-ISBN 978 0 8572 1947 3
First edition 2020

Acknowledgments
Scripture quotations are primarily taken from the Holy Bible, New International Version Anglicized. Copyright © 1979, 1984, 2011 Biblica, formerly International Bible Society. Used by permission of Hodder & Stoughton Ltd, an Hachette UK company. All rights reserved. "NIV" is a registered trademark of Biblica. UK trademark number 1448790.

Scripture quotations marked KJV are from The Authorized (King James) Version. Rights in the Authorized Version are vested in the Crown. Reproduced by permission of the Crown's patentee, Cambridge University Press.

Scripture quotations marked ESV are from The Holy Bible, English Standard Version® (ESV®) copyright © 2001 by Crossway, a publishing ministry of Good News Publishers. All rights reserved.

Scripture quotations marked NLT are taken from the Holy Bible, New Living Translation, copyright © 1996, 2004, 2007 by Tyndale House Foundation. Used by permission of Tyndale House Publishers, Inc., Carol Stream, Illinois 60188. All rights reserved.

Every effort has been made to trace copyright holders for the works reproduced in this book, and the publishers apologise for any inadvertent omissions.

Extracts from *An Ancient Mariner* by Bernard Martin, originally published by The Epworth Press,1960. Used with permission of the Trustees for Methodist Church Purposes.

A catalogue record for this book is available from the British Library

Printed and bound in the UK, April 2020, LH29

To the late Richard Francis Xavier Manning ("Brennan"), whose writings have taught me more about grace, and second chances, than anyone else's works except John Newton's.

Foreword

Life at sea can be treacherous, challenging, life threatening but also monotonous. Those who serve in the Royal Navy, the Merchant Fleet or as fishermen can be away from family and friends for many months at a time and living in cramped conditions. Living out a good and wholesome life at sea without a solid foundation based on faith can see a person falling for the dangerous currents of the wills and desires of a fallen world.

What we find in the life and writing of John Newton is one who was rescued from the turmoil of life and saved by grace. Newton's conversion proclaims the power of God: "By the grace of God, I am not what I was." Newton can speak to us today of what it means to rely not on our own moods and temperament but on the amazing grace of God who can transform and renew. The imagery that Newton uses of calmness speaks well to those in the maritime world, for there we find assurance that we will not be tossed around by the changing opinions and chances of this world. This "Through the Year" collection provides a fascinating insight into the work of John Newton, who shows the relevance to people today of a faith that transforms and renews.

The Venerable Martyn Gough QHC
Chaplain of the Fleet

Introduction

The life of John Newton has taken its place in the annals of Christendom as one that was remarkable, from a childhood marked by tragedy (the death of his beloved mother), brutality, and isolation (the inadequate care of his austere father), to a ministry as an Anglican cleric whose influence was colossal, with its hallmarks of compassion and intelligent pastoral concern.

Mention of John Newton inevitably provokes reference to his hymn "Amazing Grace" and his life-changing experience during a storm at sea. Both examples are testimonies to providential mercy, but, as this book stresses, it would be a mistake to concentrate mainly on the hymn or Newton's survival in the ocean. There was so much more to John Newton's days, not least his prolific output of letters covering an enormous breadth of spiritual counsel, his happy marriage to his childhood sweetheart, and years spent as a preacher who managed to successfully connect Scripture to hearts and heads.

Newton's passion was to establish a connection between earth and heaven, demonstrating his belief that holiness could be outworked in practical ways. His ministry shone with humility and realism, for he knew his own heart and understood the tribulations of human nature striving towards the divine.

Such was the abundance of Newton's writings, only a fraction of them are represented here, and vary in length. They do not appear in this book as a chronological, autobiographical reflection but rather as a mixture of works excavated in order to provide a devotional aid, carrying the spirit of John Newton into a modern age.[1]

My gratitude is extended to everyone whose generous co-operation has been gratefully received, not least my family, my colleagues at Lion Hudson/Monarch, and Marylynn Rouse of the John Newton Project. Any mistakes are entirely mine.

S.J.P.

1 It should be stressed and clearly understood that *Through the Year with John Newton* is not intended to be any kind of exhaustive study of John Newton's life and times. This book is purely and overtly *devotional* in nature, and does not pretend to be any kind of scholarly observation regarding Newton's testimony and ministry. To that end, an assortment of sources will provide daily readings for *devotional* purposes, but these will offer only the tiniest glimpse into the truly enormous range of such available options.

January 1st

I was blind but now I see!

(John 9:25)

Amazing grace! How sweet the sound
That saved a wretch like me!
I once was lost, but now am found;
Was blind, but now I see.

'Twas grace that taught my heart to fear,
And grace my fears relieved;
How precious did that grace appear
The hour I first believed!

Through many dangers, toils and snares,
I have already come;
'Tis grace hath brought me safe thus far,
And grace will lead me home.

The Lord has promised good to me,
His Word my hope secures;
He will my Shield and Portion be,
As long as life endures.

The earth shall soon dissolve like snow,
The sun forbear to shine;
But God, who called me here below,
Will be forever mine.[1] [2]

Truly, amazing grace! Almighty God, thank you for this hymn – what an abiding testimony to the depth of your love and mercy! Help me, gracious Father, at the beginning of this New Year, to place my own life and times firmly within these verses, and to realize, with a sense of wonder and praise, that these words are mine as well as John Newton's.

1 Arguably the most popular song ever written in the English language, this hymn represents John Newton's personal testimony of conversion (These words were sung at the funeral service of President Ronald Reagan in 2004.)

2 From http://www.cyberhymnal.org/htm/a/m/a/amazing_grace.htm

January 2nd

The Spirit of the Lord will come powerfully upon you... and you will be changed into a different person... do whatever your hand finds to do, for God is with you

(1 Samuel 10:6, 7)

All English Churchmen owe a debt of gratitude to John Newton[1]... who, while associated with the revival of which Wesley[2] and Whitefield[3] were the most conspicuous leaders, clung to their Mother Church,[4] and built up a body of faithful men who were the first to bring new life into its worship and its work. It was appropriate that the erstwhile slave-dealer should finish his course in the very year in which, after twenty years' struggle, Wilberforce at last succeeded in getting [British] Parliament to abolish the slave trade...[5]

Of all the Fathers of Evangelical Churchmanship, his history is the most remarkable; and it ought to be remembered with thankfulness to the omnipotent grace of God, which could transform such a man, given over as he was to wickedness, into a saint. A saint, too, not only saved from sin and misery himself, but privileged to exercise a notable influence on others.[6]

Gracious God, just as you transformed the life of Saul of Tarsus, so you intervened to turn a blasphemous and angry slave-trader into a minister of the gospel. Such marvellous grace! Assist me, Lord, never to doubt the life-changing power of love, but to rely upon it for the year that lies before me; to lean hard upon mercy for myself and for others. I know not what these next twelve months may have in store, but I know of a Saviour and a Redeemer who is mighty to save, who alone can transform a sinner to a saint.

1 1725–1807.
2 John Wesley (1703–91).
3 George Whitefield (1714–70).
4 That is, the Church of England.
5 William Wilberforce (1759–1833), whose campaign for the abolition of slavery succeeded with the passing of the Slavery Abolition Act in 1833, just three days before Wilberforce died. The Abolition of the Slave Trade Act first entered Parliamentary Statute in 1807.
6 From John Callis (ed.), *John Newton: Sailor, Preacher, Pastor and Poet*, London: S.W. Partridge and Co., 1908.

January 3rd

You show that you are a letter from Christ... written not with ink but with the Spirit of the living God, not on tablets of stone but on tablets of human hearts

(2 Corinthians 3:3)

In a sermon given in 1907 by the Reverend John Callis, he said: We are commemorating the life and ministry of one here who finished his work on earth a hundred years ago... 1807.[1] No fine sculptured memorial commemorates him here. But there, behind this pulpit, is the simple table bearing, by his own express wish, the inscription composed by himself for the only monument he desired to be erected for him":

JOHN NEWTON,
Clerk,
once an Infidel and libertine,
a servant of slaves in Africa
was
by the act of mercy of our Lord and Saviour
Jesus Christ
preserved, restored, pardoned,
and appointed to preach the faith
he had long laboured to destroy.[2] [3]

Lord, what will the memorial to my life say? Help me, I pray, to leave a lasting impression on the lives and hearts of those I meet – my family and friends, my colleagues and neighbours. By your Spirit's influence, bless my witness for Christ wherever I might be – at home, in the pew, or in the supermarket!

1 The Reverend John Callis was Rector of Holy Trinity Church, Norwich, England. His sermon was one of a number of sermons preached to commemorate the centenary of John Newton's death and to reflect upon his ministry and pastoral influence.

2 The monument to which Callis refers is in the Anglican church of St Mary Woolnoth, in the City of London, where Newton served as a dearly loved rector from 1779 until his death in 1807.

3 From *John Newton: Sailor, Preacher, Pastor, and Poet*

January 4th

TAKE HEED THAT YE DESPISE NOT ONE OF THESE LITTLE ONES; FOR I SAY UNTO YOU, THAT IN HEAVEN THEIR ANGELS DO ALWAYS BEHOLD THE FACE OF MY FATHER WHICH IS IN HEAVEN

(Matthew 18:10 KJV)

John Newton was a remarkable man as to his character and life-story. But he was more remarkable, perhaps, for his goodness than for his greatness; his moral qualities, rather than those of intellectual power, superiority, and brilliancy. He was a Londoner by birth,[1] the only son of a sea-captain in the merchant service,[2] the master of a ship trading in the Mediterranean; a motherless boy at seven;[3] a pupil of a schoolmaster whose treatment of him was harsh, and failed to educate him to the development of his better qualities. A sailor boy at ten, he accompanied his father on his voyages.[4] Through an ardent youthful attachment to one who afterwards became his wife,[5] he failed on more than one occasion to return to his vessel after leave of absence. When a midshipman in the Royal Navy he was once publicly whipped for desertion.[6][7]

Oh Lord, what a dreadful start in life – violence and bereavement all rolled into one horrible story that no child should ever have to suffer. This leads me to pray, Heavenly Father, for children today who are abused, trafficked, neglected, and mistreated. Help them, I pray, and bless the work of churches and charities who actively intervene and campaign. Be with those families whose lives are blighted by such horrors.

1 Newton was born in Wapping, a district in the London Docklands, in 1725.

2 John Newton, Sr.

3 Elizabeth Newton died of tuberculosis in 1732, shortly before John reached the age of seven.

4 Newton sailed at least six voyages with his father before John Newton, Sr, retired.

5 Newton married his childhood sweetheart Mary Catlett in 1750. They had first met when she was thirteen, and he seventeen.

6 In 1744, Newton was press-ganged into service with the Royal Navy, aboard HMS *Harwich*. He was punished for desertion with a public flogging of eight dozen lashes, driving him to the brink of suicide. At one point, he even contemplated murdering the ship's captain in retaliation for the humiliation he had suffered.

7 From *John Newton: Sailor, Preacher, Pastor, and Poet.*

January 5th

You shall call his name Jesus, for he will save his people from their sins

(Matthew 1:21 ESV)

How sweet the name of Jesus sounds
In a believer's ear!
It soothes his sorrows, heals his wounds,
And drives away his fear.

It makes the wounded spirit whole,
And calms the troubled breast;
'Tis manna to the hungry soul,
And to the weary rest.

Dear name! the rock on which I build,
My shield, and hiding-place,
My never-failing treasury, filled
With boundless stores of grace!

Till then I would Thy love proclaim
With every fleeting breath;
And may the music of Thy name
Refresh my soul in death![1] [2] [3] [4]

Lord Jesus, there is no other name but yours; for salvation, peace, healing, and redemption, in this life and the next. No other name will do. Thank you for this hymn. Thank you for the eternal truths in every verse.

1 From George Booth, *Primitive Methodist Hymnal*, London: Edwin Dalton, 1889.

2 Written by John Newton in 1774.

3 Throughout his days at sea, Newton developed a reputation as a curser and blasphemer, to such an extent that his language shocked even hard-bitten sailors used to foul language. This hymn, then, is all the more amazing as a testament to John Newton's experience of the transforming grace of God. In this context, it is not any sort of exaggeration to liken Newton's testimony to that of Saul of Tarsus.

4 A curious (and uncomfortable) fact is that John Newton wrote this hymn while he was still engaged in slave-trading. Undoubtedly the light of the gospel had begun to make its way into his heart, but only as dawn slowly steals upon another day. His conversion was a gradual experience.

January 6th

Those whom I love I rebuke and discipline. So be earnest and repent

(Revelation 3:19)

Afflictions do not come alone,
A voice attends the rod;
By both He to His saints is known,
A Father and a God!

Let not My children slight the stroke
I for chastisement send;
Nor faint beneath My kind rebuke,
For still I am their friend.

The wicked I perhaps may leave
Awhile, and not reprove;
But all the children I receive
I scourge, because I love.

If therefore you were left without
This needful discipline;
You might, with cause, admit a doubt,
If you, indeed, were Mine.

Break through the clouds, dear Lord, and shine!
Let us perceive Thee nigh!
And to each mourning child of Thine
These gracious words apply[1 2]

Almighty God, Heavenly Father, forgive my sins, and help me, I pray, to humbly accept your loving rebuke and discipline. Lead me into repentance. Teach me to bless the sword that cuts, if I love and trust the One who wields it.

1 From http://www.hymntime.com
2 First published in *Olney Hymns* (1779), under the heading "Love-tokens".

January 7th

Sincere faith, which first lived in your grandmother Lois and in your mother

(2 Timothy 1:5)

Newton had the inestimable privilege… of the tender, loving care, teaching and training of a godly mother.[1] She laboured to store his mind with a knowledge of those Holy Scriptures able to make wise unto salvation. But at seven her blessed influence, in life at least, was withdrawn, and he became a motherless boy at an age greatly needing the continuance of such maternal care. "I was born," he says, "in a home of godliness, and dedicated to Him in my infancy. My mother was a pious and experienced Christian. She was a Dissenter.[2] I was her only child, and almost her whole employment was the care of my education." The little son displayed some ability as a learner; he was a thoughtful lad, responding to his mother's instructions, greatly to her joy. Her ambition was to train him for the Christian ministry, if the Lord should so incline his heart; of course, naturally, in her own communion. Indifference to his religious training on the part of the father, who had received his own education at a Jesuit college in Spain,[3] the evil influences of school life of those days, and his early association with sailors – during several voyages before the age of fifteen – seemed for a time to efface the impressions of his childhood. He tells us he had learned to curse and blaspheme and was exceedingly wicked.[4]

Lord, thank you for Christian mothers and their inestimable influence. Bless them! Biological mothers, adoptive mothers, legal guardians, and those who are wise "spiritual mothers" to any number of people who come to them for counsel – bless them too! You have given them a special role, and they need your help in fulfilling it.

1 See Footnote 3, January 4th.

2 Non-conformist; not belonging to the Church of England. In years to come, when he was ordained as an Anglican priest, Newton was at pains to respect and include non-conformists within Christian friendship and fellowship.

3 Jesuits are members of The Society of Jesus, a religious congregation of the Catholic Church which originated in Spain. John Newton, Sr, adopted an austere approach to matters of religion, reflective of his upbringing.

4 From *John Newton: Sailor, Preacher, Pastor, and Poet.*

January 8th

Even if my father and mother abandon me, the Lord will hold me close

(Psalm 27:10 NLT)

The most meagre outline of [Newton's] eighty-two years is all that is either possible or befitting here. He was born in 1725, the son of a seafaring father… John's mother, a saintly Dissenter, lived devotedly for her only son, and for his temporal and eternal good. To his grievous loss she died when he was seven. But who can doubt that by her prayers she was the true Monica of this homely Augustine?[1] He was unhappy at school, and developed a dark, rebellious temper. Sent to sea, under rough conditions, he made voyage upon voyage… The pervading scepticism of the day early got hold of him, and his own deliberate and lifelong witness against himself was that, while never lustful, he became by rapid degrees flagrantly profane, and, not without compunctions now and then, habitually godless. One strange episode was his service under a West African slave-dealer, and his reduction, in the course of it, through his own recklessness, to be the practical slave of a planter and his black paramour, in an island off Sierra Leone.[2] [3]

Almighty God, Heavenly Father, I pray today for any children, teenagers, and young adults who are desperately in need of good role models as they look to shape and mould their futures; adults whose good example they can aspire to imitate. Keep your hand upon them, Lord, according to today's Bible text. Help me, in my own sphere of influence, to be kind and caring, offering support to those bereft of love and protection at home.

1 St Monica (c. 331/2–387), or Monica of Hippo, or Monica Augustine, the devout, praying mother of St Augustine of Hippo (354–430), early Christian philosopher and writer, whose great works include *Confessions* and *The City of God*. He was the bishop of Hippo Regius in North Africa

2 From *John Newton: Sailor, Preacher, Pastor, and Poet.*

3 At a particularly dreadful time in his life, Newton was more or less abandoned, at sea, to the cruel whims of a slave-trader and his mistress, who, far from taking John Newton under her wing, as might have been expected, treated him abysmally. Having transferred from the Royal Navy to a merchant ship, *Pegasus*, Newton did not get along with the crew and they left him in West Africa with Amos Clowe (or Clow), who had a marriage arrangement with an African woman, Princess Peye of the Sherbro people of Sierra Leone. Newton was treated in an appalling manner by them both and became, effectively, a slave, hiding himself whenever white slave-traders approached his vessel, ashamed of his plight and his appearance.

January 9th

Remember how the Lord your God led you all the way in the wilderness these forty years, to humble and test you in order to know what was in your heart, whether or not you would keep his commands

(Deuteronomy 8:2)

I make no doubt but you have at times had pleasing reflections upon that promise made to the Israelites in Deut. viii.2. They were then in the wilderness, surrounded with difficulties, which were greatly aggravated by their own distrust and perverseness: they had experienced a variety of dispensations, the design of which they could not as yet understand; they frequently lost sight of God's gracious purposes in their favour, and were much discouraged by reason of the way. To compose and animate their minds, Moses here suggests to them, that there was a future happy time drawing near, when their journey and warfare should be finished; that they should soon be put in possession of the promised land, and have rest from all their fears and troubles; and then it would give them pleasure to look back upon what they now found so uneasy to bear: "Thou shalt remember all the way by which the Lord thy God led thee through this wilderness."[1 2]

God of the wilderness, my prayers today are for those who feel as though they are lost or even abandoned; those in need of your confirmation and direction in their lives. Step in, Lord, and remind them of your sovereign awareness of their situation and plight, and your surrounding love. Bless them with your reassurance.

1 One of a number of letters John Newton wrote to the Reverend Thomas Haweis (1734–1820), Church of England priest and evangelist. Newton wrote an autobiography entitled *An Authentic Narrative of Some Remarkable and Interesting Particulars in the Life of — Communicated, in a Series of Letters, to the Reverend T. Haweis*, which he published anonymously.

2 From *The Life of the Rev. John Newton, Rector of St Mary Woolnoth, London*, London: The Religious Tract Society, 1868.

January 10th

If God is for us, who can be against us?... Who shall separate us from the love of Christ? Shall trouble or hardship or persecution or famine or nakedness or danger or sword?... No, in all these things we are more than conquerors through him who loved us

(Romans 8:31, 35, 37)

The importance and comfort of these words [Deuteronomy 8:2, see January 9th] is still greater, if we consider them in a spiritual sense, as addressed to all who are passing through the wilderness of this world to a heavenly Canaan; who, by faith in the promises and power of God, are seeking an eternal rest in that kingdom which cannot be shaken. The hope of that glorious inheritance inspires us with some degree of courage and zeal to press forward to where Jesus has already entered as our forerunner; and when our eye is fixed upon him, we are more than conquerors over all that would withstand our progress.[1]

Faithful God, draw close to those who feel any sense of separation from your love and goodwill towards them. Whatever the reason they are feeling like that, Lord, point them afresh to Calvary, where stands the cross as proof enough of your grace and mercy towards wanderers and the estranged. I pray for any known to me personally who are living within that category, spiritually speaking.

1 See Footnotes for January 9th.

January 11th

He which hath begun a good work in you will perform it until the day of Jesus Christ

(Philippians 1:6 KJV)

There were… occasional returns of a desire to amend.[1] [Newton's] last reform was remarkable; how like Luther[2] (in his monastery) and Bunyan,[3] under the strivings of their souls after peace and satisfaction. Newton says of this time, "After the strictest sect of our religion, I lived a Pharisee." He read the Scriptures, meditated and prayed through the greater part of the day, fasted often, abstained from all animal food for three months, almost renounced society, scarcely spoke lest he should speak amiss, and, in short, became an ascetic. He went about to establish his own righteousness, and so continued for more than two years. Then, through reading an infidel book, a change took place; faith wavered and was on the point of vanishing. "At last," he says, "I renounced the hopes and comfort of the Gospel, when every other hope was about to fail me." But for a period the admonitions of conscience, from successive repulses, had grown weaker and weaker, and at length almost entirely ceased for months, if not for years.[4]

Faithful and persistent God, I ask you to be closely alongside those who are wavering in their faith, despite their best strivings. So often, Lord, the spiritual life can be a battle and a tussle, and even something of a "to and fro" experience. Sometimes, we, your people, walk away and give up when we are tempted in some way, or when the going becomes too tough. In mercy, overcome our fickle ways with your relentless love. Lead us, moment by moment. Help those who are fighting, to battle through, despite every hurdle and obstacle. Christus Victor!

1 See Footnote 4, January 5th. John Newton's entry into an experience of grace and holiness was one that took place slowly, and gradually, in arduous stages, and was by no means an overnight event. He made several "reforms". In later life, he came to respect (and sometimes even prefer) similar testimonies of conversion in others, as he regarded them as likely to be deep and lasting, bathed in prayer and rooted in the realities of spiritual warfare.

2 Martin Luther (1483–1546), German monk, priest, and theologian; the father of the Reformation.

3 John Bunyan (1628–88), English puritan preacher and writer, probably most famous for his book *The Pilgrim's Progress*.

4 From *John Newton: Sailor, Preacher, Pastor, and Poet*.

JANUARY 12TH

LOOK ON ZION, THE CITY OF OUR FESTIVALS

(Isaiah 33:20)

Glorious things of thee are spoken,
Zion, city of our God!
He, whose Word cannot be broken,
Formed thee for His own abode;
On the Rock of Ages founded,
What can shake thy sure repose?
With salvation's walls surrounded,
Thou mayst smile at all thy foes.

See, the streams of living waters,
Springing from eternal love,
Well supply thy sons and daughters,
And all fear of want remove:
Who can faint while such a river
Ever flows their thirst t' assuage?
Grace which, like the Lord, the giver,
Never fails from age to age.

Saviour, if of Zion's city,
I through grace a member am,
Let the world deride or pity,
I will glory in Thy name;
Fading is the worldling's pleasure,
All his boasted pomp and show;
Solid joys and lasting treasure
None but Zion's children know.[1]

Eternal God, to be where you are is my prayer, within your loving presence.

1 First published in *Olney Hymns* (1779).

JANUARY 13TH

NOT AS THOUGH I HAD ALREADY ATTAINED, EITHER WERE ALREADY PERFECT: BUT I FOLLOW AFTER, IF THAT I MAY APPREHEND THAT FOR WHICH ALSO I AM APPREHENDED OF CHRIST JESUS

(Philippians 3:12 KJV)

We have not yet attained; we still feel the infirmities of a fallen nature; through the remains of ignorance and unbelief, we often mistake the Lord's dealings with us, and are ready to complain, when, if we knew all, we should rather rejoice. But to us likewise there is a time coming, when our warfare shall be accomplished, our views enlarged, and our light increased; then with what transports of adoration and love shall we look back upon the way by which the Lord led us! We shall then see and acknowledge, that mercy and goodness directed every step; we shall see, that what our ignorance once called adversaries and evils, were in reality blessings which we could not have done well without; that nothing befell us without a cause; that no trouble came upon us sooner, or pressed on us more heavily, or continued longer, than our cause required; in a word, that our many afflictions were each in their place among the means employed by Divine grace and wisdom to bring us to the possession of that exceeding and eternal weight of glory which the Lord has prepared for his people.[1]

Heavenly Father, how difficult it is sometimes, simply to trust! Forgive me, Lord, when I know, deep down, that your every move is predicated only upon love, yet have doubted. Often, hindsight is my best teacher, but help me, I pray, to exercise faith in the moment, and not only afterwards. Impress these wise words of Newton's upon my heart and soul today. Gracious Spirit, bring them to mind the next time my vision is clouded.

1 From *The Life of the Rev. John Newton*. John Newton developed an excellent and widespread reputation as a pastor and counsellor, and this brief excerpt is but one of countless examples of the wise and sympathetic counsel he dispensed to the many who came to him for help and advice.

January 14th

In every situation, by prayer and petition, with thanksgiving, present your requests to God

(Philippians 4:6)

Come, my soul, thy suit prepare;
Jesus loves to answer prayer;
He Himself has bid thee pray,
Therefore will not say thee nay.

Thou art coming to a King;
Large petitions with thee bring;
For His grace and power are such,
None can ever ask too much.

With my burden I begin;
Lord, remove this load of sin;
Let Thy blood, for sinners spilt,
Set my conscience free from guilt.

Lord, I come to Thee for rest;
Take possession of my breast;
There Thy blood-bought right maintain,
And without a rival reign.[1] [2]

Gracious God, forgive me when my prayers are small, or hesitant, or lacking in faith. I know you understand the prayer-limitations I sometimes feel, and I thank you for doing so. Nevertheless, touch my heart with increased confidence, I pray, so that I may pray boldly and with expectation. I bring my prayer list to you today. Teach me to rely upon your grace as opposed to the eloquence or frequency of my intercessions. Keep my eyes fixed on you as opposed to fixed on the problems and concerns I lay before you.

1 From *Primitive Methodist Hymnal.*

2 The popularity of this hymn is attested to by the fact that it has appeared in over 600 hymnals over many years. It speaks to everyone who is desirous of a more intimate prayer-life and a bolder dialogue, in faith, with their Heavenly Father.

January 15th

Surely goodness and mercy shall follow me all the days of my life

(Psalm 23:6 KJV)

Even in this imperfect state, though we are seldom able to judge aright of our present circumstances, yet, if we look upon the years of our past life, and compare the dispensations we have been brought through, with the frame of our minds under each successive period, if we consider how wonderfully one thing has been connected with another, so that what we now number amongst our greatest advantages, perhaps, took their first rise from incidents which we thought hardly worth our notice; and that we have sometimes escaped the greatest dangers that threatened us, not by any wisdom or foresight of our own, but by the intervention of circumstances which we neither desired nor thought of; – I say, when we compare and consider these things by the light offered us in the Holy Scriptures, we may collect indisputable proof, from the narrow circle of our own concerns, that the wise and good providence of God watches over his people from the earliest moment of their lives, overrules and guards them through all their wanderings in a state of ignorance, and leads them in a way that they know not, till at length his providence and grace concur in those events and impressions which bring them to the knowledge of him and themselves.[1]

Lord, I read these words and I am humbled in your presence, as I realize at least something of the way in which you have guided my life. I may not always have been aware of your guidance, and, truth be told, I may not even have welcomed it on occasion, but I gratefully acknowledge your providential care. I give you back that which is already yours: my moments and my days.

1 From *The Life of the Rev. John Newton*. See Footnote January 13th.

January 16th

As a dog returns to its vomit, so fools repeat their folly

(Proverbs 26:11)

I remember, when I once had the pleasure of waiting on you, you were pleased to begin an interesting conversation, which, to my concern, was soon interrupted. The subject was concerning the causes, nature, and marks of a decline in grace; how it happens that we lose that warm impression of divine things, which in some favoured moments we think it almost impossible to forget; how far this change of frame is consistent with a spiritual growth in other respects; how to form a comparative judgment of our proficiency upon the whole; and by what steps the losses we sustain from our necessary connection with a sinful nature and a sinful world may be retrieved from time to time.[1 2]

Gracious Father, how often have I wandered from the pathways of truth and righteousness back towards the familiar yet deadly pitfalls of sin. How closely my Adamic nature can sometimes threaten to overshadow my pilgrimage with Jesus. How quickly I lose sight of grace. Lord, you are a gracious and compassionate God, and you call me to a fresh dedication, time after time. Nevertheless, let me never abuse that mercy, or your "seventy times seven" forgiveness. Rather, help me to abandon those things which offend you, and to perpetually seek the blessing of a clean heart. So help me, God.

1 This brief extract, from Newton's *Cardiphonia: or, The Utterance of the Heart in the Course of a Real Correspondence, Volume One*, Edinburgh: Waugh & Innes, 1781, is from one of "Twenty Six Letters to a Nobleman" John Newton wrote in order to offer spiritual guidance to those who approached him with all manner of searching queries. We shall read more from his voluminous works, but this paragraph already clearly demonstrates that there was so much more to John Newton than only the story of his astonishing deliverance from a storm at sea and his remarkable conversion from slave-trader to minister of the gospel. For all that his testimony was certainly dramatic, highly unusual, and distinctly God-glorifying, we err if we suppose his experience of such amazing grace was confined to that alone. Newton was a learned and deeply respected clergyman as well as someone whose biography reads in part like an adventure story.

2 John Newton was a man of brilliant intellect and mental recall, as is demonstrated here, when he recounts a conversation he once had, and does so in some detail.

January 17th

Remember your leaders, who spoke the word of God to you. Consider the outcome of their way of life and imitate their faith

(Hebrews 13:7)

"Whose faith follow, considering the end of their conversation." – Heb. Xiii.7. We may render the apostolic words rather more exactly, as to their order and their diction, thus: – "Of whom, contemplating the issue of their life-walk, imitate the faith." We are here… in the centenary year of the death of John Newton. Place and time accentuate to us every impression left… Here Newton, in the vicarage garden… talked away many a summer hour under the trees, on themes wide as man and high as the promises of God… He was a strong man, but essentially a kindly one; almost notorious among his friends in London, in his later days, for his optimistic benevolence, liking to see worth, and promise, and spiritual life, where others could see none at all;[1] accessible and companionable; always ready for the friendliest conversations, in which often the highest principles and truths came up in the dress of a shrewd and sympathetic humour. It is perfectly true that Newton was a moderate, a very moderate, Calvinist[2] in his theology. But so have been some not only of the holiest but of the wisest sons of the Church, in many generations; and few who know the history of doctrine, and of the tenure and presentation of doctrine, will deny that the system of thought so indicated, held by a man who loves man and loves God, can co-exist with a spirit the very opposite of gloomy. A noble optimism is perfectly consistent with it, at least in the actual workings out of the life of faith and goodness.[3][4]

Heavenly Father, how lovely it would be, if someone wanted to imitate my faith! Holy Spirit, dwell with me, so that, by your grace, my way of life may radiate something of the charm of Christ. So help me, God. Honour my desire to be a channel of blessing in your service. I also pray for my own church leaders; bless them, Lord, with all the responsibilities, joys, and challenges that are part and parcel of their ministry.

1 John Newton carried an impressively strong personal awareness of his own weaknesses and flaws, and knew his heart to be, essentially, that of a sinner, albeit redeemed. Such humility – such realism and honesty – enabled him to deal graciously and charitably with others, not lording it over them, but mindful of his failings.

2 After the teaching of John Calvin (1509–64), French theologian, pastor, and reformer.

3 From a sermon preached by Handley Moule (1841–1920), Bishop of Durham from 1901 until his death, and Honorary Chaplain to Queen Victoria. This sermon was preached at the church of St Peter & St Paul, Olney, Buckinghamshire, England, where John Newton was curate between 1764 and 1780.

4 From *John Newton: Sailor, Preacher, Pastor, and Poet.*

January 18th

Saul was still breathing out murderous threats against the Lord's disciples. He went to the high priest and asked him for letters to the synagogues in Damascus, so that if he found any there who belonged to the Way, whether men or women, he might take them as prisoners to Jerusalem. As he neared Damascus on his journey, suddenly a light from heaven flashed around him. He fell to the ground and heard a voice say to him, "Saul, Saul, why do you persecute me?" "Who are you, Lord?" Saul asked. "I am Jesus, whom you are persecuting," he replied. "Now get up and go into the city, and you will be told what you must do"

(Acts 9:1–6)

Saul… was full of enmity against Jesus of Nazareth, and therefore he persecuted and made havoc of his disciples. He had been a terror to the church of Jerusalem, and was going to Damascus with the same views. He was yet breathing out threatenings and slaughter against all that loved the Lord Jesus. He thought little of the mischief he had hitherto done. He was engaged for the suppression of the whole sect; and hurrying from house to house, from place to place, he carried menaces in his look, and repeated threatenings with every breath. Such was his spirit and temper, when the Lord Jesus, whom he hated and opposed, checked him in the height of his rage, called this bitter persecutor to the honour of an apostle, and inspired him to preach, with great zeal and earnestness, the faith which he so lately destroyed.[1 2 3]

Lord Jesus, you dramatically arrested Saul of Tarsus at the height of his zealous persecution of Christians, a situation made all the more remarkable by the fact that he hadn't approached you for mercy. Amazing grace! With that in mind, Lord, I pray for those known to me who stand in need of your strong intervention in their lives, even if, like Saul, they have little or no intention of kneeling at your feet. Stop them in their tracks, with the full power of your mercy. Lord of the breakthrough!

1 From *The Life of the Rev. John Newton.*

2 The similarity with John Newton's own experience speaks for itself.

3 Prior to his conversion, Newton took great delight in breaking the faith of Christians, or attempting to, seeing this as a legitimate form of mischief to be carried out with ridicule and hostile interrogation. He regarded it as a victory, if he was able to persuade a Christian to sin, or even to abandon their beliefs.

A good soldier of Jesus Christ

(2 Timothy 2:3 KJV)

Nor are we without remarkable displays of the same sovereign efficacious grace in our own times.[1] I may particularly mention the instance of the late Colonel Gardiner. If any real satisfaction could be found in a sinful course, he would have met with it; for he pursued the experiment with all possible advantages. He was habituated to evil; and many uncommon, almost miraculous, deliverances made no impression upon him. Yet he likewise was made willing in the day of God's power: and the bright example of his life, illustrated and diffused by the account of him published since his death, has afforded an occasion of much praise to God, and much comfort to his people.[2 3]

Heavenly Father, my conversion story might be nowhere near as dramatic as Saul's, John Newton's, or Colonel Gardiner's (see Footnote No. 1), but I thank you that my assurance of salvation through Christ is equal and valid. I pray today, Lord, for anyone known to me who is plagued with doubts regarding their eternal destiny, even perhaps members of my own church. Help them to trust in the promises of Scripture and to launch out onto the sea of faith regarding such matters.

1 See entry for January 18th..

2 Excellent accounts of the remarkable life and conversion of Colonel James Gardiner can be found online at https://www.evangelical-times.org/27700/colonel-james-gardiner and in Philip Doddridge's very useful paperback *The Life of Colonel James Gardiner.*

3 From *The Life of the Rev. John Newton.*

January 20th

If anyone is in Christ, the new creation has come: the old has gone, the new is here!

(2 Corinthians 5:17)

The awakened soul (especially when after a season of distress and terror it begins to taste that the Lord is gracious) finds itself in a new world. No change in outward life can be so sensible,[1] so affecting. No wonder, then, that at such a time little else can be thought of; – the transition from darkness to light, from a sense of wrath to a hope of glory, is the greatest that can be imagined, and is oftentimes as sudden as wonderful. Hence the general characteristics of young converts are zeal and love. Like Israel at the Red Sea, they have just seen the wonderful works of the Lord, and they cannot but sing his praise: they are deeply affected with the danger they have lately escaped, and with the case of multitudes around them in the same alarming situation; and a sense of their own mercies, and a compassion for the souls of others, is so transporting, that they can hardly forbear preaching to every one they meet. This emotion is highly just and reasonable, with respect to the causes from whence it springs; and it is doubtless a proof, not only of the imperfection, but the depravity of our nature, that we are not always thus affected.[2] [3]

Thank you, Lord, for this opportunity – and reminder – to pray for new converts. I pray you will bless my own church with people hungry for salvation, and I pray too for those who are babes and infants in Christ. Protect them, bless them, guide them, and surround them with mature believers who can keep an eye on them and encourage spiritual growth. Lord, in many ways they are relatively easy targets for the devil and his agents, so please be as a shield to them. Make your churches welcoming, safe places, and bless those who have particular responsibility for outreach and evangelism.

1 As in, felt by the senses; sensitive.

2 From *Cardiphonia: or, The Utterance of the Heart in the Course of a Real Correspondence, Volume One.*

3 See Footnote 1, January 17th.

JANUARY 21ST

LIKE NEWBORN INFANTS, LONG FOR THE PURE SPIRITUAL MILK, THAT BY IT YOU MAY GROW UP INTO SALVATION

(1 Peter 2:2 ESV)

Such persons [new converts] are very weak in faith. Their confidence arises rather from the lively impressions of joy within, than from a distinct and clear apprehension of the work of God in Christ… Hence it comes to pass, that when the Lord varies his dispensations, and hides his face, they are soon troubled… They who are in this state of their first love, are seldom free from something of a censorious spirit. They have not yet felt all the deceitfulness of their own hearts; they are not yet well acquainted with the devices or temptations of Satan; and therefore they know not how to sympathize or make allowances, where allowances are necessary and due, and can hardly bear with any who do not discover the same earnestness as themselves. They are likewise more or less under the influence of self-righteousness and self-will. They mean well; but not being as yet well acquainted with the spiritual meaning and proper use of the law, nor established in the life of faith, a part… of their zeal spends itself in externals and non-essentials, prompts them to practise what is not commanded… and to observe various and needless austerities and singularities… However, with all their faults, methinks there is something very beautiful and engaging in the honest vehemence of a young convert.[1] Some cold and rigid judges are ready to reject these promising appearances, on account of incidental blemishes. But would a gardener throw away a fine nectarine, because it is green, and has not yet attained all that beauty and flavour which a few more showers and suns will impart?[2]

What wise, honest, brave and kind-hearted pastoral advice! Thank you, Lord, for this important counsel, which is surely worth bearing in mind in any church or Christian fellowship. I pray for those whose special responsibility it is to nurture young converts; for leaders of groups and classes, that you would help them, along these lines. Bless them with wisdom and charity.

1 Young in spiritual terms, regardless of actual physical age.

2 From *Cardiphonia: or, The Utterance of the Heart in the Course of a Real Correspondence, Volume One.*

January 22nd

Let us then approach God's throne of grace with confidence, so that we may receive mercy and find grace to help us in our time of need

(Hebrews 4:16)

Behold the throne of grace,
The promise calls us near,
There Jesus shows a smiling face
And waits to answer prayer.

That rich atoning blood,
Which sprinkled round we see,
Provides for those who come to God
An all prevailing plea.

My soul ask what thou wilt,
Thou canst not be too bold;
Since His own blood for thee He spilt,
What else can He withhold.

Beyond thy utmost wants
His love and pow'r can bless;
To praying souls He always grants,
More than they can express.

Teach me to live by faith,
Conform my will to Thine;
Let me victorious be in death,
And then in glory shine.

If Thou these blessings give,
And wilt my portion be;
Cheerful the world's poor toys I leave,
To them who know not Thee.[1]

Each verse a blessing, Lord! Thank you. Accept this hymn as my prayer today.

1 From http://www.cyberhymnal.org

January 23rd

Her many sins have been forgiven – as her great love has shown.
But whoever has been forgiven little loves little

(Luke 7:47)

Once eminent sinners proved themselves eminent Christians: much had been forgiven them; they loved much. St Paul could say, "The grace bestowed upon me was not in vain; for I laboured more abundantly than they all." Colonel Gardiner[1] likewise was as a city set upon a hill, a burning and a shining light; the manner of his conversion was hardly more singular than the whole course of his conversation from that time to his death. Here, alas! the parallel greatly fails. It has not been thus with me. I must take deserved shame to myself, that I have made very unsuitable returns for what I have received. But if the question is only concerning the patience and longsuffering of God, the wonderful interposition of his providence in favour of an unworthy sinner, the power of his grace in softening the hardest heart, and the riches of his mercy in pardoning the most enormous and aggravated transgressions; in these respects I know no case more extraordinary than my own. And indeed most persons, to whom I have related my story, have thought it worthy of being preserved.[2] [3]

Lord, help me to know my heart as Newton knew his, and to therefore realize at least something of the depth of grace you have bestowed upon my life. What strikes me today, Heavenly Father, is the power of mercy to overcome even the most resistant life. Your gift of spiritual conviction is wonderful – albeit, often, unwanted and inconvenient. Nevertheless, keep me alert to such graces. You are indeed a longsuffering and patient God.

1 See January 19th and Footnotes.
2 From *The Life of the Rev. John Newton.*
3 See Footnote 1, January 17th.

January 24th

He restoreth my soul: he leadeth me in the paths of righteousness for his name's sake

(Psalm 23:3 KJV)

When guilt is… brought upon the conscience, the heart grows hard, the hands feeble, and the knees weak; then confidence is shaken, the spirit of prayer interrupted, the armour gone, and thus things grow worse and worse, till the Lord is pleased to interpose: for though we can fall of ourselves, we cannot rise without his help. Indeed every sin, in its own nature, has a tendency towards a final apostasy; but there is a provision in the covenant of grace, and the Lord, in his own time, returns to convince, humble, pardon, comfort, and renew the soul. He touches the rock, and the waters flow. By repeated experiments and exercises of this sort (for this wisdom is seldom acquired by one or a few lessons), we begin at length to learn that we are nothing, have nothing, and can do nothing but sin. And thus we are gradually prepared to live more out of ourselves, and to derive all our sufficiency of every kind from Jesus, the fountain of grace. We learn to tread more warily, to trust less to our own strength, to have lower thoughts of ourselves, and higher thoughts of him; in which two last particulars, I apprehend, what the scripture means by a growth of grace does properly consist. Both are increasing in the lively Christian; – every day shews [sic] him more of his own heart, and more of the power, sufficiency, compassion, and grace of his adorable Redeemer; but neither will be complete till we get to heaven.[1]

Gracious God, in the light of such clear and forthright teaching, couched in gentleness and humility, I can but repeat my prayer of yesterday. I would add to that prayer, though, a note of thanks for John Newton's marvellous insights, and the eloquence with which he outlines profound spiritual matters. You are a faithful God.

1 From *Cardiphonia: or, The Utterance of the Heart; in the Course of a Real Correspondence, Volume One.*

JANUARY 25TH

I AM WRITING TO YOU WITH MY OWN HAND

(Galatians 6:11 ESV)

[William] Cowper[1] has been regarded as one of the greatest of English letter-writers. But many of Newton's letters – and they were numerous – bear a favourable comparison for raciness[2] and their admirable tone. He looked upon letter-writing as one of the greatest channels by which he might do good. A large number of Newton's letters were published by him. A volume to which he gave the title of Cardiphonia – heart breathings or voices, consisting of letters who sought his help on spiritual matters – has been widely read and greatly valued. May I add my own testimony to its excellence as a book most helpful for daily readings? The writer exhibits a profound knowledge of spiritual needs and difficulties, and affords advice and direction, marked by great sanctified common-sense, from his own life experiences.[3]

Lord of all, you have gifted some with the ability to write: letters, articles, books, and study guides. Thank you so much for every blessing such people offer, as they dedicate their gift to you – blessings of encouragement, inspiration, friendship, and education. As I read their works and benefit from doing so, I ask your blessing on them as they work and communicate in such ways.

1 William Cowper (1731–1800) was a great friend of John Newton, as well as being one of his parishioners in Olney, Buckinghamshire, England. Cowper and Newton collaborated together on a number of hymns (Cowper was a gifted poet), most notably with the publication of *Olney Hymns*. Excellent accounts of the strong friendship that existed between William Cowper and John Newton can be found at www.cowperandnewtonmuseum.org.uk – the Cowper and Newton Museum is housed at Orchard Side, Market Place, Olney, Buckinghamshire MK46 4AJ, England, and houses a wealth of materials, publications, and objects relating to this particular partnership in the gospel.

2 Energetic and full of fervour.

3 From *John Newton: Sailor, Preacher, Pastor, and Poet*. This is an extract from a sermon preached by the Reverend John Callis (see Footnote No. 5, January 3rd).

January 26th

There I will meet with thee, and I will commune with thee from above the mercy seat

(Exodus 25:22 KJV)

Approach, my soul, the mercy-seat
Where Jesus answers prayer;
There humbly fall before His feet,
For none can perish there.

Thy promise is my only plea,
With this I venture nigh;
Thou callest burdened souls to Thee,
And such, O Lord, am I.

Be Thou my Shield and Hiding-place,
That, sheltered near Thy side,
I may my fierce Accuser face
And tell him Thou hast died.

O wondrous Love, to bleed and die,
To bear the cross and shame,
That guilty sinners such as I
Might plead Thy gracious name![1] [2]

Gracious God, if this hymn needs to be mine today, then I pray it for myself. If, though, I am to pray it for someone else, then make that clear to me, so that I may have the privilege of interceding on their behalf. Whichever is the case, Lord, hear and answer prayer.

1 One of the *Olney Hymns* (1779).

2 Although the Bible refers to a particular type of mercy seat, the great American Presbyterian evangelist and revivalist preacher Charles Grandison Finney (1792–1875) introduced the concept of "the anxious bench" into his evangelistic campaigns, whereby penitent sinners, under the conviction of his preaching, would kneel before God and claim forgiveness. The Salvation Army (possibly uniquely) continues to adopt such a policy, using a "penitent form" or "mercy seat" – a wooden bench at which anyone may kneel at any time; not only for pardon, but for any prayer needs and concerns, either alone or with the support of a designated mercy seat counsellor.

January 27th

I PRAY... FOR THOSE WHO WILL BELIEVE IN ME THROUGH THEIR MESSAGE, THAT ALL OF THEM MAY BE ONE, FATHER, JUST AS YOU ARE IN ME AND I AM IN YOU

(John 17:20–21)

[Newton's] heart went forth to all men, whether Churchmen or Dissenters;[1] but he loved order, and he loved his own Church, so that he could not always act with some whom he esteemed excellent persons. And is not this the true catholic spirit? It recognises all who hold the fundamental doctrines of the Christian religion as true members of Christ's holy catholic church, Evangelical Churchmen like Newton make the plain teaching of the Gospel and Epistles the basis of their faith. At the same time they recognise other denominations holding the same principles as true branches of Christ's Church, and their right to Christian liberty in questions of church government, organisation, and forms of worship, as matters of secondary, and not of essential importance. Are there not many, an increasing number, amongst us as Churchmen who desire to see such principles more universally adopted?[2]

Lord of the church, I thank you today for my friends from other churches; those who prefer a different style of worship and spiritual expression to my own. I ask your rich blessing on them, Lord, and the various traditions and denominations in my town that come to mind as I pray. May we all witness together to reach others for the kingdom. Help us always to learn from one another, and to embrace diversity as that which is exciting, challenging, and enriching.

1 Members of the Church of England, and Christians from non-conformist denominations.

2 John Newton was well known for his strenuous efforts to work alongside both Anglicans and dissenters, without making spiritual distinctions between those two groups. In the context of his day and age, this was an unusual and refreshing enthusiasm.

January 28th

Forsake not your mother's teaching

(Proverbs 1:8 ESV)

I can sometimes feel a pleasure in repeating the grateful acknowledgment of David, "O Lord, I am thy servant, the son of thine handmaid; thou hast loosed my bonds." The tender mercies of God towards me were manifested in the first moment of my life. I was born, as it were, in his house, and dedicated to him in my infancy. My mother, as I have heard from many, was a pious, experienced Christian: she was a dissenter, in communion with the late Dr. Jennings.[1] I was her only child, and as she was of a weak constitution, and a retired temper, almost her whole employment was the care of my education. I have some faint remembrance of her care and instructions. At a time when I could not be more than three years of age, she herself taught me English; and with so much success (as I had something of a forward turn), that when I was four years old I could read with propriety… She stored my memory, which was then very retentive, with many valuable pieces, chapters, and portions of Scripture, catechisms, hymns and poems.[2]

Father God, I pray for those babies and children who will be baptized, dedicated, and christened this coming weekend, in my church or elsewhere. Place your hand upon them, Lord, even if they know little of what is happening, or understand nothing. Bless their parents, families, and guardians too, I pray, and help your church always to be welcoming and friendly to visitors and newcomers. Grant special graces to ministers who facilitate and lead services of dedication; may their words and ceremonies be backed home with your anointing and power.

1 Dr. David Jennings (1691–1762), English dissenting minister.

2 From *The Life of the Rev. John Newton*.

January 29th

As the rain and the snow come down from heaven, and do not return to it without watering the earth and making it bud and flourish, so that it yields seed for the sower and bread for the eater, so is my word that goes out from my mouth: it will not return to me empty, but will accomplish what I desire and achieve the purpose for which I sent it

(Isaiah 55:10–11)

My temper [as a child] seemed quite suitable to [my mother's] wishes: I had little inclination to the noisy sports of children, but was best pleased when in her company, and always as willing to learn as she was to teach me. How far the best education may fall short of reaching the heart, will strongly appear in the sequel of my history: yet I think, for the encouragement of pious parents to go in the good way of doing their part faithfully to form their children's minds, I may properly propose myself as an instance. Though in process of time I sinned away all the advantages of these early impressions, yet they were a great while a restraint upon me; they returned again and again, and it was very long before I could wholly shake them off; and when the Lord at length opened my eyes, I found a great benefit from the recollection of them. Further, my dear mother, besides the pains she took with me, often commended me with many prayers and tears to God; and I doubt not but I reap the fruits of these prayers.[1]

What an encouraging word this is, Lord, for mothers and fathers who pray for their children; that prayers are heard and answered, if not always when or how we think they should be. Forgive us, Lord, any impatience in prayer, and grant, instead, faith and quiet. Be with all those who are praying for their children today. Honour their love and prayerful devotion.

1 From *The Life of the Rev. John Newton.*

JANUARY 30TH

HE IS A CHOSEN VESSEL UNTO ME

(Acts 9:15 KJV)

My mother observed my early progress with peculiar pleasure, and intended from the first to bring me up with a view to the ministry, if the Lord should so incline my heart. In my sixth year I began to learn Latin; but before I had time to know much about it, the intended plan of my education was broke short. The Lord's designs were far beyond the views of an earthly parent: he was pleased to reserve for me an unusual proof of his patience, providence, and grace; and therefore overruled the purpose of my friends, by depriving me of this excellent parent when I was something under seven years old... My father was then at sea; he was a commander in the Mediterranean trade at that time: he came home the following year; and soon after married again.[1] Thus I passed into different hands. I was well treated in all other respects; but the loss of my mother's instructions was not repaired. I was now permitted to mingle with careless and profane children, and soon began to learn their ways.[2]

How wonderful, Lord, that the prayers of John Newton's mother for him to enter the ministry should be so gloriously answered in his adult years, albeit via a torturous and deeply challenging route. My prayers today are for those who feel as though you are calling them into a vocation of ministry and leadership. Speak to them, I pray, and guide their thoughts. Help them in their decision making, so that your will may be identified and accomplished. I pray too, for those in authority who handle such applications; may they be sensitive to the voice of your Spirit and careful in their handling of those matters.

1 To Thomasina (or Thomazine). The census information reads as follows: "St Mary, Whitechapel, London. John Newton, widower of St John, Wapping. Thomazine Cox of Aveley. 21st November, 1732, by licence."

2 From *The Life of the Rev. John Newton*.

January 31st

The heart of man plans his way, but the Lord establishes his steps

(Proverbs 16:9 ESV)

My friends had two daughters. The eldest, as I understood some years afterwards, had often been considered by her mother and mine as a future wife for me, from the time of her birth. I know, indeed, that intimate friends frequently amuse themselves with such distant prospects for their children, and that they miscarry much oftener than succeed. I do not say that my mother predicted what was to happen, yet there was something remarkable in the matter of its taking place. All intercourse between the families had been long broken off; I was going into a foreign country, and only called to pay a hasty visit; and this I should not have thought of, but for a message received just at that crisis, for I had not been invited at any time before. Thus the circumstances were precarious in the highest degree, and the event was as extraordinary. Almost at the first sight of this girl (for she was then under fourteen) I was impressed with an affection for her, which never abated or lost its influence in my heart from that hour. In degree, it actually equalled all that the writers of romance have imagined; in duration, it was unalterable.[1]

What a wonderful reassurance there is, Lord, in offering our hopes and dreams in submission to your will. You know what is best for us, and we can confidently surrender all that we wish for about our lives, into your loving control and wisdom. I pray today for those seeking your guidance and influence in their decision making.

1 From *The Life of the Rev. John Newton.*

February 1st

The Lord God said, "It is not good that the man should be alone; I will make him a helper fit for him"

(Genesis 2:18 ESV)

When husband and wife are happily partakers of the same faith, it seems expedient, and for their mutual good, that, besides their private devotions, and joining in family-prayer, they should pray together. They have many wants, mercies, and concerns, in common with each other, and distinct from the rest of the family. The manner in which they should improve a little time in this joint exercise cannot well be prescribed by a third person; yet I… conceive that it may prove much to their comfort to pray alternately, not only the husband with and for the wife, but the wife with and for her husband… I suppose them in private together, and then I judge it to be equally right and proper for each of them to pray with the other. Nor do I meet anything in St Paul's writings to prevent my thinking, that if he had been a married man, he would, though an apostle, have been glad of the prayers of his wife. If you ask, how often they should pray together? I think the oftener the better, provided it does not break in upon their duties; once a day at least; and if there is a choice of hours, it might be as well at some distance from their other seasons of worship. But I would observe… that in matters not expressly commanded, prudence and experience must direct.[1] [2]

Lord, on this anniversary of John Newton's wedding day, I pray for those who are embarking on their life together as married couples. Bless them as they take their very first steps on such a great adventure. Protect them from each and every ambush and assault. Be their centre.

1 From *Letters of John Newton* (Family Worship), London: The Banner of Truth Trust, 1965.

2 On February 1st, 1750, John Newton married his childhood sweetheart, Mary Catlett, in St Margaret's Church, Rochester, Kent, England. The prospect of returning to his beloved Mary one day often sustained Newton throughout long and lonely months at sea, and might even have saved him from suicide.

February 2nd

If I depart, I will send [the Comforter, the Advocate, the Holy Spirit] unto you. And when he is come, he will reprove the world of sin, and of righteousness, and of judgment

(John 16:7–8 KJV)

At school, or soon after, I had little concern about religion, and easily received very ill impressions. But I was often disturbed with convictions. I was fond of reading from a child; among other books, Bennet's "Christian Oratory"[1] often came in my way; and though I understood but little of it, the course of life therein recommended appeared very desirable, and I was inclined to attempt it; I began to pray, to read the Scriptures, and keep a sort of diary. I was presently religious in my own eyes; but, alas! this seeming goodness had no solid foundation, but passed away like a morning-cloud, or the early dew; I was soon weary, gradually gave it up, and became worse than before. Instead of prayer, I learned to curse and blaspheme, and was exceedingly wicked when from under my parent's view. All this was before I was twelve years old. About that time I had a dangerous fall from a horse: I was thrown, I believe, within a few inches of a hedgerow newly cut down. I got no hurt; but could not avoid taking notice of a gracious providence in my deliverance; for had I fallen upon the stakes, I had inevitably been killed. My conscience suggested to me the dreadful consequences if, in such a state, I had been summoned to appear before God.[2]

Gracious Spirit, you are unfailingly patient with your rebellious subjects. You bless us with the gift of conviction, whereby we are taught right from wrong. Yet, how often we persist in our rebellion! Thank you, Holy Spirit, for bearing with us when we ourselves are far from holy, and for your gentle persistence in making us more like Jesus. Grant us sensitivity when we are convicted of sin, and help us in our repentance.

1 *Devout Meditations from the Christian Oratory* by Reverend Benjamin Bennet (1674–1726).
2 From *The Life of the Rev. John Newton*.

February 3rd

It is by grace you have been saved, through faith – and this is not from yourselves, it is the gift of God – not by works, so that no one can boast

(Ephesians 2:8–9)

Though [a believer] knows that communion with God is his highest privilege, he too seldom finds it so; on the contrary, if duty, conscience, and necessity did not compel, he would leave the throne of grace unvisited from day to day. He takes up the Bible, conscious that it is the fountain of life and true comfort; yet, perhaps, while he is making the reflection, he feels a secret distaste which prompts him to lay it down, and give his preference to a newspaper. He needs not to be told of the vanity and uncertainty of all beneath the sun; and yet is almost as much elated or cast down by a trifle, as those who have their portion in this world. He believes that all things shall work together for his good, and that the most-high God appoints, adjusts, and over-rules all his concerns; yet he feels the risings of fear, anxiety, and displeasure, as though the contrary was true. He owns himself ignorant, and liable to be deceived by a thousand fallacies; yet is easily betrayed into positiveness and self-conceit. He feels himself an unprofitable, unfaithful, unthankful servant, and therefore blushes to harbour a thought of desiring the esteem and commendations of men, yet he cannot suppress it. Finally (for I must observe some bounds), on account of these and many other inconsistencies, he is struck dumb before the Lord, stripped of every hope and plea, but what is provided in the free grace of God, and yet his heart is continually learning and returning to a covenant of works.[1]

What a strange spiritual tendency this is, Lord, to revert to a dependency upon good works and thereby demonstrate some kind of reluctance to accept free grace. How often we feel as though your love is to be earned, when grace is all. Forgive us, Lord, and let that glorious truth sink in; that we are loved, forgiven, and embraced. Please don't think us ungrateful.

1 From *Cardiphonia: or, The Utterance of the Heart; in the Course of a Real Correspondence, Volume One.*

February 4th

Jesus resolutely set out for Jerusalem. And he sent messengers on ahead, who went into a Samaritan village to get things ready for him; but the people there did not welcome him, because he was heading for Jerusalem. When the disciples James and John saw this, they asked, "Lord, do you want us to call fire down from heaven to destroy them?"

(Luke 9:51–54)

Too much of that impatience which you speak of, towards those who differ from us in some religious sentiments, is observable on all sides. I do not consider it as the fault of a few individuals, or of this or that party, so much as the effect of that inherent imperfection which is common to our whole race. Anger and scorn are equally unbecoming in those who profess to be followers of the meek and lowly Jesus, and who acknowledge themselves to be both sinful and fallible; but too often something of this leaven will be found cleaving to the best characters, and mixed with honest endeavours to serve the best cause. But thus it was from the beginning; and we have reason to confess that we are no better than the apostles were, who, though they meant well, manifested once and again a wrong spirit in their zeal; Luke ix. 54.[1] [2]

O Lord! I wonder if it grieves you when Christians across various traditions and denominations focus on differences rather than that which unites. I wonder if it hurts you that doctrinal minutiae is sometimes given greater priority than mission. Help us, your people, by your Spirit, to manage those points on which we disagree, with grace and respect, without being distracted from keeping the main thing the main thing.

1 From *The Works of the Rev. John Newton (Cardiphonia Continued, Seven Letters to Mrs. ****)*, London: Hamilton, Adams, and Co., 1824.

2 Once again, we observe in this brief excerpt from a lengthy pastoral letter, John Newton's immense charity of spirit. He writes from a standpoint of humility, always willing to see the best in others and never establishing himself as "holier than thou". Likewise, we note his generous willingness to give of his time to those in need of advice and counsel.

February 5th

In your hearts honour Christ the Lord as holy, always being prepared to make a defence to anyone who asks you for a reason for the hope that is in you; yet do it with gentleness and respect

(1 Peter 3:15 ESV)

Observation and experience contribute, by the grace of God, gradually to soften and sweeten our spirits; but then there will always be ground for mutual forbearance and mutual forgiveness on this head. However, so far as I may judge of myself, I think this hastiness is not my most easy besetting sin. I am not indeed an advocate for that indifference and lukewarmness to the truths of God, which seem to constitute the candour many plead for in this present day. But while I desire to hold fast the sound doctrines of the Gospel towards the persons of my fellow-creatures, I wish to exercise all moderation and benevolence; – Protestants or Papists, Socinians[1] or Deists,[2] Jews, Samaritans, or Mahometans,[3] all are my neighbours, they have all a claim upon me for the common offices of humanity. As to religion, they cannot all be right; nor may I compliment them by allowing the differences between us are but trivial, when I believe and know they are important; but I am not to expect them to see with my eyes. I am deeply convinced of the truth of John Baptist's aphorism, John iii. 27: "A man can receive nothing, except it be given him from heaven." I well know, that the little measure of knowledge I have obtained in the things of God has not been owing to my own wisdom and docility, but to his goodness.[4]

Thank you, gracious Father, for this charming piece of spiritual logic, a blueprint for exemplary Christian witness and humility in a multicultural society. How astonishingly relevant these words are for modern society! Lord, this world sorely needs such grace and discretion. Help me, I pray, to take this advice to heart as I go about my daily business.

1 Socinianism: a system of Christian doctrine named for Fausto Sozzini, most famous for its nontrinitarian Christology but which contains a number of other unorthodox beliefs (from https://en.wikipedia.org/wiki/Socinianism).

2 Deists believe that God can only be known, or discovered, via reason, as opposed to supernatural revelation. Deists believe that God has revealed himself in nature, for example, but is non-interventionist in the affairs of humanity.

3 Or Mohammedans; followers of the prophet Mohammed.

4 From *The Works of the Rev. John Newton (Cardiphonia Continued, Seven Letters to Mrs. ****).*

FEBRUARY 6TH

MAKE EVERY EFFORT... TO BE HOLY

(Hebrews 12:14)

I... broke off from my profane practices, and appeared quite altered. But it was not long before I declined again. These struggles between sin and conscience were often repeated; but the consequence was, that every relapse sunk me into still greater depths of wickedness. I was once roused by the loss of an intimate companion. We had agreed to go on board a man of war (I think it was on a Sunday); but I providentially came too late; the boat was overset, and he and several others drowned. I was invited to the funeral of my playfellow, and was exceedingly affected, to think that by delay of a few minutes, which had much displeased and angered me, till I saw the event, my life had been preserved. However, this likewise was soon forgot.[1]

O Lord, you know us human beings! You created us, and you know us better than we know ourselves, including this annoying habit of failing in our attempts to be holy. Forgive us, and stay with us, that we might, with your help, make steady spiritual progress. Protect us from the temptation to despair. Grant us holy belligerence!

1 From *The Life of Rev. John Newton*.

February 7th

May the grace of the Lord Jesus Christ, and the love of God, and the fellowship of the Holy Spirit be with you all

(2 Corinthians 13:14)

May the grace of Christ our Saviour
And the Father's boundless love,
With the Holy Spirit's favour,
Rest upon us from above.

Thus may we abide in union
With each other and the Lord,
And possess in sweet communion,
Joys which earth cannot afford.[1 2]

Trinitarian God, you are three-in-one and one-in-three – the ultimate mystery! Thank you for this hymn, which brings with it a reminder of love and grace presented as mysterious, yet solidly real and reliable. I may not comprehend, but I believe, by faith; a Godhead of three persons, co-equal in divinity and majesty, whose name is Love. Amen!

1 From https://hymnary.org
2 Written by John Newton in 1779.

February 8th

The flesh lusteth against the Spirit, and the Spirit against the flesh: and these are contrary the one to the other: so that ye cannot do the things that ye would

(Galatians 5:17 KJV)

"Ye cannot do the things that ye would." This is an [sic] humbling but a just account of a Christian's attainments to the strongest and the weakest. The weakest need not say less, the strongest will hardly venture to say more. The Lord has given his people a desire and will, aiming at great things; without this they would be unworthy the name of Christians; but they cannot do as they would: their best desires are weak and ineffectual, not absolutely so (for He who works in them to will, enables them in a measure to do likewise). So that while they have great cause to be thankful for the desire He has given them, and for the degree in which it is answered, they have equal reason to be ashamed and abased under a sense of their continual defects, and the evil mixtures which taint and debase their best endeavours. It would be easy to make out a long list of particulars which a believer would do if he could, but in which, from first to last, he finds a mortifying inability.[1 2]

Lord Jesus, I can but cling to your cross, and in doing so, find that you are my all in all. There is nothing I can bring; no strength of my own. Yet, that stark admission need not discourage me. Rather, it is the springboard for the infilling of divine assistance and empowering. Send a new touch of power, gracious God. I kneel at the foot of your cross today.

1 From *Cardiphonia: or, The Utterance of the Heart; in the Course of a Real Correspondence, Volume One.*

2 Again, we notice John Newton's brutally honest awareness of the plight of the human heart. We would be mistaken, though, to interpret this appraisal as spiritual pessimism or despair. Quite the contrary, in fact; the more Newton came to observe and study this situation within humankind, the more he became aware of transforming grace as the only solution. We might say the darkness of the human condition led him towards the light of Christ, on his own behalf, and on behalf of others as he exercised a superb pastoral ministry of counselling and correspondence.

FEBRUARY 9TH

HUMBLE YOURSELVES THEREFORE UNDER THE MIGHTY HAND OF GOD, THAT HE MAY EXALT YOU IN DUE TIME: CASTING ALL YOUR CARE UPON HIM; FOR HE CARETH FOR YOU

(1 Peter 5:6–7 KJV)

The wonderful condescension of the great God, who humbles Himself to behold the things that are in heaven, that He should stoop so much lower, to afford His gracious ear to the supplications of sinful worms upon earth. He can bid them expect a pleasure in waiting upon the Lord, different in kind, and greater in degree than all that the world can afford. By prayer, he can say, you have liberty to cast all your cares upon Him that careth for you. By one hour's intimate access to the Throne of Grace, where the Lord causes His glory to pass before the soul that seeks Him, you may acquire more true spiritual knowledge and comfort than by a day or a week's converse with the best of men, or the most studious perusal of many folios; and in this light he would consider it and improve it for himself.[1]

Lord, you hear my prayers! Yet, you don't just hear, you listen carefully, you understand, and you allow me to repeatedly unburden my soul in your gracious presence, with all that concerns me. You are my God, my Counsellor, my Listener.

1 From *Cardiphonia: or, The Utterance of the Heart; in the Course of a Real Correspondence, Volume One.*

February 10th

A bishop must be blameless, as the steward of God; not selfwilled, not soon angry, not given to wine, no striker, not given to filthy lucre; But a lover of hospitality, a lover of good men, sober, just, holy, temperate; Holding fast the faithful word as he hath been taught, that he may be able by sound doctrine both to exhort and to convince the gainsayers

(Titus 1:7–9 KJV)

Dear and Reverend Sir, I call you dear because I love you; and I shall continue to stile [sic] you reverend as long as you dignify me with that title. I revere you, because I believe the Lord liveth in you, and has chosen you to be a temple of his presence, and an instrument of his grace…

The outward sun shines and looks pleasant, but his beams are faint, and too feeble to dissolve the frost. So it is in my heart. I have many bright and pleasant beams of truth in my view, but cold predominates in my frost-bound spirit, and they have but little power to warm me. I could tell a stranger something about Jesus, that would perhaps astonish him. Such a glorious person, such wonderful love, such humiliation, such a death… What a Son! What a Shield! What a Root! What a Life! What a friend! My tongue can run upon these mercies sometimes, and should my heart keep pace with it, I should be the happiest fellow in the country. Stupid creature! To know these things so well, and yet be no more affected with them. Indeed, I have reason to be upon ill terms with myself.[1] [2]

Lord of the church, my prayers today are with those in leadership, whatever their title or status may be. Theirs is an unenviable position, obliged to live out their Christianity in the constant spotlight of the public eye, with any faults and failings quickly pointed out. Bless leaders, Lord, especially those who, like Newton, are experiencing a coldness of heart for one reason or other. Warm them afresh with your encouraging presence. Help me, I pray, to be a good support.

---

1 From *One Hundred and Twenty Nine Letters from the Rev. John Newton*, London: Hamilton, Adams, and Co., 1847.

2 From the Preface: "The following letters were addressed to the Rev. William Bull, of Newport Pagnall [Buckinghamshire, England]… It so happened that Mr. Bull undertook the pastoral charge in the Independent congregation at Newport about the time that Mr. Newton entered the curacy at Olney [1764]. They were soon introduced to each other, and a slight acquaintance commenced. Some trifling reports, tending to lower the reputation of Mr. Bull, reached the ear of Mr. Newton, and produced a coldness between them. When, however, it was found that these reports originated in falsehood, there was a permanent renewal of that intercourse which had been for a short time suspended."

February 11th

When one says, "I follow Paul," and another, "I follow Apollos," are you not mere human beings? What, after all, is Apollos? And what is Paul? Only servants, through whom you came to believe – as the Lord has assigned to each his task. I planted the seed, Apollos watered it, but God has been making it grow. So neither the one who plants nor the one who waters is anything, but only God, who makes things grow. The one who plants and the one who waters have one purpose, and they will each be rewarded according to their own labour. For we are fellow workers in God's service; you are God's field, God's building

(1 Corinthians 3:4–9)

I think my sentiments and experience are as orthodox and Calvinistical as need be, and yet I am a sort of speckled bird among my Calvinistic brethren. I am a mighty good Churchman, but pass amongst such as a Dissenter in principle. On the other hand, the Dissenters (many of them I mean) think me defective, either in understanding or in conscience, by staying where I am, while there is a middle party called Methodists, but neither do my dimensions exactly fit with them. I am somehow disqualified for claiming a full brotherhood with any party; but there are a few among all parties who bear with me, and love me, and with this I must be content at present. But so far as they love the Lord Jesus Christ, I desire, and by his grace, I determine (with or without their leave), to love them all. Party walls, though stronger than the walls of Babylon, must come down in the general ruin, when the earth and all its works shall be burned up, if no sooner.[1]

Thank you, Lord, for different Christian denominations, whereby a variety of preferred expressions of worship are allowed to flourish. Thank you that there is room for everyone! Help us, though, to hold such things only lightly, to be flexible in denominational matters, to learn from one another. Today I pray for churches and fellowships in my area, asking you to bless their work and witness.

1 From *One Hundred and Twenty Nine Letters from the Rev. John Newton.*

FEBRUARY 12TH

BE YE DOERS OF THE WORD, AND NOT HEARERS ONLY, DECEIVING YOUR OWN SELVES

(James 1:22 KJV)

To hear a believer speak his apprehensions of the evil of sin, the vanity of the world, the love of Christ, the beauty of holiness, or the importance of eternity, who would not suppose him proof against temptation? To hear with what strong arguments he can recommend watchfulness, prayer, forbearance, and submission, when he is teaching or advising others, who would not suppose but he could also teach himself, and influence his own conduct? Yet, alas! Quam dispar sibi![1] The person who rose from his knees, before he left his chamber, a poor, indigent, fallible, dependent creature, who saw and acknowledged that he was unworthy to breathe the air or to see the light, may meet with many occasions, before the day is closed, to discover the corruptions of his heart, and to show how weak and faint his best principles and clearest convictions are in their actual exercise. And in this view, how vain is man! What a contradiction is a believer to himself! He is called a Believer emphatically, because he cordially assents to the word of God; but, alas! how often unworthy of the name![2]

What a challenging distinction, Lord! That fine line between "talking the talk and walking the walk". Help me, I pray, to do both. Fine Christian talk is all well and good, but fine Christian actions are better. I can't do this without you, Lord. I pray for your Spirit's infilling, moment by moment.

1 A basic translation from the Latin to English would be "how unlike him".

2 From *Cardiphonia: or, The Utterance of the Heart; in the Course of a Real Correspondence, Volume One.*

February 13th

Be of good cheer; I have overcome the world

(John 16:33 KJV)

The beauty of Newton's character, the salient features of which were cheerfulness, confidence in God, earnestness and courage. It was a saying with him that where the path of duty and prudence leads, there is the best situation we could possibly be in at any juncture. In his habit of rallying men of the Mr. Fearing[1] category he resembled Bunyan. The monomania that embittered the life of Cowper commenced many years before Cowper knew Newton.[2] The friendship between Newton and Cowper was one of the most delightful in the history of literature. The letters of Cowper to Newton are not, as some have alleged, forced and constrained; on the contrary, they are fluent and unconstrained, and many are humorous.[3] [4]

Grant me, Lord Jesus, a cheerful heart in your service. Draw alongside those who are finding it difficult to "be of good cheer" today. Shield and protect them from glib responses and "quick fixes".

1 A character in John Bunyan's *The Pilgrim's Progress*, most noted for his greatly troubled spirit, his preference for legalism over grace, and a lifelong tendency to doubt the promises of God pertaining to salvation. Bunyan is sympathetic to Mr. Fearing's inability to trust those promises, and the allusion here appears to reflect Newton's heart of compassion towards those who found matters of faith difficult to comprehend or accept.

2 Rumours sometimes spread that William Cowper's well-documented struggles with manic depression were aggravated by John Newton's spiritual counsel. Whereas the friendship between Newton and Cowper experienced a reasonable measure of highs and lows, there is very little evidence indeed to substantiate these rumours. On the contrary, William Cowper suffered under the weight of appalling mental health, and John Newton repeatedly proved himself a kind and able counsellor and steadfast friend.

3 From *John Newton: Sailor, Preacher, Pastor, and Poet.*

4 Extracted from a posthumous tribute to John Newton, offered by Thomas Wright, Secretary of The Cowper Society.

February 14th

Two are better than one, because they have a good return for their labour: if either of them falls down, one can help the other up

(Ecclesiastes 4:9–10)

The most remarkable circumstance of Newton's residence and ministry at Olney was his intimate friendship and association with the poet Cowper. They were men of very different temperament. The earlier years of their lives were spent in such different scenes. Newton, amid the stern, rough associations of a sailor's life; Cowper, the child of the parsonage at Birkhampstead [Berkhamsted, Hertfordshire],[1] the Westminster scholar, the student of law, the young barrister of the Temple, the welcome guest of literary and refined society. And yet, for ten years at least out of those passed in each other's companionship, and in co-operating in the pastoral work of Olney, the most sincere regard and deepest affection bound them together in delightful Christian fellowship and affection. It is most unjust to charge Newton with exercising a deleterious influence on Cowper. The one was to the other as the sturdy oak to the ivy which clings to it for strength and support. Their mutual influence was helpful and blest to each.[2]

A simple prayer today, Lord: thank you for my friends.

1 See https://www.stpetersberkhamsted.org.uk/cowpersociety/

2 From *John Newton: Sailor, Preacher, Pastor, and Poet.*

February 15th

[Wisdom's] ways are pleasant ways, and all her paths are peace

(Proverbs 3:17)

Taking care that my conversation has at no time anything in it contrary to truth, to purity, or to the peace and good nature of my neighbour, and ever endeavouring to introduce some useful remark or admonition, yet habituating myself to a constant cheerfulness of behaviour, that I may not bring an evil report upon religion, or discourage those around me from the pursuit of piety, but rather let them see that a good conscience is a continual feast, and the ways of wisdom are the ways of pleasantness… At all events I will strive to preserve a devotional frame, and that upon no occasion shall my morning and evening exercises be wholly pretermitted, for… it were safer to attempt living without food or sleep than by starving my soul and passing a whole day without presenting myself before the mercy-seat of my Heavenly Father.[1]

"I will strive to preserve a devotional frame". Gracious God, keep me in such a frame today, I ask. Keep me at the mercy seat, wherever I might be. Grant me that wisdom and blessing.

1 From Josiah Bull, *John Newton of Olney and St Mary Woolnoth. An Autobiography and Narrative, Compiled Chiefly from His Diary and Other Unpublished Documents*, London: The Religious Tract Society, 1870.

February 16th

Man shall not live on bread alone, but on every word that comes from the mouth of God

(Matthew 4:4)

As to the ordering of my conversation, I determine to choose for my companions only good people, from whom I may derive some improvement, or, if otherwise, such as I may hope to benefit by my influence. When necessarily engaged in business with others, to stand well on my guard, that I may not be seduced by their opinions or practices, and, frequently looking up to Heaven for assistance, to endeavour often to give discourse a serious turn. Whenever I hear my Maker's name blasphemed to speak boldly for His honour, yet being careful to do so without personal ill-will or comparative contempt. Not to affect a disagreeable singularity in indifferent matters, but… to become all things to all men that I may save some. When I have done everything in my power, to subscribe myself an unprofitable servant, and esteem it the greatest fault to presume that the best services I can perform would be, strictly speaking, entitled to pardon, much less acceptance, unless offered wholly in obedience to the commands and through faith in the mediation of my blessed Redeemer… which I am well assured I have in myself no ability to perform; but that since He has promised His Holy Spirit to such as sincerely ask it, I therefore humbly put in my claim.[1]

Lord, I love John Newton's humility! A tremendous sense of his own spiritual vulnerability permeates these words and shines through; his awareness that even his best efforts might not amount to much, relatively speaking, and are in any case entirely dependent upon your Spirit's guidance and enabling. Grant me such humble wisdom, I pray, in the hope that I may be of some use to the kingdom this day.

1 From *John Newton of Olney and St Mary Woolnoth. An Autobiography and Narrative.*

February 17th

You shall have no other gods before me

(Exodus 20:3)

[The Christian] believes [the Scriptures] to be the word of God: he admires the wisdom and grace of the doctrines, the beauty of the precepts, the richness and suitableness of the promises; and therefore, with David, he accounts it preferable to thousands of gold and silver, and sweeter than honey or the honey comb. Yet while he thinks of it, and desires that it might dwell in him richly, and be his meditation night and day, he cannot do as he would. It will require some resolution to persist in reading a portion of it every day; and even then his heart is often less engaged than when reading a pamphlet. Here again his privilege frequently dwindles into a task. His appetite is vitiated, so that he has but little relish for the food of his soul. He would willingly have abiding, admiring thoughts of the person and love of the Lord Jesus Christ. Glad he is, indeed, of those occasions which recall the Saviour to his mind; and with this view, notwithstanding all discouragements, he perseveres in attempting to pray and read, and waits upon the ordinances. Yet he cannot do as he would. Whatever claims he may have to the exercise of gratitude and sensibility towards his fellow creatures, he must confess himself mournfully ungrateful and insensible towards his best friend and benefactor. Ah! what trifles are capable of shutting Him out of our thoughts, of whom we say, He is the beloved of our souls, who loved us, and gave Himself for us, and whom we have deliberately chosen as our chief good and portion. What can make us amends for the loss we suffer here?[1] [2]

Lord, it's not that I mean to neglect my times of prayer and Bible reading. It's more a case of "drifting" and allowing my concentration to wander; more a case of failing to fix my thoughts on you, when so much else vies for my attention. Forgive me, and help me, lest I deprive myself of blessings. In your mercy, stay with me.

1 From *Cardiphonia: or, The Utterance of the Heart; in the Course of a Real Correspondence, Volume One.*

2 It might be thought, on reading these words, that John Newton had adopted a superior attitude, one of criticism. Nothing could be further from the truth. His heartbeat was always that of a kind pastor and a shepherd, hence this strong pastoral concern for those who are robbed of blessings by any failure to observe spiritual disciplines. Newton's intention was always to point believers to the One whose grace is sufficient, and to thereby offer a solution to their dilemma.

February 18th

What shall it profit a man, if he shall gain the whole world, and lose his own soul?

(Mark 8:36 KJV)

We find Mr. Newton praying for grace to entertain a proper veneration and awe of the great and tremendous name of God… He complains of the distractions of business… and he prays God to help him to consider how poor a bargain he should make if all his wishes were effected, even were he to gain the whole world, but in the end his success were to endanger his mortal soul… "Lord," he prays, "Thou hast heaped many benefits upon me, be pleased to add one more – the blessing of an ingenuous and thankful heart. Without this all the rest is but lost… Could my whole life be passed in a continual act of praise, it would at best be a very poor return for what great things Thou hast done for me. But alas! a day or an hour is more than I can employ as I ought in this glorious service."[1]

Thank you, Lord, for your mercy in prompting me to spend "quiet times" in your presence. This is kind of you, and so indicative of your faithfulness and steadfast love towards me. I too pray for the grace of a thankful heart.

1 From *John Newton of Olney and St Mary Woolnoth. An Autobiography and Narrative.*

February 19th

"Suppose one of you has a servant ploughing or looking after the sheep. Will he say to the servant when he comes in from the field, 'Come along now and sit down to eat'? Won't he rather say, 'Prepare my supper, and wait on me; after that you may eat and drink'? Will he thank the servant because he did what he was told to do? So you also, when you have done everything you were told to do, should say, 'We are unworthy servants; we have only done our duty'"

(Luke 17:7–10)

Though we aim at... good, evil is present with us; we find we are renewed but in part, and have still cause to please the Lord's promise, to take away the heart of stone, and give us a heart of flesh. [The Christian] would willingly acquiesce in all the dispensations of divine Providence. He believes that all events are under the direction of infinite wisdom and goodness, and shall surely issue in the glory of God, and the good of those who fear Him. He doubts not but the hairs of his head are all numbered, that the blessings of every kind which he possesses were bestowed upon him, and are preserved to him, by the bounty and special favour of the Lord whom he serves; that afflictions spring not out of the ground, but are fruits and tokens of Divine love, no less than His comforts:– that there is a need-be, whenever for a season he is in heaviness. Of these principles he can no more doubt than of what he sees with his eyes, and there are seasons when he thinks they will prove sufficient to reconcile him to the sharpest trials. But often when he aims to apply them in an hour of present distress, he cannot do what he would. He feels a law in his members warring against the law in his mind: so that, in defiance of the clearest conviction, seeing as though he perceived not, he is ready to complain, murmur, and despond. Alas! how vain is man in his best estate! How much weakness and inconsistency, even in those whose hearts are right with the Lord! And what reason have we to confess that we are unworthy, unprofitable servants![1] [2]

Gracious God, you are faithful even when we are not! Thank you. We have to confess our fickle behaviour at times, when we can blow hot or cold, and when even our best efforts are only reasonable service, in the light of your great love and sacrifice. Thankfully, you do not give up on us! What a blessing! Help me, I pray, to mature in consistency as I walk with you.

1 From *Cardiphonia: or, The Utterance of the Heart; in the Course of a Real Correspondence, Volume One.*

2 John Newton would no doubt have remembered his own struggles during what we might refer to as his season(s) of conversion, when he seemed to take two steps forward and one back, before his eventual breakthrough to full commitment. His battle(s) to do right, and his failures, would have marked his deeply sympathetic understanding of such matters in the lives of Christian people.

February 20th

Peter got down out of the boat, walked on the water and came towards Jesus. But when he saw the wind, he was afraid and, beginning to sink, cried out, "Lord, save me!" Immediately Jesus reached out his hand and caught him. "You of little faith," he said, "why did you doubt?"

(Matthew 14:28–31)

A word from Jesus calms the sea,
The stormy wind controls;
And gives repose and liberty
To tempest-tossed souls.

To Peter on the waves he came,
And gave him instant peace;
Thus he to me revealed his name,
And bid my sorrows cease.

The storm increased on every side,
I felt my spirit shrink;
And soon, with Peter, loud I cried,
Lord, save me, or I sink.

Kindly he caught me by the hand,
And said, Why dost thou fear?
Since thou art come at my command,
And I am always near.

Upon my promise rest thy hope,
And keep my love in view;
I stand engaged to hold thee up,
And guide thee safely through.[1]

This day, Lord Jesus, help me to keep my eyes fixed on you. Likewise, my faith, especially if and when the waters run deep and storms are brewing.

1 From *Olney Hymns* (1779).

February 21st

Righteousness exalteth a nation

(Proverbs 14:34 KJV)

In an interesting volume entitled The Later Evangelical Fathers (Seeley),[1] there is an admirable sketch of Newton. The writer says, when Mr. Newton began his work in London it was just ten years before the French Revolution. Most terrible times were therefore at hand; but we can see now that it was the will of God to preserve England from joining in the sins and suffering from the political earthquake which was about to shake all Europe; and still more we can see that it was the will of God that our country should be singled out as His chief instrument for freeing the slave, for leading the way in many a reform by which the human race was to be benefitted, and, above all, to be herald of peace through the blood of Christ's Cross in many of the dark places of the earth.[2 3]

Almighty God, I pray for my country today.

1 Mary Seeley..

2 See Footnotes 4 and 5, January 3rd.

3 From *John Newton: Sailor, Preacher, Pastor, and Poet.*

February 22nd

My thoughts are not your thoughts, neither are your ways my ways, saith the Lord. For as the heavens are higher than the earth, so are my ways higher than your ways, and my thoughts than your thoughts

(Isaiah 55:8–9 KJV)

The Lord has reasons, far beyond our ken, for opening a wide door, while he stops the mouth of a useful preacher. John Bunyan would not have done half the good he did, if he had remained preaching in Bedford, instead of being shut up in Bedford prison.[1 2]

Grant me faith, Lord, when I don't understand what you are doing. Help me to trust, when your ways seem baffling. I pray for anyone today who is finding it difficult to trust you; bless them with your peace. You aren't of course under any obligation to explain yourself, but have mercy upon us when we struggle to comprehend what's going on.

1 From *The Life of Rev. John Newton.*
2 John Bunyan was arrested and imprisoned for his refusal to attend Church of England services, and for repeatedly preaching in public (as opposed to within the confines of a designated place of worship), despite being warned not to. He was held in Bedford Prison, England, from 1661 to 1672, during which time he wrote *The Pilgrim's Progress.*

February 23rd

Whoever derides their neighbour has no sense, but the one who has understanding holds their tongue

(Proverbs 11:12)

Professors, who own the doctrines of free grace, often act inconsistently with their own principles, when they are angry at the defects of others. A company of travellers fall into a pit, one of them gets a passenger to draw him out: now he should not be angry with the rest for falling in, nor because they are not yet out, as he is; he did not pull himself out: instead, therefore, of reproaching them, he should show them pity; he should avoid, at any rate, going down upon their ground again, and show how much better and happier he is upon his own. We should take care that we do not make our profession of religion a receipt in full for all other obligations. A man truly illuminated will no more despise others, than Bartimeus, after his own eyes were opened, would take a stick, and beat every blind man he met.[1]

O Lord, save me today from looking down on anyone, especially as I probably don't know anything much at all about their circumstances or their background. Help me to remember that I have no claim on grace, and that we are all seeking the same Saviour. Help me always to look with pity, not with blame.

1 From *The Life of Rev. John Newton.*

February 24th

Restore to me the joy of your salvation and grant me a willing spirit, to sustain me

(Psalm 51:12)

Ever anxious that his religious life should suffer no decline, and conscious of some degree of spiritual deadness, we find Mr. Newton engaged… in an exercise of diligent self-examination, confession, and prayer before God… "O most gracious Saviour, hear my prayers, which I am only emboldened to make in dependence upon Thy gracious promise. I am weary and heavy laden with the sense of my corruption; and to such Thou hast promised rest. Fulfil Thy own work in me. Thy mercy prevented my ruin when I was Thy utter and avowed enemy. Suffer me no longer to lie helpless, now I would willingly be Thy servant. Oh, let Thy wonderful love constrain me to close with Thee in the manner I ought to do. Increase my faith. Inspire me with humility, and enable me to fulfil the engagements by which I have so often and so solemnly found myself to Thy service. Lord, I repent and abhor myself in dust and ashes for my frequent backslidings. Restore unto me the influences of Thy Holy Spirit, whom I have by my carelessness provoked to withdraw from me, and assist me from this day to labour with redoubled earnestness in the way of my duty, that I may at length begin to live to Thy honour and glory, and my own comfort. Amen."[1]

Gracious Spirit, stay with me.

1 From *John Newton of Olney and St Mary Woolnoth. An Autobiography and Narrative.*

February 25th

Study to shew thyself approved unto God, a workman that needeth not to be ashamed, rightly dividing the word of truth

(2 Timothy 2:15 KJV)

Mr. Newton spent several weeks in succession in London, for the purpose of hearing the word, and of enjoying occasions of religious conference. The following extracts from his diary, which he kept with great regularity, will give some idea of these engagements: "… At the society of Mr. M—'s. After prayer, etc, spent evening in discourse, chiefly upon doctrinal points… At Pinner's Hall.[1] Mr. Rawlins on the everlasting covenant. Afterwards at the A. Coffee-house. Heard some very remarkable cases of cures performed by unction with oil, in compliance with James v. 14, which I propose to inquire further into… This evening heard Mr. Heyward at the Lecture for Cases of Conscience… Heard Mr. Romaine[2] on Ephes. vi. 14. May God increase the number of faithful labourers where they are so much wanted, and give success to their ministry… Rose at five. Went to the Tabernacle, and heard Mr. Adams[3] on Matt. v. 6; a very comfortable sermon. The forenoon at Mr. Brewer's. In the afternoon heard Dr. Jennings."[4][5]

What enthusiasm for studying the Bible, Lord! Help me to learn from this; maybe even to pursue lectures and studies with as much energy, in order to feed on your word and nourish my spirit.

1 Old Broad Street, London, where weekday lectures were given by leading dissenters.
2 Rector of St Ann's, Blackfriars, London.
3 Reverend Thomas Adams.
4 The other names referred to here were leading dissenters of their day – lecturers, preachers, and writers.
5 From *John Newton of Olney and St Mary Woolnoth. An Autobiography and Narrative.*

February 26th

God demonstrates his own love for us in this: while we were still sinners, Christ died for us. Since we have now been justified by his blood, how much more shall we be saved from God's wrath through him!

(Romans 5:8–9)

The depravity of the heart… impedes us when we would do good, and pollutes our best intended services with evil… yet we need not sorrow as they who have no hope. The Lord has provided His people relief under those complaints, and teaches us to draw improvement from them. If the evils we feel were not capable of being overruled for good, He would not permit them to remain in us. This we may infer from His hatred of sin, and the love which He bears to His people. As to the remedy, neither our state nor His honour are affected by the workings of indwelling sin, in the hearts of those whom He has taught to wrestle, strive, and mourn, on account of what they feel. Though sin wars, it shall not reign; and though it breaks our peace, it cannot separate from His love. Nor is it inconsistent with His holiness and perfection to manifest His favour to such poor defiled creatures, or to admit them to communion with Himself; for they are not considered as in themselves, but as one with Jesus, to whom they have fled for refuge, and by whom they live a life of faith. They are accepted in the Beloved, they have an Advocate with the Father, who once made an atonement for their sins, and ever lives to make intercession for their persons. Though they cannot fulfil the law, He has fulfilled it for them; though the obedience of the members is defiled and imperfect, the obedience of the head is spotless and complete; and though there is much evil in them, there is something good, the fruit of His own gracious Spirit.[1 2]

Father, what a wonderful insight this is, showing me a glimpse of your redemptive love. You do not ostracize. You do not give up on your people. You bless. You hope. Though we sin, you love, and in Christ, you have arranged a solution saturated in mercy. Thank you, Heavenly Father.

---

1 From *Cardiphonia: or, The Utterance of the Heart; in the Course of a Real Correspondence, Volume One.*

2 It might be worth noting here, a lovely glimpse of John Newton as not only a kind and gracious pastor, but a gifted theologian too, with an ability to translate sound Christian doctrine into its practical and humane manifestation. Newton's was always *applied* theology, and never that which was abstract or irrelevant.

February 27th

If God is for us, who can be against us?

(Romans 8:31)

The gracious purposes to which the Lord makes the sense and feeling of our depravity subservient are manifold. Hereby His own power, wisdom, faithfulness, and love, are more signally displayed; His power, in maintaining His own work in the midst of much opposition, like a spark burning in the water, or a bush unconsumed in the flames; His wisdom, in defeating and controlling all the devices which Satan, from his knowledge of evil in our nature, is encouraged to practise against us. He has overthrown many a fair professor, and, like Goliath, he challenges the whole army of Israel; yet he finds there are some against whom, though he thrusts sorely, he cannot prevail; notwithstanding any seeming advantage he gains at some seasons, they are still delivered, for the Lord is on their side. The unchangeableness of the Lord's love and the riches of His mercy are likewise more illustrated by the multiplied pardons he bestows upon His people than if they needed no forgiveness at all. Hereby the Lord Jesus is more endeared to the soul; all boasting is effectually excluded, and the glory of a full and free salvation is ascribed to Him alone.[1]

"The Lord is on their side". How marvellous! Grace personified. Help me, gracious Father, to keep that truth tucked away in my heart today.

1 From *Cardiphonia: or, The Utterance of the Heart; in the Course of a Real Correspondence, Volume One.*

February 28th

I will select some of them also to be priests

(Isaiah 66:21)

I estimate a minister's character from combining what he is in the pulpit, with what he is when out of it; and they stand highest upon my scale, whose conduct is most expressive of the doctrines they preach.[1 2]

Once again today, Lord, I pray for my minister.

1 From *One Hundred and Twenty Nine Letters from the Rev. John Newton.*

2 John Newton developed a tremendous reputation as what we might call a minister among ministers; someone to whom other members of the clergy could turn for pastoral counsel. He maintained a tremendous empathy with those in Christian ministry, and was only too aware of their needs and challenges. Newton respected, but often avoided, denominational boundaries, in favour of personal relationships.

March 1st

I have learned to be content whatever the circumstances. I know what it is to be in need, and I know what it is to have plenty. I have learned the secret of being content in any and every situation

(Philippians 4:11–12)

I still find my mind unsettled; but I hope that trust in God, and a desire to seek his face, is in the bottom of my heart, though my duty engages me this week early and late, and leaves me little time that I can call my own; yet it gives me great comfort to consider it as God's appointment,[1] and while I act in it as in his view, I am in a remoter manner serving him. How wonderful is His condescension, that is pleased to esteem my taking care of my own interest in the world as His service! I esteem it my privilege and my mercy that nothing here is capable of satisfying me; and yet I hope I can say I am contented, and see reason to be thankful for my present lot, which though it has its inconveniences (and where is the state of life without them?), yet frees me from greater which are incident to the sea.[2]

Heavenly Father, I ask you to bless those whose lives are so busy that they struggle to devote much time to prayer, or as much time as they would prefer. With so many demands upon their time, Lord, a devotional life is thin and poorly maintained. Help them, I pray. Likewise, please help us each to serve you wherever we might be; in our witness and conduct, even if more formal devotions aren't always possible every day.

1 Newton was appointed as Tide Surveyor (tax collector) for the English port of Liverpool, in 1755. Liverpool was an integral location to slave ships coming and going from Great Britain.

2 From *John Newton of Olney and St Mary Woolnoth. An Autobiography and Narrative.*

March 2nd

A time is coming and has now come when the true worshippers will worship the Father in the Spirit and in truth, for they are the kind of worshippers the Father seeks. God is spirit, and his worshippers must worship in the Spirit and in truth

(John 4:23–24)

Mr. Newton would gladly have entered into closer communion with Mr. Johnson's church;[1] but he found that this could not be done except upon "full terms" (namely, baptism by immersion), of which he says, "as I do not see the necessity myself, I cannot at present submit. However, I desire thankfully to receive so much of the ordinances under him as I can obtain. Oh, that the happy time was come when all the sincere worshippers of God were of one heart and mind!"[2]

Heavenly Father, the honest reality is, not one single Christian denomination has a monopoly on truth! Forgive us, I pray, if ever we think we have! Dismantle any such arrogance, I pray, in favour of hearts and attitudes that enable us to learn from one another, in humility and gratitude. You are God, and beyond comprehension, so it is unlikely we will come anywhere near a complete grasp of your truth, and your nature, until we see you face to face. Until that day, help us to appreciate and savour Christian fellowship – including our differences of opinion! – and all that it has to teach us.

1 "Mr. Johnson" was connected with the Baptist ministry in Liverpool, England. Although John Newton was to become an ordained Anglican minister, he was, in heart and spirit, so to speak, by no means confined to one particular denomination, but always eager to learn from other traditions.

2 From *John Newton of Olney and St Mary Woolnoth. An Autobiography and Narrative.*

March 3rd

Lord, I believe; help thou mine unbelief

(Mark 9:24 KJV)

How happy should we be, could we always believe the glorious things which are spoken to us as children, in the word of him who cannot fail of accomplishing his promise. But are we not fools and slow of heart in this matter? At least I am, and hence proceed my many complaints – alas! what a hard heart have I, that can doubt, and repine, and limit the Lord, after all the great things he had shown me! Wretched heart, that can stand it out still, against oaths, and promises, and blood. Methinks I may sum up all my wants and prayers in one sentence – Lord, give me faith! Oh, if faith was in daily exercise, how little would the world, and the things of time and sense, seem in my eyes! What a dreadful thing that would appear, that spilt my Saviour's blood! And how would my very heart rejoice at the sound of Jesus' name! If I had faith to pierce within the veil, and see what is going forward in yon blessed world, how earnestly should I spend and be spent for the Gospel's sake! However, though it is not with us as we would wish, we have reason to bless God it is so well with us as it is; that we are not altogether dead in trespasses and sins, strangers and enemies to the glorious Gospel of the blessed God. We have reason to be thankful that we know something of our disease and our physician. He who has taken our case in hand will in his own time, perfect the cure.[1]

How strange it is, Lord, and what a mystery – my seeming proclivity towards a lack of faith and unbelief, when all the time I have umpteen promises before me! How odd my behaviour is at times, when the spilt blood of Christ speaks solidly and consistently of pardon and peace! This day, Lord, I pray the prayer of Mark 9:24. Bear with me, forgive me, and impart fresh confidence to my soul. Draw alongside others who experience similar conflicts and contradictions; bless them too, I ask.

1 From *The Works of the Rev. John Newton (Cardiphonia Continued, Seven Letters to Mrs. ****)*.

March 4th

Paul and Silas were praying and singing... suddenly there was a great earthquake, so that the foundations of the prison were shaken... the jailer... rushed in, and trembling with fear he fell down before Paul and Silas... "Sirs, what must I do to be saved?"

(Acts 16:25–31 ESV)

A believer, free from care,
May in chains, or dungeons, sing,
If the Lord be with him there;
And he happier than a king:
Paul and Silas thus confined,
Though their backs were torn by whips,
Yet possessing peace of mind,
Sung his praise with joyful lips.

Suddenly the prison shook,
Open flew the iron doors;
And the jailer, terror-struck,
Now his captives' help implores:
Trembling at their feet he fell,
Tell me, Sirs, what must I do
To be saved from guilt and hell?
None can tell me this but you.

Look to Jesus, they replied,
If on Him thou canst believe;
By the death which he has died,
Thou salvation shalt receive:
While the living word he heard,
Faith sprung up within his heart;
And released from all he feared,
In their joy his soul had part.[1] [2]

Lord, you stop at nothing to impart grace and salvation! Bless those who today are trapped in a spiritual prison. Shake foundations and bring release!

1 Originally entitled "The Trembling Jailer" and published in *Olney Hymns* (1779).
2 This hymn speaks clearly of Newton's intention of translating Scripture into "everyday" language.

March 5th

He will command his children and his household after him, and they shall keep the way of the Lord

(Genesis 18:19 KJV)

Happy is that family where the worship of God is constantly and conscientiously maintained. Such houses are temples, in which the Lord dwells, and castles garrisoned by a divine power. I do not say, that by honouring God in your house, you will wholly escape a share in the trials incident to the present uncertain state of things. A measure of such trials will be necessary for the exercise and manifestation of your graces, to give you a more convincing proof of the truth and sweetness of the promises made to a time of affliction, to mortify the body of sin, and to wean you more effectually from the world. But this I will constantly say, that the Lord will both honour and comfort those who thus honour him. Seasons will occur in which you shall know, and probably your neighbours shall be constrained to take notice, that he has not bid you seek him in vain. If you meet with troubles, they shall be accompanied by supports, and followed by deliverance; and you shall upon many occasions experience, that he is your protector, preserving you and yours from the evils by which you will see others suffering around you.[1]

Heavenly Father, my prayers today are for Christian families; those precious units whereby so much is taught, learned, imitated, and imbibed regarding the spiritual life. Bless parents who are doing their best to raise their children as Christians, and bless those children too, I pray, as they grow up and take their place in the world. I think of my own family and loved ones, and ask your gracious blessing there too, according to their needs and circumstances.

1 From *Letters of John Newton*.

MARCH 6TH

WE KNOW THAT IN ALL THINGS GOD WORKS FOR THE GOOD OF THOSE WHO LOVE HIM, WHO HAVE BEEN CALLED ACCORDING TO HIS PURPOSE

(Romans 8:28)

Satan… hates the Lord's people, grudges them all their privileges and all their comforts; and will do what he can to disquiet them, because he cannot prevail against them. And though the Lord sets such bounds to his rage as he cannot pass, and limits him to discover his malice to a considerable degree; not to gratify Satan, but to humble and prove them; to show them what is in their hearts, to make them truly sensible of their immediate and absolute dependence upon himself, and to quicken them to watchfulness and prayer. Though temptations, in their own nature, are grievous and dreadful, yet when, by the grace of God, they are productive of these effects, they deserve to be numbered among "all things which are appointed to work together for the good of those who love him".[1 2]

Almighty God, I pray for any who are engaged in a bitter spiritual fight; those who feel as though their very footsteps are relentlessly dogged by Satan and his demons. Surround them with your strong protection, Lord. Be a tower around them, and impart words such as these above to their souls. Help them not to tremble, but to trust, not in their own might, but in yours. Handle Satan on their behalf, according to your superior power. When your people feel weakest and most vulnerable, Lord, rush to their aid and intervene.

1 From *Letters of John Newton.*

2 John Newton had a very real belief in Satan and the forces of evil, believing them to be literal and permanently busy in opposition to Christ and his kingdom. His counsel, though, was not alarmist or rooted in fear, but perfectly reasonable, brave, and logical. He applied a sharply forensic mind to such matters, always proclaiming the victory of Jesus over the opposing powers of death and hell. His was a sensible faith, and a confident one.

March 7th

I was given a thorn in my flesh, a messenger of Satan, to torment me. Three times I pleaded with the Lord to take it away from me. But he said to me, "My grace is sufficient for you"

(2 Corinthians 12:7–9)

It is pure mercy that negatives a particular request. A miser would pray very earnestly for gold, if he believed prayer would gain it; whereas, if Christ had any favour to him, he would take his gold away. A child walks in the garden in spring, and sees cherries; he knows they are good fruit, and therefore asks for them. "No, my dear," says the father, "they are not yet ripe: stay till the season." If I cannot take pleasure in infirmities, I can sometimes feel the profit of them. I can conceive a king to pardon a rebel, and take him into his family, and then say, "I appoint you for a season to wear a fetter. At a certain season I will send a messenger to knock it off. In the meantime this fetter will serve to remind you of your state; it may humble you, and restrain you from rambling."[1]

O Lord, how often your answers to prayer seem to be shrouded in mystery! How often your responses seem to be delayed! Help me to place my prayers into your hands and then to leave them there, trusting that your way is perfect and that you know best. Grant me grace to trust your timing. Thank you for the prayers you answer. Thank you too for those that you deny. Thank you for your revelations. Thank you too for what you keep hidden, for my own good.

1 From *The Life of Rev. John Newton*.

March 8th

Every beast of the forest is mine, and the cattle upon a thousand hills

(Psalm 50:10 KJV)

I feel like a man who has no money in his pocket, but is allowed to draw for all he wants upon one infinitely rich: I am, therefore, at once both a beggar and a rich man. I went one day to Mrs. G—'s, just after she had lost all her fortune: I could not be surprised to find her in tears, but she said, "I suppose you think I am crying for my loss, but that is not the case; I am now weeping to think I should feel so much uneasiness on this account." After that I never heard her speak again upon the subject as long as she lived.[1]

Jehovah Jireh, God my Provider, you are aware this day of all my needs. Not one of them has escaped your loving attention. You are my God. You are no one's debtor. Help me to relax in these truths today.

1 From *The Life of Rev. John Newton.*

March 9th

THERE WAS A RICH MAN WHO LIVED IN LUXURY EVERY DAY. AT HIS GATE WAS LAID A BEGGAR NAMED LAZARUS, COVERED WITH SORES AND LONGING TO EAT WHAT FELL FROM THE RICH MAN'S TABLE. THE BEGGAR DIED AND THE ANGELS CARRIED HIM TO ABRAHAM'S SIDE. THE RICH MAN ALSO DIED. IN HADES, WHERE HE WAS IN TORMENT, HE LOOKED UP AND SAW ABRAHAM FAR AWAY, WITH LAZARUS BY HIS SIDE. SO HE CALLED TO HIM, "FATHER ABRAHAM, HAVE PITY ON ME AND SEND LAZARUS TO DIP THE TIP OF HIS FINGER IN WATER AND COOL MY TONGUE, BECAUSE I AM IN AGONY IN THIS FIRE." BUT ABRAHAM REPLIED, "SON, REMEMBER THAT IN YOUR LIFETIME YOU RECEIVED YOUR GOOD THINGS, WHILE LAZARUS RECEIVED BAD THINGS, BUT NOW HE IS COMFORTED HERE AND YOU ARE IN AGONY"

(Luke 16:19–25)

This woman, I know not for what reason, was strangely prejudiced against me from the first; and what made it still worse for me, was a severe fit of illness, which attacked me very soon… At first I was taken some care of; but as I did not recover very soon, she grew weary, and entirely neglected me. I had sometimes not a little difficulty to procure a draught of cold water when burning with a fever. My bed was a mat spread upon a board or chest, and a log of wood my pillow. When my fever left me, and my appetite returned, I would gladly have eaten, but there was no one gave unto me. She lived in plenty herself, but hardly allowed me sufficient to sustain life, except now and then, when in the highest good humour, she would send me victuals in her own plate after she had dined; and this, so greatly was my pride humbled, I received with thanks and eagerness, as the most needy beggar does an alms. Once, I well remember, I was called to receive this bounty from her own hand; but being exceeding weak and feeble, I dropped the plate. Those who live in plenty can hardly conceive how this loss touched me; but she had the cruelty to laugh at my disappointment; and though the table was covered with dishes (for she lived much in the European manner), she refused to give me any more.[1 2]

Almighty God, I pray today for those who suffer and starve as a result of inhumanity, deliberate cruelty, thoughtless selfishness, and greed. I pray for the "haves", that you would soften their hearts, and I pray for the "have nots", that you would look upon them in mercy. Lord of justice, I ask for your intervention on behalf of those who are denied access to the plenty that others enjoy. Grant me a heart of compassion, ruled by the impulses of love.

1 From *The Life of Rev. John Newton.*
2 See Footnote 3, January 8th.

March 10th

I am in deep distress. Let us fall into the hands of the Lord, for his mercy is great

(2 Samuel 24:14)

It is often darkest just before dawn. On the voyage in which came the great crisis in his spiritual life, he [Newton] says his daily course was one of the most horrid impiety and profaneness. "I know not that I have since met so daring a blasphemer." In March 1748, sailing towards England, [Newton's] ship was overtaken by a terrific storm. The sea breaking over, the cry was raised that it was sinking. He says that on March 21 he laboured at the pumps from three in the morning till near noon. Nearly spent with cold and labour, going to speak with the captain, he said, "If this will not do, the Lord have mercy upon us! This thought, spoken without much reflection, was the first desire I had breathed for mercy for many years. It directly answered, 'What mercy can there be for me?'"[1]

God of great and surprising mercy, not many of us will cry out to you in a literal storm at sea (though some might). Nevertheless, please draw alongside those who cry out for mercy at times of deep and overwhelming distress in their lives. Human nature being what it is, Lord, we often only remember you when we are afraid, or turn to you in moments of peril. Forgive us our self-reliance. Have mercy. I pray especially for those known to me personally who are desperate and at their wits' end.

1 From *John Newton: Sailor, Preacher, Pastor, and Poet.*

March 11th

They that go down to the sea in ships, that do business in great waters; These see the works of the Lord, and his wonders in the deep.

(Psalm 107:23–29 KJV)

About six in the evening the hold was free from water, and there came a gleam of hope. "I thought," said Newton, "I saw the hand of God displayed in our favour. I began to pray. I could not utter the prayer of faith. I could not draw near to a reconciled God and call him Father. My prayer was like the prayer of the ravens, which yet the Lord Jesus does not disdain to hear."[1]

On the night of March 10th, a dreadful storm almost swamped John Newton's terribly battered slave-trading ship, Greyhound, as it drifted tantalizingly close towards the coast of Ireland, making its way home to England via the Atlantic triangle trade route. So violent was the storm it caused Newton to pray for the first time in many a year. In a state of sheer panic, Newton was terrified and feared for his life, with the realization striking his heart that, if the Christian faith were true and he drowned, he would plunge headlong not only into the ocean, but also into eternity without any assurance of his sins forgiven. In blind terror, both physical and spiritual, with the ferocious elements ceaselessly lashing his vessel, those sins flashed dramatically and forcefully across his memory, tormenting him; his blasphemies, his cruel mocking of the Christian faith, his persecution of believers, his shocking and inhumane treatment of slaves in his charge… After four days, the storm was stilled, by which time crucial provisions were almost exhausted and Newton himself, though still alive, was a cowering wreck, shocked to his very core. He thereafter attributed his deliverance from a storm he hadn't expected to survive, to divine providence – truly, his deeply personal experience of "amazing grace". Consequently, John Newton began to read the New Testament, and was struck by the astonishing parallels he noticed, between his life and that of the prodigal son, as outlined in Luke 15.[2]

Heavenly Father, First Sea Lord, what strikes me about these accounts is the importance and worth of a human soul in your estimation; the lengths to which you are prepared to go in order to confront someone with the realities of eternity. In John Newton's context, a wild storm was a gracious blessing – albeit heavily disguised! Thank you, Almighty God, for a love that constantly strives to grab our attention, so that we might be saved.

1 From *John Newton: Sailor, Preacher, Pastor, and Poet.*

2 This is my brief personal summary of John Newton's experience in March 1748 (see Footnotes 2 & 3, March 12th).

March 12th

"Return to me," declares the Lord Almighty, "and I will return to you"

(Zechariah 1:3)

The ship drifted for a month. Provisions were running out. The captain blamed Newton's blasphemy for the problems and considered throwing Newton overboard, like Jonah. The crippled ship finally made its way to Northern Ireland just in time before another great wind began to blow. Newton acknowledged that God had answered his prayer. Upon reaching shore, Newton resolved to swear no more. He even went back to church. However, he was not yet a Christian. He said later, "I consider this as the beginning of my return to God, or rather of his return to me; but I cannot consider myself to have been a believer (in the full sense of the word) till a considerable time afterwards."[1 2 3]

Lord, your mercy is astonishing. You would be entitled to reject any of us, yet you do not treat us as our sins deserve. Rather, you entreat us to come to you for forgiveness and pardon. You would be entitled to turn your back on any of us, yet you persist in amazing grace. What a truly lovely Bible text you have given for today. You are gracious and compassionate. You are my God.

1 From *Saved by Amazing Grace, the John Newton Story* (https://israelmyglory.org).

2 These last three pages touch upon one of several key moments in the life of John Newton. While the storm at sea was the most dramatic of these, I have chosen not to dwell overmuch upon this famous incident, because there is much more to Newton's story that is sometimes overlooked. I do not belittle the account of the storm, but neither do I wish that singular event to potentially obscure other examples of equally significant grace in Newton's years. This brevity is intentional, but not dismissive (see Footnote No. 1, January 16th).

3 Numerous books detailing the life and ministry of Reverend John Newton are available. A wealth of biographical material is available from the John Newton Project (https://www.johnnewton.org).

March 13th

Thou desirest truth in the inward parts

(Psalm 51:6 KJV)

Smuggling was common throughout the nine years that Newton was in the Customs Service[1] and for a long time afterwards; nor was it considered immoral or unpatriotic to take advantage of this dangerous activity. James Woodforde, a respectable clergyman,[2] refers in his diary to "the honest Smuggler, Richd [sic] Andrews", and in his cash accounts writes "paid my smuggler", as simply as we should put "paid my grocer." The Isle of Man had not yet been brought within the fiscal kingdom, and ships from America and the West Indies landed goods there duty-free. Smugglers had a fine chance to bring across to the mainland rum, brandy and tobacco and make a handsome profit. "Leverpoole", as it was known in Customs records, was considered a difficult and dangerous area. Customs boats patrolled coastal waters; all incoming vessels were boarded and searched, while a close watch was kept on the docks and their environs; and a mounted patrol operated some ten miles inland. A Collector at Liverpool was responsible for the whole area.[3]

Lord, you are full of grace and truth, yet here is a "grey area" – what we might call the bending of the rules, as opposed to the breaking of them. Grant me wisdom, I pray, to love truth, even when the boundaries might not be crystal clear, or when I am tempted towards compromise. I pray too, for Christians seeking to maintain a witness in countries, or situations, where dishonesty and corruption is the norm, or where bribes are routinely expected. Strengthen their convictions and help them.

1 John Newton was Surveyor of Tides in the Customs Service in Liverpool, England, from 1755 until he was ordained as an Anglican curate in 1764.

2 Reverend James Woodforde (1740–1803), author of *The Diary of a Country Parson*.

3 From Bernard Martin, *An Ancient Mariner*, London: Wyvern Books, The Epworth Press, 1960.

March 14th

Joses, who by the apostles was surnamed Barnabas, (which is, being interpreted, The son of consolation)

(Acts 4:36 KJV)

Mr. Newton was indeed "a son of consolation." He had a peculiar talent for entering into the feelings and the views of the distressed. Much of the word of God is applicable to a state of trouble, and can only be understood in circumstances of trial. The gospel of Christ throws light on the most mysterious events of time. He who so loved us as to give himself a sacrifice for our sins, when we were sunk in rebellion, can never cease to care for us. In the midst of all the trials and conflicts of the wilderness, he is showing us the utter emptiness and vanity of the present world, and the insufficiency of the soul to its own happiness, that he may draw us to himself, and lead us to repose on him as our ultimate rest and satisfying portion. And what blessings are the most painful and complicated troubles, if the heart is thereby weaned from the transitory objects of sense, and if every stroke of affliction impels the soul more powerfully towards him who is the inexhaustible fountain of all genuine enjoyment.[1]

Lord, I thank you for those you have gifted with listening ears, caring hearts, and wise counsel. They have such a lovely ministry; one which is increasingly important in a pressurized world. Bless them, I pray, as they handle and absorb the problems and needs of others. Equip them, strengthen them, and be with those to whom they minister.

1 From *Cardiphonia: or, The Utterance of the Heart in the Course of a Real Correspondence, Volume One* (Introductory Essay by Reverend David Russell of Dundee, Scotland, who was himself a prolific author).

March 15th

Despisest thou the riches of his goodness and forbearance and longsuffering; not knowing that the goodness of God leadeth thee to repentance?

(Romans 2:4 KJV)

Not only does the Saviour appeal to our love, he also interposes his authority. "Ye are my friends," says he, "if ye do whatsoever I command you," John xv. 14. It is clear then, that while we are treated, not merely as servants, but as friends, we are enjoined obedience by authority. Hence such expressions as the following: – "Ye know what commandments were given by the Lord Jesus," 1 Thess. iv. 2. "These things commend and teach," 1 Tim. iv. 11. "Charge them that are rich in this world, that they do good, that they be rich in good works, ready to distribute, willing to communicate," 1 Tim. vi.17, 18. Now here a being ready and willing to do what is right is represented as a matter of charge or command, because, along with the charge, suitable service and sufficient motives to obedience are suggested. Why then oppose one to the other? The authority of God is not only blended with kindness, it is in fact a display of kindness, for it is employed the more effectually to preserve us from that which is our ruin.[1]

Have your own way in my life, Lord. You are the potter, while I am but as clay in your hands – pliable and in daily need of your friendship and gracious moulding. Exercise your Lordship and authority over me this day, for I know I am in the care of one who loves me and has my very best interests at heart. You are the Lord of my today.

1 From *Cardiphonia: or, The Utterance of the Heart in the Course of a Real Correspondence, Volume One* (Introductory Essay by Reverend David Russell).

March 16th

The dream is certain, and the interpretation thereof sure

(Daniel 2:45 KJV)

Those who acknowledge Scripture will allow that there have been monitory and supernatural dreams, evident communications from Heaven, either directing or foretelling future events: and those who are acquainted with the history and experience of the people of God are well assured that such intimations have not been totally withheld in any period down to the present times. Reason, far from contradicting this supposition, strongly pleads for it, where the process of reasoning is rightly understood and carefully pursued. So that a late eminent writer,[1] who I presume is not generally charged with enthusiasm, undertakes to prove, that the phenomenon of dreaming is inexplicable at least, if not absolutely impossible, without taking in the agency and intervention of spiritual things, to us invisible. I would refer the incredulous to him. For my own part, I can say, without scruple, "The dream is certain, and the interpretation thereof sure."[2]

Lord of time and eternity, today I pray for dreamers – those who dream, literally, and have a ministry of prophecy, and those who dream, metaphorically, in terms of hopes and ambitions. Grant your prophets courage and wisdom in sharing messages you have imparted. And for those who lay their ideas and plans at your feet, bless them and help them. May your will be done in all things. Thank you for the exciting gift of holy imagination!

1 Andrew Baxter (b. 1686 or 1687), Scottish metaphysician, philosopher, writer, and private tutor, at some time famous for his publication *An Enquiry into the Nature of the Human Soul, Wherein its Immateriality is Evinced from the Principles of Reason and Philosophy*.

2 From *The Life of the Rev. John Newton*.

March 17th

WE HAVE THIS TREASURE IN JARS OF CLAY TO SHOW THAT THIS ALL-SURPASSING POWER IS FROM GOD AND NOT FROM US

(2 Corinthians 4:7)

On Mr. Newton descending the pulpit on one occasion, a person who had felt the force of the sermon leaned over and said: "A most excellent discourse, sir." Mr. Newton, conscious of the temptation to self-approval, replied, "The devil told me that, sir, before you."[1]

O Lord! What an insight! What humility! Help me, I pray, to quickly deflect any praise or glory to its rightful source. Help me not to linger on compliments, lest pride sneaks in and is given a root. Help me not to worry about who receives the credit, just so long as you receive honour due.

1 From *John Newton: Sailor, Preacher, Pastor, and Poet.*

MARCH 18TH

IN EVERYTHING SET THEM AN EXAMPLE

(Titus 2:7)

Mr. Whitefield[1] is, as he was formerly, very helpful to me. He warms up my heart, makes me more indifferent to cares and crosses, and strengthens my faith. I have had more of his company here than would have come to my share at London in a twelvemonth. Though some of the wags of my acquaintance have given me the name of young Whitefield, from my constant attendance upon him when he was here, it does not grieve me; and perhaps if they would speak the truth, they do not think the worse of me in their hearts. I find I cannot be consistent and conscientious in my profession without incurring the charge of singularity. I shall endeavour to act with prudence, and not give needless offence; but I hope I shall never more be ashamed of the gospel.[2]

Thank you, Lord, for friends and colleagues who exert a positive influence. Thank you for those people you have placed across my path, who encourage me and affirm me in my faith. I pray to be that sort of friend to those around me.

1 George Whitefield (also Whitfield) (1714–70), Anglican cleric and an outstanding evangelist of his day. He was one of the founders of Methodism, and had a marvellous influence over John Newton. Newton heard him preach, and they established a friendship whereby Whitefield became some kind of mentor. They met as friends and colleagues, spending time together in London and Liverpool.

2 From *John Newton of Olney and St Mary Woolnoth. An Autobiography and Narrative.*

March 19th

James and John, the sons of Zebedee, came to him. "Teacher," they said, "we want you to do for us whatever we ask." "What do you want me to do for you?" he asked. They replied, "Let one of us sit at your right and the other at your left in your glory"... Jesus called them together and said, "You know that those who are regarded as rulers of the Gentiles lord it over them, and their high officials exercise authority over them. Not so with you. Instead, whoever wants to become great among you must be your servant, and whoever wants to be first must be slave of all. For even the Son of Man did not come to be served, but to serve, and to give his life as a ransom for many"

(Mark 10:35–37, 42–45)

When some people talk of religion, they mean they have heard so many sermons and performed so many devotions, and thus mistake the means for the end. But true religion is an habitual recollection of God and intention to serve him, and this turns everything into gold. We are apt to suppose that we need something splendid to evince our devotion; but true devotion equals things – washing plates and cleaning shoes is a high office, if performed in a right spirit. If three angels were sent to earth, they would feel perfect indifference who should perform the part of prime minister, parish minister, or watchman.[1]

Lord Jesus, your humility puts mine to shame, when I reflect on some of my ambitions, which have little or nothing to do with servanthood. Forgive me, and place within my heart an altruistic desire to serve, and not to be served. Make me a cleaner of shoes!

1 From *John Newton: Sailor, Preacher, Pastor, and Poet.*

March 20th

Moses said to the Lord, "Pardon your servant, Lord. I have never been eloquent, neither in the past nor since you have spoken to your servant. I am slow of speech and tongue." The Lord said to him, "Who gave human beings their mouths? Who makes them deaf or mute? Who gives them sight or makes them blind? Is it not I, the Lord? Now go; I will help you speak and will teach you what to say"

(Exodus 4:10–12)

Newton went to a meeting where the members made public confession. "I had an opportunity to speak of God's great goodness to me but found myself contracted and irresolute: my pride had been criticizing upon the expressions and delivery of some that had spoken before me, but I believe I performed much worse myself"... One day he took a quiet country walk to compose his mind, and then... "endeavoured to say something suitable... but was remarkably tongue tied". Another day, "in ye afternoon visited Mrs. D. but my tongue was tied so that I said nothing as I ought". [1]

Lord God, you call some people to be preachers and public speakers. Bless them, I pray, in the proclamation of the gospel. Bless too, though, those of us whose witness is made in a car journey, or across the office, in a café, or over the garden fence; a conversation, a word in season. How easy it is to talk about football, or the weather, or politics! Help me to also speak of Jesus, despite any reservations or hesitation.

1 From *An Ancient Mariner*.

Prepare to meet your God

(Amos 4:12)

Before dawn on the 10th March 1748, John Newton was awakened... by the force of a violent sea, which broke on board the fast driving ship. So much water came below as almost to fill the cabin where he slept. The first crash, occasioned by a great wave, and the noisy swirling of water and displaced articles, gave place to a silence in which every living creature aboard seemed to be straining to hear what had happened and what was to come... The sea had torn away the upper timbers on one side of the ship so that wave after wave flushed the deck and the vessel filled rapidly. The pumps could not keep the water level from rising. Newton joined a dozen of the crew in the almost hopeless task of baling with buckets. Had The Greyhound carried a common cargo, she must have sunk; but fortunately there was a large quantity of beeswax and dyer's wood in the holds, both of which commodities are lighter than water, and thereby kept her afloat... As he staggered back to the pump he was "instantly struck"... Would the Lord have mercy upon the ship, upon his comrades, upon him? If, indeed, there was a God, a father of mankind who showed mercy, as the Christians affirmed, what mercy could there be for such a blasphemer as John Newton?... He was physically exhausted and so sure of imminent death that he felt what he described as "a sullen frame, a mixture of despair and impatience." Like a character in Roderick Random[1] he was "bound for the other world but... damnably ill provided for the voyage"... When The Greyhound made her final plunge into the dark waters he would go to everlasting torment. And, as had been written by the poet George Herbert:[2] None shall in Hell such bitter pangs endure, As those who mock at God's way of salvation.[3][4]

Today, Lord, help me to pray specifically for family, loved ones, and friends who do not (yet) know you as their Lord and Saviour. In your mercy, hear my prayers. Grant me time reserved for prayer, and bring their names to mind. I owe them my prayerful interest.

1 *The Adventures of Roderick Random*, a 1748 novel by Tobias Smollett (1721–71), based upon his experiences in the Royal Navy.
2 George Herbert (1593–1633), poet and Church of England priest.
3 From Herbert's poem "The Church Porch".
4 From *An Ancient Mariner.*

March 22nd

"Woe to me!" I cried. "I am ruined! For I am a man of unclean lips, and I live among a people of unclean lips"

(Isaiah 6:5)

A remarkable fact was that Newton no longer blasphemed. From the moment during the height of the storm when he had uttered an unthinking prayer for mercy, the curses which had rippled his tongue and the oaths which had punctuated his every sentence were forgotten. He found his "principles of infidelity deeply riveted" but his tongue was cleansed without any conscious effort… For nearly four weeks the damaged ship drifted, and then, when hope was almost gone, the wind came about to the desired quarter… The fair breeze remained until land was seen. It was Tory Island off the coast of Donegal. "Our very last victuals was boiling in the pot," observed Newton. Two hours after the anchor was dropped the wind veered and began to blow with such violence that if The Greyhound had been still at sea she must have sunk. The ship's company of The Greyhound were received by the Irish with "the great kindness" due to shipwrecked mariners; for although their vessel was not a total wreck it took six weeks to patch her sufficiently for the further short passage to Liverpool. Newton went to Londonderry, and as he lay in a decent shore bed for the first night in over three years, and listened to the rising gale, every gust of wind spoke to him of Providence.[1]

Gracious God, our sins and weaknesses do not hinder your great love towards us. Our waywardness is no deterrent. You are offended, but not discouraged in your relentless efforts to change those ways of ours that grieve you. Thank you, Lord, for steadfast mercy, even in the midst of life's storms and gales.

1 From *An Ancient Mariner.*

March 23rd

"All things are lawful", but not all things are helpful. "All things are lawful", but not all things build up

(1 Corinthians 10:23 ESV)

Settled in his new occupation, and his wife with him,[1] and having all that his heart desires, Mr. Newton complains that he is now ready to take up his rest, though he is well aware it cannot be here. "I know," he says, "the reason of this want of spiritual life. Perimus licitis.[2] The devil attacks some by storm, with violent temptations within or without, but he lays against me, as it were, by sap, in a more secret way, but not less dangerous, by beguiling my affections. But why do I say the devil? Alas! my own heart is weak and wicked enough to ruin me. This it is that sets up idols against the Lord, and brings me under the power of lawful things."[3]

Thank you, Lord, for this insight into those things which are not "sins" as such, but are, nevertheless not particularly edifying; habits that are innocuous in themselves, but don't necessarily build me up in a spiritual sense, and which might inadvertently open doors to a way of life that leads me away from you. Watch me, Lord, I pray, and teach me about myself.

1 In Liverpool.

2 From the Latin, roughly translating as "We come to ruin by permitted things" or "Death in a good cause".

3 From *John Newton of Olney and St Mary Woolnoth. An Autobiography and Narrative.*

March 24th

How good and pleasant it is when God's people live together in unity! It is like precious oil poured on the head, running down on the beard, running down on Aaron's beard, down on the collar of his robe. It is as if the dew of Hermon were falling on Mount Zion. For there the Lord bestows his blessing, even life for evermore

(Psalm 133:1–3)

It is with pleasure I hear of a work of revival going on in so many different parts of the kingdom; and, as an inhabitant of this town,[1] I am grieved to think that we should be as yet excluded from a share in it. It is true, we have the truth preached in the Baptist Meetings; but I believe you know the particular disadvantages they are both under, so that, though they are useful to their own people (I trust, through grace, to me also), yet they seem not calculated for general usefulness. The unhappy bigotry of Mr. Wesley's people[2] here is another great disadvantage to the cause. They have the best house in the place, yet they will neither suffer any but their own people to preach in it, nor will they keep it supplied themselves.[3] [4] [5]

O Lord, how it must frustrate you when possibilities of revival are hampered, or possibly even squandered, by denominational rivalries. Forgive your church, Lord, for these unnecessary barriers, and turn our eyes (and our hearts) towards priorities. I pray for revival in my area, and for church unity to facilitate that.

1 Liverpool.
2 Methodists/Wesleyans.
3 With preachers, on a regular basis. The unavailability or absence of a preacher sometimes meant that a church was unable to open its doors on a Sunday.
4 From a letter Newton wrote to his friend and mentor George Whitefield.
5 From *John Newton of Olney and St Mary Woolnoth. An Autobiography and Narrative.*

March 25th

I LONG TO SEE YOU SO THAT I MAY IMPART TO YOU SOME SPIRITUAL GIFT TO MAKE YOU STRONG – THAT IS, THAT YOU AND I MAY BE MUTUALLY ENCOURAGED BY EACH OTHER'S FAITH

(Romans 1:11–12)

What a mercy is it to be separated in spirit, conversation, and interest, from the world that knows not God, where all are alike by nature! Grace makes a happy and unspeakable difference. Believers were once under the same influence of that spirit who still worketh in the children of disobedience, pursuing different paths, but all equally remote from truth and peace; some hatching cockatrice[1] eggs, others weaving spiders' webs. These two general heads of mischief and vanity include all the schemes, sins, and achievements of which man is capable, till God is pleased to visit the heart with his grace.[2] The busy part of mankind are employed in multiplying evils and miseries; the more retired, speculative, and curious, are amusing themselves with what will hereafter appear as unsubstantial, unstable, and useless as a cobweb.[3]

Thank you, Heavenly Father, for the gift and privilege of Christian fellowship. Help me always to value and seek the company of my Christian friends. I pray for those friends today, asking you to bless them. Thank you for their influence and encouragement along the way.

1 A mythical double-headed creature whose glance was said to be deadly; part rooster, part dragon, part crocodile, hatched by a serpent from a cock's egg.

2 Once again, we observe John Newton's strong awareness of the base condition of the human heart; its deceptiveness, its weakness and its sinfulness, save for the grace of God.

3 From *Cardiphonia: or, The Utterance of the Heart in the Course of a Real Correspondence, Volume One.*

March 26th

I consider everything a loss because of the surpassing worth of knowing Christ Jesus my Lord, for whose sake I have lost all things. I consider them garbage, that I may gain Christ

(Philippians 3:8)

Well then may the believer say; let them laugh, let them rage, let them, if they please, point at me for a fool as I walk the streets; if I do but take up the Bible, or run over in my mind the inventory of the blessings with which the Lord has enriched me, I have sufficient amends. Jesus is mine; in him I have wisdom, righteousness, sanctification, and redemption, an interest in all the promises and in all the perfections of God; he will guide me by his counsel, support me by his power, comfort me with his presence, while I am here; and afterwards, when flesh and heart fail, he will receive me to his glory.[1]

What a marvellous perspective, Lord! To regard this world's passing pleasures as merely temporal, and even at best, of little or no consequence when compared to my relationship with you. Help me to live in this light today.

1 From *Cardiphonia: or, The Utterance of the Heart in the Course of a Real Correspondence, Volume One.*

MARCH 27TH

THOUGH THE FIG-TREE DOES NOT BUD AND THERE ARE NO GRAPES ON THE VINES, THOUGH THE OLIVE CROP FAILS AND THE FIELDS PRODUCE NO FOOD… YET I WILL REJOICE IN THE LORD, I WILL BE JOYFUL IN GOD MY SAVIOUR

(Habakkuk 3:17–18)

The time you were down was a harvest season with me. The Lord enlarged my heart to hear His word from your mouth, but, for the most part, I have been since then in the valley, dull, contracted, and unuseful; but, as though Divine grace I have been led to live above and beyond my frames upon the everlasting righteousness of my dear Redeemer, to which my best obedience can add no value, and from which all my infirmities can take nothing away, so those things, though they take from my pleasure, have no considerable effect upon my peace. Therefore, though I have not yet attained, I am pressing on.[1 2]

Heavenly Father, you are the Lord of each and every season of my life: the "harvest" times when all seems well, and those days "in the valley" which can be dark and cold. Help me always, Lord, to trust in your abiding presence. I pray today for anyone I know who is struggling through "dull" moments, when all seems gloomy and maybe even hopeless. Help them, I pray.

1 From a letter to George Whitefield.

2 From *John Newton of Olney and St Mary Woolnoth. An Autobiography and Narrative.*

March 28th

May God himself, the God of peace, sanctify you through and through. May your whole spirit, soul and body be kept blameless at the coming of our Lord Jesus Christ

(1 Thessalonians 5:23)

If deliverance out of trouble or danger is a mercy of great value, it is something more extraordinary and indulgent to be kept from the very appearance of evil; to be preserved weeks, months, and years successively unhurt either in my person or best enjoyments in a world such as this, when there are so many arrows continually flying, and so many persons continually suffering – to observe them falling before, behind, and on every hand, and yet I and mine (though daily provoking the Lord and leaning to idols) escaping without a wound, may, without an alarm – this is surprising and distinguishing indeed. How loudly does this call me to do more than others; yet, alas! on the contrary, what sloth, insensibility, unbelief, worldliness, pride, and self-indulgence must I charge myself with![1]

Gracious God, your love is patient and steadfast – likewise, your ongoing work of sanctification in the life of the believer. You save, and then you sanctify. Help me, Lord, by sustaining grace, to always allow your "work in progress" to remain active in my life!

1 From *John Newton of Olney and St Mary Woolnoth. An Autobiography and Narrative.*

March 29th

TAKE... NO THOUGHT FOR THE MORROW: FOR THE MORROW SHALL TAKE THOUGHT FOR THE THINGS OF ITSELF. SUFFICIENT UNTO THE DAY IS THE EVIL THEREOF

(Matthew 6:34 KJV)

Sometimes I compare the troubles which we have to undergo in the course of the year to a great bundle of fagots,[1] far too large for us to lift. But God does not require us to carry the whole at once; he mercifully unties the bundle, and gives us first one stick, which we are to carry today, and then another, which we are to carry tomorrow, and so on. This we might easily manage, if we would only take the burden appointed for us each day; but we choose to increase our troubles by carrying yesterday's stick over again today, and adding tomorrow's burden to our load, before we are required to bear it.[2]

Our prayer today is from the pen of St Francis de Sales.[3] It seems appropriate to use it here:

Do not look forward to what might happen tomorrow; the same everlasting Father who cares for you today will take care of you tomorrow, and every day. Either He will shield you from suffering, or He will give you unfailing strength to bear it. Be at peace then and put aside all anxious thoughts and imaginations.

1 Old English: a bundle of sticks used for fuel.
2 From *The Life of Rev. John Newton.*
3 1567–1622, Roman Catholic Bishop of Geneva.

MARCH 30TH

WHAT THE LAW WAS POWERLESS TO DO BECAUSE IT WAS WEAKENED BY THE FLESH, GOD DID BY SENDING HIS OWN SON IN THE LIKENESS OF SINFUL FLESH TO BE A SIN OFFERING

(Romans 8:3)

Ah, what can I do, or where be secure?
If justice pursue, what heart can endure?
When God speaks in thunder and makes himself known,
The heart breaks asunder though hard as a stone.

With terror I read my sins' heavy score,
The numbers exceed the sands on the shore;
Guilt makes me unable to stand or to flee,
So Cain murdered Abel, and trembled like me.

Each sin, like his blood, with terrible cry,
Calls loudly to God to strike from on high:
Nor can my repentance, extorted by fear,
Reverse the just sentence; 'tis just, though severe.

And must I then go, forever to dwell
In torments and woe with devils in hell?
Oh where is the Saviour I scorned in times past?
His word in my favour would save me at last.

A case such as mine will honour Thy power;
All hell will repine, all Heav'n will adore;
If in condemnation strict justice takes place,
It shines in salvation more glorious than grace.[1 2]

The demands of the law fulfilled by grace, in Christ. And what grace!

1 From http://www.traditionalmusic.co.uk/john-newton/ah-what-can-i-do-john-newton.htm
2 Penned by John Newton in 1779.

March 31st

LIVE IN HARMONY WITH ONE ANOTHER. DO NOT BE PROUD, BUT BE WILLING TO ASSOCIATE WITH PEOPLE OF LOW POSITION. DO NOT BE CONCEITED

(Romans 12:16)

If two angels were sent from heaven to execute a Divine command, one to conduct an empire, and the other to sweep a street in it, they would feel no inclination to change employments.[1]

What a delightful way of putting it, Lord! Help me, I pray, to be lowly of heart, whatever my status in the eyes of the world. Yet, simultaneously, to always realize I am the child of a King! Fit that spiritual balance within me today.

1 From *The Life of Rev. John Newton.*

April 1st

The wisdom of this world is foolishness with God

(1 Corinthians 3:19 KJV)

I am persuaded we have many plain people here, who, if a wise man of the world was to suggest that the Bible is a human invention, would be quite at a loss how to answer him, by arguments drawn from this blessed book, that they would be no more moved by the insinuation, that if they were told, that a cunning man, or set of men, invented the sun, and placed it in the firmament. So, if a wise Socinian[1] was to tell them that the Saviour was only a man like themselves, they would conceive just such an opinion of his skill in divinity, as a philosopher would do of a clown's skill in astronomy, who should affirm that the sun was no bigger than a cart-wheel. It remains therefore a truth, in defiance of all the cavils of the ignorant, that the Holy Spirit does influence the hearts of all the children of God, or, in other words, they are inspired, not with new revelations, but with grace and wisdom to understand, apply, and feed upon the great things already revealed in the scriptures, without which the scriptures are as useless as spectacles to the blind.[2]

Thank you, Holy Spirit, for your gracious gifts of supernatural revelation and wisdom. Thank you for imparting the truth of the gospel, all because of mercy. My prayers today, Lord, are for those in my family who don't know you as their God and Saviour. I ask you to open their eyes and reveal Jesus to their hearts. As I pray, I bring them to your throne of grace.

---

1 See Footnote 1, February 5th, .

2 From *Cardiphonia: or, The Utterance of the Heart in the Course of a Real Correspondence, Volume One.*

April 2nd

If you remain in me and I in you, you will bear much fruit; apart from me you can do nothing

(John 15:5)

What is weaker than a worm? Yet the Lord's worms shall, in his strength, thresh the mountains, and make the hills as chaff. But this life of faith, this living and acting by a power above our own, is an inexplicable mystery, till experience makes it plain. I have often wondered that St Paul had obtained so much quarter at the hands of some people as to pass with them for a man of sense; for surely the greatest part of his writings must be in the last degree absurd and unintelligible upon their principles. How many contradictions must they find, for instance, if they give any attention to what they read in that one passage, Gal. ii. 20, "I am crucified with Christ: nevertheless I live; yet not I, but Christ liveth in me: and the life which I now live in the flesh I live by faith in the Son of God, who loved me, and gave himself for me." And as believers are thus inspired by the Holy Spirit, who furnishes them with desires, motives and abilities, to perform what is agreeable to his will; so I apprehend, that they who live without God in the world, whom the apostle styles sensual, not having the Spirit, are in greater or less degree… under what I call a black desperation.[1]

Gracious God, you do not leave us alone in this world. Neither do you expect us to live the Christian life unaided. On the contrary, you offer enabling grace and the presence of your indwelling Spirit. Thank you. I pray, Lord, for those who struggle on without you and even resist your intervention – the blind leading the blind, as it were, spiritually speaking. Reach out to them in mercy.

1 From *Cardiphonia: or, The Utterance of the Heart in the Course of a Real Correspondence, Volume One.*

April 3rd

How much better to get wisdom than gold, to get insight rather than silver!

(Proverbs 16:16)

We have an account of a remarkable providential deliverance. "I rose early," says Mr. Newton, and went to the watch-house[1] till eight o'clock. At ten a most violent storm came on, doing considerable damage while it lasted. In the afternoon when I returned to the watch-house I found the roof beaten in by the fall of the chimney, and the chair in which I usually sit broken to pieces. Had the storm happened two hours sooner, or at many other times, I should have been crushed in a place where I should have thought myself in safety"… We have a very striking meditation on his great deliverance. Subsequently we find these observations: "There is a great grace with which some have been favoured – an abstracted mind in the midst of a crowd, so as to converse with God while surrounded and seemingly engaged with the busy world. Such an attainment methinks I should prize beyond thousands of gold and silver."[2]

What a skill, Lord – to be in fellowship with you even in the midst of a busy and sometimes chaotic world! What a lovely gift – to be able to live with heart to God and hand to humankind, as it were. Bless me, I pray, as I go about my business today, to walk with you while I do all that needs to be done in an everyday way. Grant me practical holiness!

1 In Liverpool, where John Newton worked as a Tide Surveyor for several years. Every dock had such a house, more formally referred to as a Customs Watch-House. This was either a house in isolation (something like a small cottage), or part of a larger dock building.

2 From *John Newton of Olney and St Mary Woolnoth. An Autobiography and Narrative.*

April 4th

The joy of the Lord is your strength

(Nehemiah 8:10)

Prayer is the great engine to overthrow and rout my spiritual enemies, the great means to procure the graces of which I stand in hourly need… I generally find all my other tempers and experiences to be proportioned to the spirit of my prayers. When prayer is a burden, nothing does me good; but as long as the door of access is kept open and duly attended I find the joy of the Lord to be my strength, and nothing is suffered to harm me.[1][2]

Grant me, Lord, a spirit of prayer. Give me constantly to know that fellowship with you whereby "the door of access is kept open" in each and every circumstance. Teach me how to pray.

1 From *John Newton of Olney and St Mary Woolnoth. An Autobiography and Narrative.*

2 Part of John Newton's regular daily routine (in the normal run of things) was to spend two hours in rayer and Bible reading every morning, in addition to "keeping short accounts" throughout the day.

April 5th

I am ordained a preacher

(1 Timothy 2:7 KJV)

We find Mr. Newton entertaining his first definite thoughts of the ministry. Some happy results had followed his efforts to do good, and he had received several hints from friends upon the subject. Henceforth this important question is constantly upon his mind, and he is almost morbidly anxious lest unworthy motives should influence him… He expresses himself as "in doubt, not knowing whether the views I have of late aspired to are the notions of His gracious Spirit, or the fruits of self-will and sufficiency. I commit myself to the Lord, who will perhaps in one way or other determine for me."[1] [2]

Heavenly Father, I pray that you would help those who are considering their future, whether that includes a call to ordained ministry or another sphere of service. Bless them with your Holy Spirit's guidance and honour their sincere intention to follow your will. Speak clearly to those who stand at the threshold of decision-making, that they may know your voice of reassurance.

1 From *John Newton of Olney and St Mary Woolnoth. An Autobiography and Narrative.*

2 John Newton agonized for a great length of time as to whether or not he had received a call to ordained ministry. He was, as ever, acutely aware of his own heart and its capacity to deceive, and was therefore anxious to investigate this matter thoroughly.

April 6th

Trust in the Lord with all your heart and lean not on your own understanding; in all your ways submit to him, and he will make your paths straight

(Proverbs 3:5–6)

O Lord, the fountain of wisdom, and the sure guide of those who depend on thee; thou hast promised that if we commit our ways to thee, thou wilt establish them, and if we trust in thee with all our hearts, thou wilt direct our steps – Lord I rely on this thy good word which has been tried and found faithful in every age. Vouchsafe to direct me by thy Spirit in the course of my present deliberations, and do thou lead me so to determine, as may be most agreeable to thy will, most conducive to thy glory. May my heart be divested of all prepossession and self-seeking, may I be enabled to see and to follow my duty; and may I maintain the comfortable testimony of a sincere, teachable and obedient conscience in thy sight. O may thy Spirit witness in my heart, and my conversation witness in the world, that I am indeed thy disciple, thine without reserve, thine and not another's, thine and not my own. Amen.[1 2 3]

Guiding God, you can see the way ahead – we can't! You are Alpha and Omega, beginning and end, whereas we can barely see the way ahead from day to day. Shine your light on our searching, I pray, so that our steps receive your blessing and approval. I pray for anyone who is specifically seeking a way forward. Visit them with protection, reassurance, and peace.

1 See Footnote 2, April 5th.

2 From *Ministry on my mind* (a booklet on John Newton on entering pastoral ministry). Transcribed by Marylynn Rouse as part of *The Complete Works of John Newton*, Stratford-upon-Avon: The John Newton Project, 2010.

3 A prayer written by Newton at the commencement of his great "heart search" regarding ministry.

April 7th

You will be like a well-watered garden

(Isaiah 58:11)

A garden contemplation suits,
And may instruction yield,
Sweeter than all the flow'rs and fruits
With which the spot is filled.

Eden was Adam's dwelling place,
While blest with innocence;
But sin o'erwhelmed him with disgrace,
And drove the rebel thence.

Oft as the garden-walk we tread,
We should bemoan his fall;
The trespass of our legal head
In ruin plunged us all.

The garden of Gethsemane,
The second Adam saw,
Oppressed with woe, to set us free
From the avenging law.

His church as a fair garden stands,
Which walls of love enclose;
Each tree is planted by his hand,
And by his blessing grows.

Such themes to those who Jesus love,
May constant joys afford;
And make a barren desert prove
The garden of the Lord.[1]

Lord Jesus, divine keeper of the garden of my heart.

---

1 From http://www.traditionalmusic.co.uk/john-newton

APRIL 8TH

COMMIT TO THE LORD WHATEVER YOU DO

(Proverbs 16:3)

A Christian should never plead spirituality for being a sloven; if he be a shoe-cleaner, he should be the best in the parish.[1]

Thank you, Heavenly Father, for today's tasks and responsibilities. Thank you for washing up that needs to be done, for it means I have eaten today. Thank you for my employment, for it means I have an income. Thank you for a lawn to mow, for it means I have a garden to enjoy. Thank you for journeys to make, for they mean I have a purpose to my day. Thank you for groceries to be chosen and brought home, for it means I have my daily provisions. And so on…

1 From *The Life of Rev. John Newton.*

April 9th

You, dear children, are from God and have overcome them, because the one who is in you is greater than the one who is in the world

(1 John 4:4)

Satan's malice is not abated; and though he has met with millions of disappointments, he still, like Goliath of old, defies the armies of God's Israel; he challenges the stoutest, and "desires to have them that he may sift them as wheat". Indeed he is far an overmatch for them, considered as in themselves: but though they are weak, their Redeemer is mighty, and they are for ever secured by his love and intercession. "The Lord knows them that are his, and no weapon formed against them can prosper." That this may appear with the fullest evidence, Satan is allowed to assault them. We handle vessels of glass or china with caution, and endeavour to preserve them from falls and blows, because we know they are easily broken. But if a man had the art of making glass malleable, and, like iron, capable of bearing the stroke of a hammer without breaking, it is probable that, instead of locking it carefully up, he would rather, for the commendation of his skill, permit many to attempt to break it, when he knew their attempts would be in vain. Believers are compared to earthen vessels, liable in themselves to be destroyed by a small blow; but they are so strengthened and tempered by the power and supply of divine grace, that the fiercest efforts of their fiercest enemies against them may be compared to the dashing of waves against a rock. And that this may be known and noticed, they are exposed to many trials; but the united and repeated assaults of the men of the world, and the powers of darkness, afford but the more incontestable demonstration, that the Lord is with them of a truth, and that his strength is made perfect in their weakness. Surely, this thought, my friend, will afford you consolation; and you will be content to suffer, if God may be glorified by you and in you.[1]

Almighty God, you are greater and mightier than any opponent. I pray for any who are experiencing direct spiritual attack or conflict. May the words of today's reading be their experience as you protect them from every assault. Deliver them from evil.

1 From *Letters of John Newton*.

April 10th

David, after he had served the purpose of God in his own generation, fell asleep and was laid with his fathers

(Acts 13:36 ESV)

John Newton's change of occupation from the slave trade to Tide Surveyor coincided... with notable changes in the social life of England. The eighteenth century was one of almost continuous change, but about the seventeen-fifties a momentum was clearly visible. Whatever date historians assign for the beginning of the Industrial Revolution, it was during the second half of the century that industrial changes became really marked. Manufacturing began to move from cottage to factory and cheap articles of all sorts found their way into workmen's homes. At the same time a no less remarkable change was taking place in agriculture. Land was being enclosed into small fields for the scientific rotation of crops and for the better breeding of cattle. While the material life of the people was undergoing such drastic changes, literary and artistic reformers... stirred complacent minds, and organised religion was turned topsy-turvy by a small group of Oxford University men.[1 2]

Lord of all ages, I pray for the witness of your church in a modern world. Change is inevitable, even if it isn't always welcome! Please help your church to present timeless truths in a way that is relevant. Deliver us from irrelevance!

1 From *An Ancient Mariner*.

2 The winds of evangelical fervour were stirring within certain groups of Oxford University students. The Wesley brothers, John and Charles, were hugely influential in this revival of interest in personal faith.

April 11th

THE TIME WILL COME WHEN PEOPLE WILL NOT PUT UP WITH SOUND DOCTRINE. INSTEAD, TO SUIT THEIR OWN DESIRES, THEY WILL GATHER ROUND THEM A GREAT NUMBER OF TEACHERS TO SAY WHAT THEIR ITCHING EARS WANT TO HEAR

(2 Timothy 4:3)

At the beginning of the century the best of the Anglican clergy were scholarly men, broad-minded and mildly pious. They preached, or rather read, carefully composed sermons which were strictly orthodox and innoxious; usually with a few classical tags to impress the squire and any satellites in his pew. They played their part in village life but had little desire to reform their parishioners. But many clergy were lazy. "Livings" were let to curates at stipends which showed a handsome profit to the absent incumbent. The generally lukewarm nature of the parsons resulted all too often in empty churches. A character in Congreve's Love for Love[1] observes, "Oh prayers will be said in empty churches at the usual hours." And some clergy were dissolute: Then unbelieving Priests reformed the nation, and taught more pleasant methods of salvation.[2 3]

Father, forgive. Forgive your church when it is weak and insipid. Forgive your church when it is boring and layered with dust. Forgive your clergy when learned individuals are emptying churches by degrees. Father, forgive. I pray for my own church. I pray for my own minister. Send the fire!

1 A comedy play by the British playwright William Congreve. Its first performance was in London in 1695.

2 A quotation from Alexander Pope's *Essay on Criticism.*

3 From *An Ancient Mariner.*

April 12th

EVERYONE BORN OF GOD OVERCOMES THE WORLD. THIS IS THE VICTORY THAT HAS OVERCOME THE WORLD, EVEN OUR FAITH

(1 John 5:4)

There are three things attributed to faith: (1) it works by love; (2) it purifies the heart; (3) it overcomes the world.[1]

Loving God, I pray that you would add to my faith: (1) a loving spirit; (2) a pure heart; (3) a life that overcomes. None of this is possible without your help and blessing. I come to you.

1 From *John Newton: Sailor, Preacher, Pastor, and Poet.*

April 13th

He which hath begun a good work in you will perform it until the day of Jesus Christ

(Philippians 1:6 KJV)

The Lord was pleased to lead me in a secret way. I had learned something of the evil of my heart; I could read the Bible over and over, with several good books, and had a general view of gospel truths; but my conceptions were, in many respects, confused, not having in all this time met with one acquaintance who could assist my inquiries… I found a captain of a ship from London, whose conversation was greatly helpful to me. He was… a man of experience in the things of God, and of a lively communicative turn. We discovered each other by some casual expressions in mixed company, and soon became, so far as business would permit, inseparable… I was all ear; and, what was better, he not only informed my understanding, but his discourse inflamed my heart. He encouraged me to open my mouth in social prayer; he taught me the advantage of Christian converse; he put me upon an attempt to make my profession more public, and to venture to speak for God. From him, or rather from the Lord by his means, I received an increase of knowledge; my conceptions became clearer and more evangelical.[1] [2]

Thank you, Heavenly Father, for those people you have graciously sent into my life from time to time, whose spiritual influence has been positive and significant. I pray that I would be such a person to others. Thank you too, that in your sovereign love, you bless our lives with tokens of encouragement and help along the way.

1 From *The Life of Rev. John Newton.*

2 John Newton's experience of conversion was slow, steady and gradual, and by no means what we might call a "road to Damascus" change of heart. His pathway to a lasting experience of faith and sanctification was littered with setbacks and times of stagnation. It is therefore greatly to his credit that he persevered and eventually came to a deep knowledge of grace. His life stands as a testimony to God's faithfulness and unrelenting interest in his children. (See Footnote 1, January 11th.)

April 14th

Now know I that the Lord saveth his anointed; he will hear him from his holy heaven with the saving strength of his right hand

(Psalm 20:6 KJV)

I began to understand the security of the covenant of grace, and to expect to be preserved, not by my own power and holiness, but by the mighty power and promise of God, through faith in an unchangeable Saviour.[1]

O Lord! Deliver me from any futile thoughts of self-reliance, especially when it comes to salvation and eternal life. Help me to stand on your promises, and those alone. I have no other argument.

1 From *The Life of Rev. John Newton*.

April 15th

Our Lord Jesus, that great Shepherd of the sheep

(Hebrews 13:20)

The Redeemer of sinners must be mighty; he must have a personal dignity to stamp such a value upon his undertakings, so that thereby God may appear just, as well as merciful, in justifying the ungodly for his sake; and he must be all-sufficient to bless, and almighty to protect, those who come unto him for safety and life. Such a one is our Shepherd. This is he of whom we, through grace, are enabled to say, we are his people and the sheep of his pastures. We are his by every tie and right; he made us, he redeemed us, he reclaimed us from the hand of our enemies, and we are his by our own voluntary surrender of ourselves; for though we once slighted, despised, and opposed him, he made us willing in the day of his power: he knocked at the door of our hearts; but we (at least I) barred and fastened it against him as much and as long as possible. But when he revealed his love, we could stand out no longer. Like sheep, we are weak, destitute, defenceless, prone to wander, unable to return, and always surrounded with wolves. But all is made up in the fullness, ability, wisdom, compassion, care, and faithfulness of our great Shepherd. He guides, protects, feeds, heals, and restores, and will be our guide and our God, even until death. Then he will meet us, receive us, and present us unto himself, and we shall be near him, and like him, and with him for ever.[1]

What a wonderful description, Lord Jesus, of my plight and your plan! The sinner and the Shepherd meet! Glue these words to my heart and soul, I pray.

1 From *Cardiphonia: or, The Utterance of the Heart in the Course of a Real Correspondence, Volume One.*

April 16th

WHO IS A GOD LIKE UNTO THEE, THAT PARDONETH INIQUITY, AND PASSETH BY THE TRANSGRESSION OF THE REMNANT OF HIS HERITAGE? HE RETAINETH NOT HIS ANGER FOR EVER, BECAUSE HE DELIGHTETH IN MERCY

(Micah 7:18 KJV)

How wonderful is the patience of God towards sinful men! In him they live, and move, and have their being; and if he were to withdraw his support for a single moment, they must perish. He maintains their lives, guards their persons, supplies their wants, while they employ the powers and faculties they receive from him in a settled course of opposition to his will. They trample upon his laws, affront his government, and despise his grace; yet he still spares. To silence all his adversaries in but a moment, would require no extraordinary assertion of his power; but his forbearance towards them manifests his glory, and gives us cause to say, Who is a God like unto thee?[1]

Lord God, just as you are patient with me, I pray that you would exercise similar restraint towards those members of my family, and my friends, who do not yet know you as their loving Saviour. I pray for your "forbearance towards them" until the day comes when they turn to you.

1 From *Cardiphonia: or, The Utterance of the Heart in the Course of a Real Correspondence, Volume One.*

APRIL 17TH

WHERE THE SPIRIT OF THE LORD IS, THERE IS LIBERTY

(2 Corinthians 3:17 KJV)

Mr. Newton went to supply a destitute congregation at Bolton – as he says, "to assist the poor forsake flock at Bolton."[1] "I spent the Sabbath comfortable amongst them, through the Lord's tender mercy. Though unbelief pressed me sore at times, I was favoured with freedom, and found acceptance."[2]

A straightforward prayer today, Lord, for those who will be preaching this Sunday, whether in their own church or as a guest elsewhere. May they too, under your hand, find freedom and acceptance. Bless them, and bless too, those who will receive their messages, with open hearts and ears.

1 Lancashire, north-west England.

2 From *John Newton of Olney and St Mary Woolnoth. An Autobiography and Narrative.*

April 18th

What has been will be again, what has been done will be done again; there is nothing new under the sun

(Ecclesiastes 1:9)

The last entry in Newton's Journal, when The African came back safely to Liverpool in the year 1754, was a Latin phrase, Soli Deo Gloria, which means Give all the Glory to God. To us there can be no thanks for a voyage which enslaved men, women and children, but at that time only a few English Quakers condemned slavery. To other folk it seemed right to thank God for the safe return of the ship and the success of the trading. A year later one of the English bishops preached a sermon against slavery and the Quakers again warned their members – as they had done twenty-eight years earlier – that keeping slaves was, "not a commendable or allowed practice". Later they disowned any of their members who still had slaves. But the great majority of English people had never heard of these protests. They were glad to have such good things as sugar and tobacco and cotton for clothes and they never thought about the slaves who produced these crops.[1]

Lord, how lovely it would be if slave-trading had vanished entirely. Yet, there is still so much work to be done. I pray your blessing upon groups and businesses engaged in promoting anti-human trafficking, fairer trading, decent pay-packets, and so on. As they campaign on behalf of the poor and downtrodden, give strength to their efforts. Alert your church to its responsibilities and help it always to find its voice.

1 From Bernard Martin, *John Newton and the Slave Trade*, London: Longmans, Green and Co., Ltd., 961.

April 19th

The Spirit of the Lord is on me, because he has anointed me to proclaim good news to the poor. He has sent me to proclaim freedom for the prisoners and recovery of sight for the blind, to set the oppressed free

(Luke 4:18)

John Newton… joined H.M. Customs Service. He was made what was called a Tide Surveyor at Liverpool. He had an office and a staff or more than fifty men under him and a fine six-oared boat with a coxswain to row about the river and visit ships entering the port. He had to search them for smuggled goods… Newton tried to catch smugglers, and the records show that he had some successes… About the same time a young lawyer, named Granville Sharp,[1] rescued a… slave in the streets of London. This slave had been badly knocked about by his master until he was useless for work and so had been abandoned. Sharp looked after him until he was cured and found him a job as a messenger. After two years the slave's former master saw him in a street, seized him and sold him for £30 to a planter who meant to ship him to Jamaica. Sharp appealed to the Lord Mayor and got the slave set free.[2]

God of mercy, look with pity upon those who are modern-day captives and slaves; those still being captured and tricked into horrific situations. Look too upon their captors. May justice prevail.

1 1735–1813. The son of a clergyman and one of the first English campaigners against the slave trade. He was a social activist engaged in a number of political campaigns. Sharp vigorously promoted the idea of repatriation for African slaves, and was chairman of The Society for Effecting the Abolition of the Slave Trade.

2 From *John Newton and the Slave Trade.*

April 20th

Jesus said, "Father, forgive them, for they do not know what they are doing"

(Luke 23:34)

"Father, forgive," the Saviour said
"They know not what they do";
His heart was moved when thus He prayed
For me, my friends, and you.

He saw, that as the Jews abused
And crucified His flesh,
So He, by us, would be refused,
And crucified afresh.

We knew not what a law we broke,
How holy, just and pure!
Nor what a God we durst provoke,
But thought ourselves secure.

But Jesus all our guilt foresaw,
And shed His precious blood
To satisfy the holy law,
And make our peace with God.

My sin, dear Saviour, made Thee bleed,
Yet didst Thou pray for me!
I knew not what I did, indeed,
When ignorant of Thee.[1]

God of mercy, this hymn is my prayer. It is the prayer of every sinner – sinners who go to church, sinners who don't, and sinners who, even nowadays, trade in the lives of their fellow human beings. We're all seeking the same Saviour.

1 From http://www.traditionalmusic.co.uk/john-newton/pdf/father-forgive-the-savior-said

April 21st

I will have mercy on whom I will have mercy, and I will have compassion on whom I will have compassion

(Exodus 33:19)

Sometimes… there are striking instances of [God's] displeasure against sin. When such events take place, immediately upon a public and premeditated contempt offered to Him that sitteth in the heavens, I own they remind me of the danger of standing, if I may so speak, in the Lord's way: for though his long-suffering is astonishing, and many dare him to his face daily, with seeming impunity, yet he sometimes strikes an awful and unexpected blow, and gives an illustration of that solemn word, "Whoever hardened himself against the Lord and prospered?" But who am I to make the observation? I ought to do it with the deepest humiliation, remembering that I once stood (according to my years and ability) in the foremost rank of his avowed opposers; and with a determined and unwearied enmity, renounced, defiled, and blasphemed him. "But he will have mercy on whom he will have mercy;" and therefore I was spared, and reserved to speak of his goodness.[1 2]

Lord, I sometimes wonder if I have even begun to plumb the depths of your mercy. Forgive me for those times when I begin to think my sins may be beyond the reach of your compassion, when any such thoughts must distress you, such is the magnitude of your heart. Your grace is sufficient.

1 From *Cardiphonia: or, The Utterance of the Heart in the Course of a Real Correspondence, Volume One.*

2 This excerpt is yet another example of John Newton's humility of heart, and his insistence on preaching to himself long before he preached to others. He was, as we have observed previously, acutely aware of his own sins and his corresponding need of grace.

APRIL 22ND

NO ONE CAN FATHOM WHAT GOD HAS DONE FROM BEGINNING TO END

(Ecclesiastes 3:11)

Many have puzzled themselves about the origin of evil. I observe there is evil, and that there is a way to escape it, and there I begin and end.[1]

God of mystery, many are the things I cannot understand. Teach me, I pray, the value of saying "I do not know". Let my heart be content today, in the knowledge that you know all things. That will suffice.

1 From *John Newton: Sailor, Preacher, Pastor, and Poet.*

April 23rd

When you pass through the waters, I will be with you; and when you pass through the rivers, they will not sweep over you

(Isaiah 43:2)

My connexions with sea-affairs have often led me to think, that the varieties observable in Christian experience may be properly illustrated from the circumstances of a voyage. Imagine to yourself a number of vessels, at different times, and from different places, bound to the same port; there are some things in which all these would agree – the compass steered by, the port in view, the general rules of navigation, both as to the management of the vessel and determining their astronomical observations, would be the same in all. In other respects they would differ; perhaps no two of them would meet with the same distribution of winds and weather. Some we see set out with a prosperous gale; and when they almost think their passage secured, they are checked by adverse blasts; and, after enduring much hardship and danger, and frequent expectations of shipwreck, they just escape, and reach the desired haven. Others meet the greatest difficulties at first; they put forth in a storm, and are often beaten back; at length their voyage proves favourable, and they enter the port with a rich and abundant entrance. Some are hard beset with cruisers and enemies, and obliged to fight their way through; others meet with little remarkable in their passage. Is it not thus in the spiritual life? All true believers walk by the same rule, and mind the same things; the word of God is their compass; Jesus is both their polar star and their sun of righteousness; their hearts and faces are all set Sion-ward. Thus far they are as one body, animated by one spirit; yet their experience, formed upon those common principles, is far from being uniform. The Lord, in his first call, and his following dispensations, has a regard to the situation, temper, and talents of each, and to the particular services or trials he has appointed them for. Though all are exercised at times, yet some pass through the voyage of life much more smoothly than others. Be he "who walketh upon the wings of the wind, and measures the waters in the hollow of his hand," will not suffer any of whom he has once taken charge to perish in the storms, though for a season, perhaps, many of them are ready to give up hopes.[1]

Almighty God, Heavenly Father, your love surrounds me in each and every circumstance of life. Whatever happens to me today, your love will be all around me. Help me always to trust in that, however the voyage goes.

1 From *The Life of Rev. John Newton*.

April 24th

The grass withers and the flowers fall, but the word of our God endures for ever

(Isaiah 40:8)

I have an imperfect remembrance of an account I read when I was a boy, of an ice-palace, built one winter at Petersburg.[1] The walls, the roof, the floors, the furniture, were all of ice, but finished with taste; and everything that might be expected in a royal palace was to be found there; the ice, while in the state of water, being previously coloured, so that to the eye of all seemed formed of proper materials; but all was cold, useless, and transient. Had the frost continued… the palace might have been standing; but with the returning spring it melted away, like the baseless fabric of a vision. Methinks there should have been one stone in the building, to have retained the inscription Sic transit gloria mundi![2] for no contrivance could exhibit a fitter illustration of the vanity of human life.[3]

Lord of eternity, help me this day to see the bigger picture, to work for the long term, and to take these words to heart.

1 St Petersburg, Russia.
2 From Latin to English: "Thus passes the glory of the world."
3 From *Cardiphonia: or, The Utterance of the Heart in the Course of a Real Correspondence, Volume One.*

April 25th

If the Spirit of him who raised Jesus from the dead is living in you, he who raised Christ from the dead will also give life to your mortal bodies because of his Spirit who lives in you

(Romans 8:11)

I assent to our Lord's declaration, "Without me ye can do nothing;" not only upon the authority of the speaker, but from the same irresistible and experiential evidence, as if he had told me, that I cannot make the sun to shine, or change the course of the seasons. Though my pen and my tongue sometimes move freely, yet the total incapacity and stagnation of thought I labour under at other times, convinces me, that in myself I have not sufficiency to think a good thought; and I believe the case would be the same if that little measure of knowledge and abilities, which I am too prone to look upon as my own, were a thousand times greater than it is. For every new service I stand in need of a new supply, and can bring forth nothing of my supposed store into actual exercise, but by his immediate assistance. His gracious influence is that to those who are best furnished with gifts, which the water is to the mill, or the wind to the ship, without which the whole apparatus is motionless and useless.[1]

Lord Jesus, by your Spirit's grace, please preserve my life from being either motionless or useless.

1 From *Cardiphonia: or, The Utterance of the Heart in the Course of a Real Correspondence, Volume One.*

April 26th

Return to your God; maintain love and justice, and wait for your God always

(Hosea 12:6)

If believers in Jesus, however unworthy in themselves, are the temples of the Holy Ghost; if the Lord lives, dwells, and walks in them; if he is their life and their light; if he has promised to guide them with his eye, and to work in them to will and to do of his own good pleasure; methinks… that line in the hymn, "Help I every moment need",[1] is not a hypocritical expression, but strictly and eternally true, not only in great emergencies, but in our smoother hours, and most familiar paths. This gracious assistance is afforded in a way imperceptible to ourselves, to hide pride from us, and to prevent us from being indolent and careless with respect to the use of appointed means; and it would be likewise more abundantly, and perhaps more sensibly afforded, were our spirits more simple in waiting upon the Lord.[2]

Abide with me, gracious God. Today and every day.

1 From the hymn "Son of God, Thy Blessing Grant".
2 From *Cardiphonia: or, The Utterance of the Heart in the Course of a Real Correspondence, Volume One.*

April 27th

One thing I ask from the Lord

(Psalm 27:4)

I hope your soul prospers, that the Lord comforts, refreshes, and strengthens you in your inner man and your outward labours. I hope the house you have built to His name is filled with His glory. Happy they that know the grace of our Lord Jesus Christ; but happy above all others are those who receive appointment and power to proclaim this grace to poor sinners, and who feel the Lord confirming their word by signs following. To be thus engaged among a few faithful, lively people, to dispose all my faculties, studies, and time to this service, is the one thing that I continually desire of the Lord, and which I think I could, without hesitation, prefer to the honours and possessions of a lord or a prince.[1]

Lord of my life, if I could ask one thing of you, what might that be? Speak to me today, I pray, and let that one priority rise to the surface of my mind. Blend my will with yours. Help me to know your voice.

1 From *John Newton of Olney and St Mary Woolnoth. An Autobiography and Narrative.*

April 28th

Thou fool, this night thy soul shall be required of thee: then whose shall those things be?

(Luke 12:20 KJV)

What a poor acquisition to be what is usually called a thriving man for a few years, and then to drop unawares into an unknown eternity! What a contrast between living today in affluence and pleasure, regardless of that great God who has made us, and tomorrow, perhaps, to be summoned away to appear, naked and alone, before His tribunal, to give account what we have made of the talent so long entrusted to us!… I have tried both ways, and find that religion – I mean the true inward religion which is so generally scorned and opposed – does not destroy, but greatly heightens the relish of temporal things. It teaches me to live comfortably here, as well as enables me to look with comfort beyond the grave. In this way I possess peace, which in every other way I sought in vain.[1]

God of eternity, once again I pray for those known to me whose focus in life has been everything except spiritual matters, and the welfare of their souls. In your mercy, Lord, speak to them about such things, before it is too late. My friends and family, my nearest and dearest: Lord, I come to you on their behalf.

1 From *John Newton of Olney and St Mary Woolnoth. An Autobiography and Narrative.*

April 29th

God saw all that he had made, and it was very good

(Genesis 1:31)

In writing to his friend… Mr. Newton says, "I have lately been a journey into Yorkshire. That is a flourishing country indeed, like Eden, the garden of the Lord, watered on every side by the streams of the gospel. There the voice of the turtle is heard in all quarters, and multitudes rejoice in the light. I have a pretty large acquaintance there among various denominations, who, though they differ in some lower things, are all agreed to exalt Jesus and His salvation. I do not mean that the truth is preached in every church and meeting throughout the county, but in many – perhaps in more, proportionately, than in any other part of the land, and with greater effect, both as to numbers and as to the depth of the work in particular persons. It is refreshing to go from place to place and find the same fruits of love, joy, and peace.[1]

Thank you, Creator God, for a beautiful world. Thank you for county after county, and for country after country, where your handiwork is on display. Bless those who work and campaign for the betterment and care of this planet.

1 From *John Newton of Olney and St Mary Woolnoth. An Autobiography and Narrative.*

April 30th

When he comes, he will convict the world concerning sin

(John 16:8 ESV)

Just exactly when Newton realised that slavery was wrong is not known. Looking back in his old age, he said that while he was a Trader in Africa and at sea he never had any thought that what he was doing was wrong, nor did any friend ever suggest such a thing to him. He said that some part of his work as a slave ship captain was "disagreeable" and that when he gave it up and became a custom's officer he was glad to have done with chains and shackles and such appurtenances of the slave trade, but this does not mean that he thought the trade was wicked. At some time later he changed his mind completely and came to see that it was absolutely wrong and to hate his own part in it.[1]

Lord, how easy it can be to believe that what we are doing is the right thing – even in the name of Christ – when it can sometimes be nothing of the sort. Forgive me, Lord, those ways of mine that have more to do with ignorance and culture than authentic spirituality. Gracious Holy Spirit, thank you for that special blessing of conviction and revelation, whereby your light shines into my heart. Come to my heart today.

1 From *John Newton and the Slave Trade.*

May 1st

A good person leaves an inheritance

(Proverbs 13:22)

We are unwilling to believe that the name of John Newton has lost its charm, or that the Christian public has forgotten his writings. There are those, we are sure, to whom his memory is still dear, and who, in spite of various attractions elsewhere, yet love to linger over the pages which provide wise and pleasant things which flowed from his prolific pen.[1]

Thank you, Lord, for those whose legacy in my life is good, and lasting. Help me, I pray, to invest in the lives of others: with prayer and a Christ-like influence.

1 From *John Newton of Olney and St Mary Woolnoth. An Autobiography and Narrative* (Foreword).

May 2nd

Is not this the fast that I choose: to loose the bonds of wickedness, to undo the straps of the yoke, to let the oppressed go free, and to break every yoke?

(Isaiah 58:6 ESV)

We have [John Newton's] views on fasting. After speaking generally of his reasonableness and Scriptural authority, he concludes with these remarks: "Upon the whole I would not confine myself to a fast absolutely of such a determined number of hours, which often degenerate into superstition; I would rather habituate myself to a constant and orderly abstemiousness and moderation in the enjoyment of God's temporal blessings. Yet at some times, when most agreeable to my temper, frame, and opportunities, in order to be perfecting myself in this mastery over the fleshly appetites, and to keep a sense of dependence upon God's bounty and the free grace of the Saviour, and the just forfeiture I have often made of the commonest of his favours, I will look upon fasting as amongst the means of grace and improvement which I enjoy, and in some measure or manner as a duty to be frequently observed. And for the most part I dare say I should find a profit in setting apart one day in every week for this purpose."[1] [2]

God of law, God of grace, help me, I pray, to find a balance between observing the requirements of Scripture yet living within a spirit of liberty. Help me to avoid Phariseeism and legalism, while at the same time honouring that which is written in your word.

1 From *John Newton of Olney and St Mary Woolnoth. An Autobiography and Narrative.*

2 John Newton, in keeping with his entire character and generosity of spirit, was at pains to preserve Christian unity by looking for that which united believers, for the gospel's sake. He would not, of course, overlook heresy or doctrinal error, but on what we might call "lower" matters, Newton was unfailingly prepared to make allowances. He was never so arrogant as to assume that he had any personal monopoly whatever on Christian truth.

May 3rd

Our struggle is not against flesh and blood, but against the rulers, against the authorities, against the powers of this dark world and against the spiritual forces of evil

(Ephesians 6:12)

Though there is a principle of consciousness, and a determination of the will sufficient to denominate our thoughts and performances our own, yet I believe mankind in general are more under an invisible agency than they apprehend. The Lord, immediately from himself, and perhaps by the ministry of his holy angels, guides, prompts, restrains, or warns his people. So there undoubtedly is what I may call a black inspiration, the influence of the evil spirits who work in the hearts of the disobedient, and not only excite their wills, but assist their faculties, and qualify as well as incline them to be more assiduously wicked, and more extensively mischievous, than they could be of themselves. I consider Voltaire, for instance, and many writers of the same stamp, to be little more than secretaries and amanuenses of one who has unspeakably more wit and adroitness in promoting infidelity and immorality, than they themselves can justly pretend to. They have, for a while, the credit (if I may so call it) of the fund from whence they draw; but the world little imagines who is the real and original author of that philosophy and poetry, of those fine terms and uprightly inventions, which are so generally admired. Perhaps many now applauded for their genius, would have been comparatively dolts, had they not been engaged in a cause which Satan had so much interest in supporting.[1]

Lord Jesus, the truth of the matter is, I haven't a hope of living the Christian life without your protection and enabling grace. This is a daily battle, and I need all the spiritual help there is, lest I stumble and fall. Temptations are all around: please keep me steadfast, wise, and strong.

1 From *Cardiphonia: or, The Utterance of the Heart in the Course of a Real Correspondence, Volume One.*

May 4th

[Zacchaeus] ran ahead and climbed a sycamore-fig tree to see him, since Jesus was coming that way

(Luke 19:4)

Zaccheus climbed the tree,
And thought himself unknown;
But how surprised was he
When Jesus called him down!
The Lord beheld him, though concealed,
And by a word his pow'r revealed.

Thus where the gospel's preached,
And sinners come to hear;
The hearts of some are reached
Before they are aware:
The word directly speaks to them,
And seems to point them out by name.

'Tis curiosity
Oft brings them in the way,
Only the man to see,
And hear what he can say;
But how the sinner starts to find
The preacher knows his inmost mind.

While thus distressing pain
And sorrow fills his heart,
He hears a voice again,
That bids his fears depart;
Then like Zaccheus he is blest,
And Jesus deigns to be his guest.[1 2]

Lord Jesus, you seek and save.

1 From *Olney Hymns* (1779).
2 Written by John Newton in 1779..

May 5th

Freely you have received; freely give

(Matthew 10:8)

The vast satisfaction of mind I possess makes me generally desirous to impart the same to everyone, but chiefly to my best friends, and for this reason I have enjoined it as a rule to myself never to write a letter when I have any knowledge or intimacy without inserting a few lines that may either tend to the benefit of my correspondent, or to the honour of the Divine goodness and mercy that has been pleased to make a vile apostate an example of His patience and an instrument of His praise.[1 2]

Help me, Lord, never to be reluctant to share any of the blessings you bestow upon my life. Show me today what I might be able to impart to someone I meet – an encouraging word, maybe. Let me be grateful for blessings received, but always willing to pass them along.

1 John Newton was a prolific letter writer, and exercised a unique ministry of pastoral care and counsel in this way. His correspondents included a wide range of people from all walks of life.

2 From *John Newton of Olney and St Mary Woolnoth. An Autobiography and Narrative.*

May 6th

Moses said to them, "It is the bread the Lord has given you to eat. This is what the Lord has commanded: 'Everyone is to gather as much as they need. Take an omer for each person you have in your tent.'" The Israelites did as they were told; some gathered much, some little. And when they measured it by the omer, the one who gathered much did not have too much, and the one who gathered little did not have too little. Everyone had gathered just as much as they needed. Then Moses said to them, "No one is to keep any of it until morning"

(Exodus 16:15–19)

Moses, when speaking of the methods the Lord used to humble Israel, mentions his feeding them with manna, as one method. I could not understand this for a time. I thought they were rather in danger of being proud, when they saw themselves provided for in such an extraordinary way – but the manna would not keep, they could not hoard it up; and were therefore in a state of absolute dependence from day to day: this appointment was well suited to humble them. Thus it is with us in spirituals. We should be better pleased, perhaps, to be set up with a stock or sufficiency at once, such an inherent portion of wisdom and power, as we might depend upon, at least for common occasions, without being constrained by a sense of indigence, to have continual recourse to the Lord for everything we want. But his way is best. His own glory is most displayed, and our own safety best secured, by keeping us quite poor and empty in ourselves, and by supplying us from one minute to another, according to our need. This, if anything, will prevent boasting, and keep a sense of gratitude awake in our hearts. This is well adapted to quicken us to prayer, and furnishes us with a thousand occasions for praise, which would otherwise escape our notice.[1]

Thank you, God my Provider, for daily blessings. Thank you too, for the important principles outlined here. Grant me faith to trust you for today, one day at a time, and in doing so, to prove you faithful.

1 From *Cardiphonia: or, The Utterance of the Heart in the Course of a Real Correspondence, Volume One.*

May 7th

THE BOUNDARY LINES HAVE FALLEN FOR ME IN PLEASANT PLACES

(Psalm 16:6)

When at London, I lived at the fountain-head, as it were, for spiritual advantages. When I was in Kent it was very different; yet I found some serious[1] persons there: but the fine variegated woodland country afforded me advantages of another kind. Most of my time, at least some hours every day, I passed in retirement, when the weather was fair; sometimes in the thickest woods, sometimes on the highest hills, where almost every stop varied the prospect… The country between Rochester and Maidstone, bordering upon the Medway,[2] was well suited to the turn of my mind; and were I to go over it now, I could point to many a place where I remember to have either earnestly sought, or happily found, the Lord's comfortable presence with my soul.[3 4]

Lord, guide me this day so that I am in the right place at the right time, so that my usefulness in your service is not hindered. I pray today for anyone who feels as though they are in the wrong place; anyone who has a sense of unease about where they are in life, literally or metaphorically. Bless us all with your guidance.

1 Thoughtful, not humourless.

2 All in the county of Kent, south-east England.

3 John Newton became well known in Christian circles, and he was often the guest of friends in different parts of the country, sometimes as a visiting preacher, but at other times as a visitor. We sense in this excerpt his very real experience of daily communion with God, wherever he happened to be. Having travelled the world in the course of his time aboard ships, it seemed geography was of little importance to him, as long as he was where he felt God wanted him to be.

4 From *The Life of the Rev. John Newton*.

May 8th

You will be blessed in the city and blessed in the country

(Deuteronomy 28:3)

It has been my custom, for many years, to perform my devotional exercises sub die,[1] when I have opportunity; and I always find… rural scenes have some tendency both to refresh and to compose my spirits. A beautiful diversified prospect gladdens my heart. When I am withdrawn from the noise and petty works of men, I consider myself as in the great temple which the Lord has built for his own honour.[2]

Lord, teach me that habit of praying wherever I might be. Help me to realize your gracious presence in every circumstance of life. You have promised never to leave me, so I believe you to be there; heighten my senses to appreciate the fact that you are present each and every moment.

1 The literal translation of this phrase, from Latin to English, is "under the". In context, then, John Newton may be saying something like "wherever I am" or "in any situation". In other words, he was not dependent upon, say, a church building or a fixed location for his devotional life, nor any set form of service.

2 From *The Life of the Rev. John Newton*.

May 9th

WHO IS SUFFICIENT FOR THESE THINGS?

(2 Corinthians 2:16 KJV)

The Greek word for sufficient here used has two or three significations in the New Testament – Matthew 3:11 – Luke 22:38; Acts 20:37; Luke 23:9 – 2 Timothy 2:2. In this place the question may be considered as twofold: Who is worthy to bear the gospel message? or, Who is able to dispense it? Well may each be asked with respect to the best of men. Lord what can I answer to either?[1]

Lord, the truth of the matter is, no one is worthy! Likewise, no one can dispense the gospel message; no one, that is, by virtue of their own merit. However, your enabling grace imparts such worthiness and ability. Keep me aware of that, Lord: this is your calling and your gifting – but my unmerited privilege and honour.

1 From *Ministry on my mind.*

May 10th

THE LOVE OF MONEY IS THE ROOT OF ALL EVIL: WHICH WHILE SOME COVETED AFTER, THEY HAVE ERRED FROM THE FAITH, AND PIERCED THEMSELVES THROUGH WITH MANY SORROWS

(1 Timothy 6:10 KJV)

During the first week of his service [as a Tide Surveyor], Newton made a seizure. He discovered aboard a ship goods – chiefly tobacco and coffee, valued at £1 2" 3'.[1] – over and above the Captain's declaration. They were "condemned" in a special court of law, and half their value awarded to Newton. Such seizures were not made frequently, however, and there are only twelve credited to "J. Newton Esq" in The Register of Seizures of H.M. Customs Department during his nine years' service. Married men in their early thirties are often anxious to increase their income. A week after Newton began his job he wrote in his diary: "Pretty much engag'd in business today tho not so hurrying a kind as last week; began to reap some of the profits of my new office and to my grief and surprise found too much of the love of money, which is the root of all evil, spring up in my heart."[2 3]

Thank you, Lord, for the money you have given me. Thank you for my income. Protect my heart this day, I pray, from greed, envy, and avarice. I am richer than some, and poorer than others. Give me a grateful heart that counts its blessings.

1 Pre-decimal British currency: One pound, two shillings and three pence.

2 From *An Ancient Mariner*.

3 Once again, we are privy to an insight into the sensitive heart and mind of John Newton. His was quite a unique sensitivity to sin and temptation, emanating from his close daily walk with the Holy Spirit.

May 11th

This is how you can show your love to me: everywhere we go, say of me, "He is my brother"

(Genesis 20:13)

Newton wrote a little book, Thoughts Upon the African Slave Trade, which denounced slavery in a cool way, without abusing anyone.[1] He wrote simply of what he had seen. He admitted frankly that there were some sides of slavery of which he had not much experience. But what he recalled from memory was sufficient. All through the eighteenth century there was great cruelty in England – cruel punishments for criminals, pleasure in watching the antics of lunatics, and many sports in which rich and poor alike delighted in seeing animals suffer – so that it is not surprising that many Englishmen could feel no pity for black men on the other side of the world. But Newton's book was effective with those who were capable of feeling. It made the reader see what slavery was like.[2]

O Lord, forgive me when I have been cold-hearted towards my fellow human beings – unkind or thoughtless. Grant me a heart that will love, then love again, and love where love is not returned.

1 Some Abolitionists went too far in what they said, speaking angrily and personally about their opponents, instead of focusing on the slave trade itself. Newton thought it wiser – and more effective – to abstain from such insults and attacks.

2 From *John Newton and the Slave Trade.*

May 12th

Righteousness exalteth a nation

(Proverbs 14:34 KJV)

In the first half of the 18th century England was in a state of religious and moral decay. For many years the land had been sinking into darkness and paganism. Intemperance and immorality, crime and cruelty were increasingly becoming the characteristics of the age. The National Church was in such a dead condition that instead of being the salt, preserving the nation from corruption, she was only adding to the immorality by weakening the restraints which Christianity imposed upon the lusts of men. The teaching from the pulpit consisted of natural theology and cold morality which were utterly impotent to awaken the Church or to stem the flood of iniquity. If the nation was to be saved the Church would first have to be revived. And this is what took place.[1]

Heavenly Father, I pray for my nation. I pray for its leaders. Hear my prayers today for my home country – the land of my birth or the land in which I live. Have mercy and bestow your blessings.

1 From *Letters of John Newton* (Introduction).

May 13th

God has not forsaken us... He has shown us kindness... He has granted us new life

(Ezra 9:9)

What the arm of flesh could not do the arm of omnipotence accomplished. God was pleased to send a mighty revival which in the course of fifty years transformed the religious and moral life of the land. Although this great awakening was entirely the work of the Holy Spirit yet God used human instruments to effect the change. Some of the leaders of the movement are well known to us, such as George Whitefield and John Wesley. They were the early leaders in the awakening and, because of their widespread labours, overshadowed such eminent contemporaries as William Grimshaw,[1] John Berridge,[2] Daniel Rowlands[3] and William Romaine.[4] As the revival movement spread, a second generation of leaders emerged. Chief among them was John Newton, the once infidel mariner and servant of slaves, who became, through the grace of God, a humble Christian and devoted minister of Christ.[5] [6]

Lord, you revived the spiritual condition of Great Britain in years gone by, by raising up evangelists and preachers. Show Britain your kindness once again by granting new life. Not just Great Britain, though, Lord: each and every nation that once called itself a Christian country, but is now in need of revival. Send your Spirit afresh. In your mercy, do not forsake us.

1 Reverend William Grimshaw (1708–63) of Haworth, Yorkshire, England.

2 Reverend John Berridge (1716–93), Anglican evangelical.

3 Reverend Daniel Rowlands (also Rowland) (c.1711–90), ordained a Church of England clergyman but foremost leader of the Welsh Calvinistic Methodists. (Methodism was not originally a separate denomination, so it was perfectly possible to be an Anglican and a Methodist at the same time.)

4 Reverend William Romaine of Hartlepool (1714–95), County Durham, England.

5 From *Letters of John Newton* (Introduction).

6 Each of the characters referred to was hugely instrumental in facilitating the move of God's Spirit in national revival, but they were charged with fanning the spiritual embers within their own denomination before any flames could spread across the country.

May 14th

THEY ARE PLANTED IN THE HOUSE OF THE LORD; THEY FLOURISH IN THE COURTS OF OUR GOD

(Psalm 92:13 ESV)

I have had an increasing acquaintance in the West Riding of Yorkshire, where the gospel flourishes greatly. This has been a good school to me: I have conversed at large among all parties, without joining any; yet the Lord has enabled me to profit by my mistakes. In brief, I am still a learner, and the Lord still condescends to teach me. I begin at length to see that I have attained but very little; but I trust in him to carry on his own work in my soul, and by all the dispensations of his grace and providence to increase my knowledge of him, and of myself.[1]

Lord of the church, I pray for anyone trying to find the right fellowship to belong to. Guide them by your Spirit, I pray, so that they can find a church that suits them, and where they can best be of service in membership. Help all our churches, Lord, to be inclusive and welcoming.

1 From *The Life of the Rev. John Newton.*

May 15th

The Spirit you received does not make you slaves, so that you live in fear again; rather, the Spirit you received brought about your adoption to sonship. And by him we cry, "*Abba*, Father"

(Romans 8:15)

A spirit of adoption is the spirit of a child. He may displease his father, yet is not afraid of being turned out of doors. The union is not dissolved, though the commerce is. He is not well with his father, therefore must be unhappy, as their interests are inseparable.[1]

My God. My Father.

1 From *John Newton: Sailor, Preacher, Pastor, and Poet.*

May 16th

Godly sorrow brings repentance that leads to salvation and leaves no regret

(2 Corinthians 7:10)

The nature and effects of that unhappy and disgraceful branch of commerce, which has long been maintained on the Coast of Africa, with the sole, and professed design of purchasing our fellow-creatures, in order to supply our West-India islands and the American colonies, when they were ours, with slaves; is now generally understood. So much light has been thrown upon the subject, by many able pens; and so many respectable persons have already engaged to use their utmost influence, for the suppression of a traffic, which contradicts the feelings of humanity; that it is hoped, this stain on our national character will soon be wiped out.[1 2]

Gracious God, my prayer today is for anyone who is feeling remorse and contrition for their past sins and misdeeds. Heavenly Father, reassure them of forgiveness. Guard their hearts and thoughts when the devil would like to heap condemnation into their situation. Reassure them of divine pardon.

1 From *Thoughts Upon the African Slave Trade*.

2 On 25 March 1807, the Abolition of the Slave Trade Act entered the statute books. Nevertheless, although the Act made it illegal to engage in the slave trade throughout the British colonies, trafficking between the Caribbean islands continued, regardless, until 1811 (www.nationalarchives.gov.uk/pathways/blackhistory/rights/abolition.htm).

May 17th

A broken and a contrite heart, O God, thou wilt not despise

(Psalm 51:17 KJV)

If I attempt… to throw my mite into the public stock of information, it is less from an apprehension that my interference is necessary, than from a conviction, that silence, at such a time, and on such an occasion, would, in me, be criminal. If my testimony should not be necessary, or serviceable, yet, perhaps, I am bound, in conscience, to take shame to myself by a public confession, which, however sincere, comes too late to prevent, or repair, the misery and mischief to which I have, formerly, been accessory. I hope it will always be a subject of humiliating reflection to me, that I was, once, an active instrument, in a business at which my heart now shudders.[1] [2]

Heavenly Father, God of grace, I pray you will impress today's Bible text upon the lives of those who have repented of their sins. Teach them, Lord, that the cross is greater than any sin. Bless those who are seeking to depart from wrongdoing and walk uprightly.

1 Once more, we witness the astonishing contrast between the early stages of John Newton's adulthood, and the remainder of his years, transformed by grace from sinner to saint. Likewise, we sense again the testimony of a heart that was constantly aware of such a transformation. Newton revelled in amazing grace, yet never lost his awareness of his daily dependence upon the mercy of God.

2 From *Thoughts Upon the African Slave Trade.*

May 18th

What is mankind that you are mindful of them, human beings that you care for them? You have made them a little lower than the angels

(Psalm 8:4–5)

It is the future promised privilege of believers in Jesus, that they shall be as the angels; and there is a sense in which we should endeavour to be as the angels now. This is intimated to us where we are taught to pray, Thy will be done on earth, as it is in heaven. I have sometimes amused myself with supposing an angel should be appointed to reside awhile upon earth in a human body; not in sinful flesh, like ours, but in a body free from infirmity, and still preserving an unabated sense of his own happiness in the favour of God, and of his unspeakable obligation to his goodness; – and then I have tried to judge, as well as I could, how such an angel would comport himself in such a situation. I know not that I ever enlarged upon the thought, either in preaching or writing… Were I acquainted with this heavenly visitor, I am willing to hope I should greatly reverence him; and, if permitted, be glad in some cases to consult him. In some, but not in all; for I think my fear would be equal to my love. Methinks I could never venture to open my heart freely to him, and unfold my numberless complaints and infirmities; for, as he could have no experience of the like things himself, I should suppose he would not know how fully to pity me, indeed hardly how to bear with me, if I told him all. Alas! What a preposterous, strange, vile creature should I appear to an angel if he knew me as I am! It is well for me that Jesus was made lower than the angels, and that the human nature he assumed was not distinct from the common nature of mankind, though secured from the common depravity.[1][2]

What an interesting speculation, Lord! All the celestial beings worship you as Almighty God, so, while I may not understand the divine order of such matters, or even realize a fraction of what exists in the heavenlies, I offer my adoration too, humble as it might be. As you receive the homage of angelic choirs this day, Lord God, be pleased to receive mine too. You are my God.

1 From *Cardiphonia: or, The Utterance of the Heart in the Course of a Real Correspondence, Volume One.*

2 This little discourse gives us an insight into John Newton's sense of humour. He used his gentle wit from time to time, to illustrate serious points.

May 19th

FOR WE DO NOT HAVE A HIGH PRIEST WHO IS UNABLE TO FEEL SYMPATHY FOR OUR WEAKNESSES, BUT WE HAVE ONE WHO HAS BEEN TEMPTED IN EVERY WAY, JUST AS WE ARE – YET HE DID NOT SIN

(Hebrews 4:15)

Though he [Jesus] was free from sin himself, yet sin and its consequences, being (for our sakes) charged upon him, he acquired, in the days of his humiliation, an experimental sympathy with his poor people. He knows the effects of sin and temptation upon us, by that knowledge whereby he knows all things; but he knows them likewise in a way more suitable for our comfort and relief, by the sufferings and exercises he passed through for us. Hence arises encouragement. We have not an [sic] high priest who cannot be touched with a feeling of our infirmities, but was in all points tempted even as we are. When I add to this, the consideration of his power, promises, and grace, and that he is exalted on purpose to pity, relieve, and save, I gather courage. With him I dare be free, and am not sorry, but glad, that he knows me perfectly, that not a thought of my heart is hidden from him. For without this infinite and exact knowledge of my disease, how could he effectually administer to my cure?[1]

Thank you, Heavenly Father, for that unique tenet of Christianity: God seeking sinners, God taking the initiative to reach a fallen world. Thank you, Lord, that this glorious fact distinguishes the Christian faith from any other: Jesus came down!

1 From *Cardiphonia: or, The Utterance of the Heart in the Course of a Real Correspondence, Volume One.*

May 20th

First of all, then, I urge that supplications, prayers, intercessions, and thanksgivings be made for all people, for kings and all who are in high positions, that we may lead a peaceful and quiet life, godly and dignified in every way

(1 Timothy 2:1–2 ESV)

The Righteous Lord loveth Righteousness, and he has engaged to plead the cause, and vindicate the wrongs of the oppressed. It is righteousness that exalteth a nation; and wickedness is the prudent reproach, and will, sooner or later, unless repentance intervene, prove the ruin of any people. Perhaps what I have said of myself may be applicable to the nation at large. The Slave Trade was always unjustifiable; but inattention and interest prevented, for a time, the evil from being perceived. It is otherwise at present; the mischiefs and evils, commended with it, have been, of late years, represented with such undeniable evidence, and are now so generally known, that I suppose there is hardly an objection can be made, to the wish of thousands, perhaps of millions, for the suppression of this Trade, but upon the ground of political expedience. Tho' I were even sure, that a principal branch of the public revenue depended upon the African Trade (which, I apprehend, is far from being the case), if I had access and influence, I should think myself bound to say to Government, to Parliament, and to the Nation, "It is not lawful to put into the Treasury, because it is the price of blood".[1] [2]

Today, Almighty God, I pray for my government. Whatever political allegiances I may have, I bring the leaders of my nation before you in prayer. Help them, Lord, to pursue policies based upon honesty, decency, and integrity.

1 From *Thoughts Upon the African Slave Trade.*

2 John Newton's ambition to influence Parliament was achieved thanks to his friendship with William Wilberforce. For a more detailed analysis of this political collaboration, please visit https://johnnewton.org/Groups/69920/The_John_Newton/archive/The_Complete_Works/Correspondence/William_Wilberforce/William_Wilberforce.aspx

May 21st

The heart of the discerning acquires knowledge, for the ears of the wise seek it out

(Proverbs 18:15)

When… my business would afford me much leisure time, I considered in what manner I should improve it. And… I devoted my life to the prosecution of spiritual knowledge, and resolved to pursue nothing but in subservience to this main design. This resolution divorced me… from the classics and mathematics. My first attempt was to learn so much Greek as would enable me to understand the New Testament and Septuagint; and when I had made some progress in this way, I entered upon Hebrew the following year; and two years afterwards, having surmised some advantages from the Syriac version, I began with that language. You must not think that I have attained, or ever aimed at, a critical skill in any of these: I had no business with them, but as in reference to something else. I never read one classic author in the Greek; I thought it too late in life to take such a round in this language as I had done in the Latin. I only wanted the signification of scriptural words and phrases… In the Hebrew, I can read the historical books and Psalms. With tolerable ease.[1 2]

Lord of my life, here and now I invite you to realign my priorities – those things which I think matter, but may not. Speak quietly to my heart this day and grant me that grace whereby I may move closer to your will for me.

1 From *The Life of the Rev. John Newton.*

2 John Newton was a scholar of rare intelligence, fluent in several languages and a lifelong student, yet always anxious to employ his intelligence in the cause of the gospel. He had little time for academic research that didn't serve this aim.

May 22nd

For since the law has but a shadow of the good things to come instead of the true form of these realities, it can never, by the same sacrifices that are continually offered every year, make perfect those who draw near... in these sacrifices there is a reminder of sins every year. For it is impossible for the blood of bulls and goats to take away sins...We have been sanctified through the offering of the body of Jesus Christ once for all. And every priest stands daily at his service, offering repeatedly the same sacrifices, which can never take away sins. But when Christ had offered for all time a single sacrifice for sins, he sat down at the right hand of God... For by a single offering he has perfected for all time those who are being sanctified

(Hebrews 10:1–4, 10–12, 14 ESV)

Consecrated things under the law were first sprinkled with blood, and then anointed with oil, and thenceforward were no more common. Thus under the gospel, every Christian has been a common vessel, for profane purposes; but when sprinkled and anointed, he becomes separated and consecrated to God.[1]

"He has perfected for all time": what a Saviour!

1 From *The Life of the Rev. John Newton.*

May 23rd

Be sure to fear the Lord and serve him faithfully with all your heart

(1 Samuel 12:24)

As to [an angel's] concernment, all his aims and desires would be to fulfil the will of God. All situations would be alike to him; whether he was commanded, as in the case of Sennacherib, to destroy a mighty army with a stroke; or, as in the case of Hagar, to attend upon a woman, a servant, a slave: both services would be to him equally honourable and important, because he was in both equally pleasing the Lord; which would be his element and his joy, whether he was appointed to guide the reins of empire, or to sweep the streets.[1]

Help me to trust, Heavenly Father, that I am where you want me to be, and doing what you want me to do, according to your will and purpose. If I'm not, then move me! Like the angels in your service, I place myself at your disposal. All I ask is that you confirm this for me.

1 From *Cardiphonia: or, The Utterance of the Heart in the Course of a Real Correspondence, Volume One.*

May 24th

Are not all angels ministering spirits sent to serve those who will inherit salvation?

(Hebrews 1:14)

The will and glory of God being the angel's great view, and having a more lively sense of the realities of an unseen world than we can at present conceive, he would certainly, in the first and chief place, have the success and spread of the glorious gospel at heart. Angels, though not redeemed with blood, yet feel themselves nearly[1] concerned in the work of redemption. They admire its mysteries. We may suppose them well informed in the works of creation and providence. But (unlike too many men, who are satisfied with the knowledge of astronomy, mathematics or history) they search and pry into the counsels of redeeming love, rejoice at the conversion of a sinner, and think themselves well employed to be ministering spirits, to minister to the heirs of salvation. It would therefore be his chief delight to espouse and promote their cause, and to employ all his talents and influences in spreading the savour and knowledge of the name of Jesus, which is the only and effectual means of bringing sinners out of bondage and darkness into the glorious liberty of the sons of God.[2]

May I pray, Lord, to become more like an angel?

1 Closely, intimately.
2 From *Cardiphonia: or, The Utterance of the Heart in the Course of a Real Correspondence, Volume One.*

May 25th

Christ in you, the hope of glory

(Colossians 1:27)

Alas! most gracious Lord, what shall I say? I have nothing to offer for all Thy goodness but new confessions of my guilt. That thou art kind to the unthankful and the evil I am one of the most remarkable instances. Forgive me, I beseech Thee, this year of misspent life, and charge me not with the long abuse of Thy bounty. I owe Thee ten thousand talents, and have nothing to pay, yet I entreat Thee to have patience with me; not for that it will be ever in my power to make any amends by the best I can do, but because my Saviour Jesus Christ, Thy beloved Son, has done and suffered more than sufficient to atone for all my offences, and to supply all my defects. Let me plead his merits.[1] [2]

I have no claim on grace. Christ is all.

1 From *John Newton of Olney and St Mary Woolnoth. An Autobiography and Narrative.*

2 Perhaps one of the secrets of John Newton's spiritual strength lay in his deep awareness of his weakness. This paradox caused him to rely more and more upon his Saviour. As he realized his own condition of helplessness, he leant increasingly upon Christ.

May 26th

The Lord added to the church daily such as should be saved

(Acts 2:47 KJV)

A prodigious multitude of people, so that, besides those who stood in the yard, many hundreds were forced to go away, though the place is supposed to contain five thousand. [The] discourse was suited to the audience – an offer and pressing invitation to the gospel, from Rev. xxi. 6,[1] and with great life and power.[2]

Three prayers, Lord:
Please send converts to my church.
Please grant your ministers and preachers words in season.
Please grant their messages life and power.

1 "He said to me: 'It is done. I am the Alpha and the Omega, the Beginning and the End. To the thirsty I will give water without cost from the spring of the water of life." (*NIV*).

2 From *John Newton of Olney and St Mary Woolnoth. An Autobiography and Narrative* (an extract from John Newton's reflections after he had visited a particular church).

May 27th

Keep this Book of the Law always on your lips; meditate on it day and night, so that you may be careful to do everything written in it

(Joshua 1:8)

I have kept up a course of reading of the best writers in divinity that have come to my hand, in the Latin and English tongues, and some French; for I picked up the French at times while I used the sea. But… I have accustomed myself chiefly to writing, and have not found time to read many books besides the Scriptures. I am the more particular in this account, as my case has been something singular; for in all my literary attempts I have been obliged to strike out my own path, by the light I could acquire from books, as I have not had a teacher or assistant since I was ten years of age.[1 2]

Lord, you have called some people to the ministry of teaching. Bless them, help them, as they apply their knowledge and diligence for the benefit of others. As they seek to help other people better understand the Bible, may they too reap not only intellectual benefits, but spiritual ones too. I pray also for those who have no teachers, or little opportunity of formal education.

1 From *The Life of the Rev. John Newton.*

2 See Footnote 2, May 21st.

May 28th

Another dieth in the bitterness of his soul

(Job 21:25 KJV)

Bitter, indeed, the waters are,
Which in this desert flow;
Though to the eye they promise fair,
They taste of sin and woe.

Of pleasing draughts I once could dream,
But now, awake, I find,
That sin has poisoned every stream,
And left a curse behind.

But there's a wonder-working wood,
I've heard believers say,
Can make these bitter waters good,
And take the curse away.

The cross on which the Saviour died,
And conquered for his saints;
This is the tree, by faith applied,
Which sweetens all complaints.

Thousands have found the blest effect,
Nor longer mourn their lot;
While on his sorrows they reflect,
Their own are all forgot.

When they, by faith, behold the cross,
Though many griefs they meet;
They draw again from every loss,
And find the bitter sweet.[1]

Transforming God, you alone can take that which is bitter and change it to something sweet: our souls, our lives, our relationships, our daily lot. Thank you, Lord. This day, I place my times and my needs in your hands.

1 First published in *Olney Hymns* (1779).

May 29th

Do not love the world or anything in the world. If anyone loves the world, love for the Father is not in them

(1 John 2:15)

From pole to pole let others roam,
And search in vain for bliss;
My soul is satisfied at home,
The Lord my portion is.

Jesus, who on his glorious throne
Rules heav'n and earth and sea;
Is pleased to claim me for his own,
And give himself to me.

His person fixes all my love,
His blood removes my fear;
And while he pleads for me above,
His arm preserves me here.

For him I count as gain each loss,
Disgrace, for him, renown;
Well may I glory in his cross,
While he prepares my crown!

Let worldlings then indulge their boast,
How much they gain or spend!
Their joys must soon give up the ghost,
But mine shall know no end.[1] [2]

Lord, how empty and shallow this world really is! Yet, despite that, how attractive and seductive! Hold my heart in your hands, Lord, lest I should foolishly mistake dross for gold.

1 First published in *Olney Hymns* (1779).

2 Having sailed on a number of voyages, it is possible John Newton found his greatest fulfilment and contentment as an established minister in Olney and London. He refers here, of course, to the spiritual rest of a life in Christ, but may also be alluding to the fact that his travelling days were over.

May 30th

But encourage one another daily, as long as it is called "Today" so that none of you may be hardened by sin's deceitfulness.

(Hebrews 3:13)

In the midst of the hurries and changes of this unsettled state, we glide along swiftly towards an unchangeable world, and shall soon have as little connection with the scenes we are now passing through, as we have with what happened before the flood. All that appears great and interesting in the present life, abstracted from its influence upon her internal character, and our everlasting allotment, will soon be as unreal as the visions of the night. This we know and confess; but though our judgments are convinced, it is seldom our hearts are duly affected by the thought. And while I find it easy to write in this moralising strain, I feel myself disposed to be seriously engaged about trifles, and trifling in the most serious concerns, as if I believed the very contrary. It is with good reason the Lord challenges, as his own prerogative, the full knowledge of the deceitfulness, desperate wickedness, and intent depths of the human heart, which is capable of making even his own people so shamefully inconsistent with themselves, and with their acknowledged principles.[1]

God of truth, help me, I pray, only ever to accept your verdict on matters, regardless of what my heart may whisper to the contrary, and however persuasive those whispers may be. Grant me the humility to submit to your judgments and standards.

1 From *Cardiphonia: or, The Utterance of the Heart in the Course of a Real Correspondence, Volume One.*

May 31st

Much dreaming and many words are meaningless. Therefore fear God

(Ecclesiastes 5:7)

I find that, when I have something agreeable in expectation… my imagination paints and prepares the scene beforehand; hurries me over the intervening space of time, as though it were a useless blank, and anticipates the pleasure I propose. Many of my thoughts of this kind are mere waking dreams; for, perhaps, the opportunity I am eagerly waiting for never happens, but is swallowed up by some unforeseen disappointment; or if not, something from within or without prevents its answering the idea I had formed of it. Nor does my fancy confine itself within the narrow limits of probabilities; it can bust itself as eagerly in ranging after chimeras and impossibilities, and engage my attention to the ideal pursuit of things which are never likely to happen. In these respects my imagination travels with wings; so that if the wildness, the multiplicity, the variety of the phantoms which pass through my mind in the space of a winter's day were known to my fellow-creatures, they would probably deem me, as I am ready to deem myself, but a more sober and harmless kind of lunatic.[1]

Daydreaming, Lord! Flights of fancy that raise my hopes and engage my attention on matters that are neither here nor there! Take my imagination, I pray, so that my hopes, visions, and ambitions are in accordance with your plans for my life. Lead me to invest in heavenly imaginations!

1 From *Cardiphonia: or, The Utterance of the Heart in the Course of a Real Correspondence, Volume One.*

June 1st

Do not be hasty in the laying on of hands

(1 Timothy 5:22)

We often seek to apply cordials when the patient is not prepared for them; and it is the patient's advantage that he cannot take a medicine when prematurely offered.[1]

God whose timing is always perfect, guide me by your Spirit to follow your lead in all matters; in evangelism, in counsel, in praying for healing, whatever the issue might be. This is your work, Lord. Help me to remember that.

1 From *The Life of the Rev. John Newton.*

June 2nd

Let anyone who thinks that he stands take heed lest he fall

(1 Corinthians 10:12 ESV)

There are critical times of danger. After great services, honours, and consolations, we should stand upon our guard. Noah, Lot, David, and Solomon fell in these circumstances. Satan is a footpad. A footpad[1] will not attack a man going to the bank, but in returning with his pocket full of money.[2]

I ask your protection today, Almighty God, on those who are making good headway in their relationship with you. Surround them and protect them, I pray, reminding them always to stay within the shadow of your wings. Help me too, to follow this good advice.

1 A highwayman operating on foot, without a horse.

2 From *John Newton: Sailor, Preacher, Pastor, and Poet.*

June 3rd

I gave you milk, not solid food, for you were not yet ready for it

(1 Corinthians 3:2)

The state of new believers, compared with that of others, is always blessed. If they are born from above, and united to Jesus, they are delivered from condemnation, and are heirs of eternal life, and may therefore well be accounted happy. But I consider now, not their harvest, but their first fruits; not their portion in reversion, but the earnest attainable in this life; not what they shall be in heaven, but what, in an humble attendance upon the Lord, they may be while upon earth. There is even at present a prize of our high calling set before us. It is much to be desired, that we had such a sense of its value as might prompt us so to run that we might obtain.[1]

Father of all, I pray for any new converts in my church, or known to me personally; those young in their faith. There is of course, Lord, a long way ahead of them as their experience of your love matures and develops. However, help them to grow steadily in their understanding, so that their roots form well. Help churches, too, I pray, to carefully and patiently nurture those in their care, not overloading anyone who is not ready.

1 From *Cardiphonia: or, The Utterance of the Heart in the Course of a Real Correspondence*, Volume One.

June 4th

PREACH THE WORD; BE PREPARED IN SEASON AND OUT OF SEASON; CORRECT, REBUKE AND ENCOURAGE – WITH GREAT PATIENCE AND CAREFUL INSTRUCTION

(2 Timothy 4:2)

If a man be informed of the birth of his child, or that his house is on fire, the message takes up his thoughts, and he is seldom much disgusted with the manner in which it is delivered. But what an insuperable bar is the refined taste of many to their profiting by the preaching of the gospel, or even to their hearing it. Though the subject of a discourse be weighty, and some just representation given of the evil of sin, the worth of the soul, and the love of Christ; yet, if there be something amiss in the elocution, language, or manner of the preacher, people of taste must be possessed, in a good measure, of grace likewise, if they can hear him with tolerable patience. And perhaps three-fourths of those who are accounted the most sensible and judicious in the auditory, will remember little about the sermon, but the tone of the voice, the awkwardness of the attitude, the obsolete expressions, and the like; while the poor and simple, not being encumbered with this hurtful accomplishment, receive the message as the Lord's servant, and the truth as the Lord's word, and are comforted and edified.[1] [2]

Lord of the Word, once again I ask for your blessing on all who are faithfully preaching the gospel in churches up and down the land. By the same token, I pray for those of us who receive their messages: help us, Lord, to discern your voice over and above everything else, and not to be distracted by details that are irrelevant. Make us receivers, rather than critics!

1 From *Cardiphonia: or, The Utterance of the Heart in the Course of a Real Correspondence, Volume One.*

2 John Newton lived under the strong conviction that the Christian gospel must connect with the human heart, or else it was worthless. He was frustrated by clergy who preached empty messages that were based more upon show and intellect than conviction, and whose messages carried little weight. Newton had little time for preaching that made no difference to the human condition.

June 5th

... HE HAS GIVEN US HIS VERY GREAT AND PRECIOUS PROMISES, SO THAT THROUGH THEM YOU MAY PARTICIPATE IN THE DIVINE NATURE

(2 Peter 1:4)

Christ has taken our nature into heaven to represent us, and has left us on earth with His nature to represent Him.[1 2]

Lord Jesus, this is a remarkable exchange – the epitome of redemptive grace. Help me to understand it more, so that my gratitude may only ever increase.

1 From *John Newton: Sailor, Preacher, Pastor, and Poet.*

2 We can only imagine the weight of this statement in John Newton's life, given his sensitive awareness of his own sins. He would not have written these words lightly. Likewise, none of us who have participated in the divine exchange will consider this anything but a remarkable declaration of gospel truth.

June 6th

Then Hadad said to Pharaoh, "Let me go, that I may return to my own country." "What have you lacked here that you want to go back to your own country?" Pharaoh asked. "Nothing," Hadad replied, "but do let me go!"

(1 Kings 11:21–22)[1]

In a letter to Mrs. Newton [John Newton's] work as a tide-surveyor is thus described: "My duty is one week to attend the tides, and visit the ships that arrive, and such as are in the river, and the other week to inspect the vessels in the docks, and these alternately the year round. The latter is little more than a sinecure, but the former requires pretty constant attendance both by day and night. I have a good office, with fire and candle, fifty or sixty people under my direction, with a handsome six-oared boat and coxswain to row me about in form." He adds the following particulars, in a letter to his brother-in-law, Mr. Catlett: "Last week I acted as boarding surveyor, that is, going on board ships on their first arrival, some at the rock, some nearer land. The weather was bad, and there were a good many fresh arrivals, so that I entered upon my new office under its worst appearance; but I went through it cheerfully and with pleasure, got no cold, and received no damage. But being obliged to attend tides by night as well as by day, I found myself a little fatigued at the week's end. I have now entered upon my quiet week, which is only to visit and clear the ships in the docks, without going into a boat at all, and have time enough upon my hands. This too is my week of harvest, as the former was my seed-time. When it is finished I may probably let you know the quality of corn one crop produces, for as yet I have only an earnest sheaf. However, I am richer and easier than if I had been a land-waiter, as at first proposed."[2][3]

Heavenly Father, I ask you to guide those who are in one line of work, when they would prefer to be in another; those who appreciate your provision, but lack a deeper sense of conviction. Place your hand upon their lives and lead them into the future you have planned for them.

1 John Newton's years as a Tide Surveyor in Liverpool were rewarding insofar as he thanked God for the provision of secure employment, but somewhat frustrating too as he sought God's will for a line of work that better represented a more fulfilling vocation.

2 From *John Newton of Olney and St Mary Woolnoth. An Autobiography and Narrative.*

3 See March 1st.

June 7th

You strain out a gnat but swallow a camel

(Matthew 23:24)

Went to tea… and was drawn into an unprofitable dispute about baptism. I wish I was able to decline this controversy, for of late I have not been able to hear or say anything new upon the subject, and I find risings of pride and passion often tempting me to sin. I fear I usually forget the main thing, and have my thoughts chiefly taken up with vindicating proud, corrupt, deceitful self. It is not sufficient to be acquitted by my own conscience, but I must aim to appear right in the judgment of others. It were a valuable piece of self-denial to be content to be thought mistaken in some things, without wasting time and words to clear myself, when the opinion can have no bad consequence, and especially amongst people who, I must confess, do more overrate me in some things than mistake me in others.[1]

Lord, forgive me when I stand on a point of theology or doctrine at the expense of fellowship and charity. Forgive me too, I pray, for forgetting the main thing. Likewise, I seek your pardon for those days on which I allow my reputation to take an inappropriate place in my thinking or motivation.

1 From *John Newton of Olney and St Mary Woolnoth. An Autobiography and Narrative.*

June 8th

Then Saul dressed David in his own tunic. He put a coat of armour on him and a bronze helmet on his head. David fastened on his sword over the tunic and tried walking around, because he was not used to them. "I cannot go in these," he said to Saul, "because I am not used to them"

(1 Samuel 17:38–39)

For an old Christian to say to a young one, "Stand in my evidence," is like a man who has with difficulty climbed by a ladder or scaffolding to the top of the house, and cries to one at the bottom, "This is the place for a prospect – come up at a step."[1]

Father God, help me always to respect another's walk with you, even if their steps might not be ones I personally would have taken. Teach me the grace of wise encouragement, but help me to resist imposition or interference!

1 From *The Life of the Rev. John Newton*.

June 9th

Enter through the narrow gate. For wide is the gate and broad is the road that leads to destruction, and many enter through it. But small is the gate and narrow the road that leads to life, and only a few find it

(Matthew 7:13–14)

Destruction's dangerous road
What multitudes pursue!
While that which leads the soul to God,
Is known or sought by few.

Believers enter in
By Christ, the living gate;
But they who will not leave their sin,
Complain it is too strait.

If self must be denied,
And sin forsaken quite;
They rather choose the way that's wide,
And strive to think it right.

Obey the Gospel call,
And enter while you may;
The flock of Christ is always small,
And none are safe but they.

Lord, open sinners' eyes
Their awful state to see
And make them, ere the storm arise,
To Thee for safety flee.[1]

Once again today, Lord, I pray for my friends and loved ones who do not know you as their Saviour. Hear me as I name them before you in prayer.

1 First published in *Olney Hymns* (1779).

June 10th

WHEN TEMPTED, NO ONE SHOULD SAY, "GOD IS TEMPTING ME." FOR GOD CANNOT BE TEMPTED BY EVIL, NOR DOES HE TEMPT ANYONE

(James 1:13)

The word temptation, taken at large, includes every kind of trial. To tempt, is to try or prove. In this sense, it is said, the Lord tempted Abraham, that is, he tried him; for God cannot tempt to evil. He proposed such as an act of obedience to him, as was a test of his faith, love, dependence, and integrity. Thus, all our afflictions, under his gracious management, are appointed to prove, manifest, exercise, and purify the graces of his children. And not afflictions only; prosperity likewise is a state of temptation: and many who have endured sharp sufferings, and came off honourably, have been afterwards greatly hurt and ensnared by prosperity.[1]

Lord, shield my heart this day from all manner of temptation – the obvious and the blatant, as well as that which is more subtle and seductive. Stay close.

1 From *Cardiphonia: or, The Utterance of the Heart in the Course of a Real Correspondence, Volume One.*

June 11th

[Jesus] got up, rebuked the wind and said to the waves, "Quiet! Be still!" Then the wind died down and it was completely calm. He said to his disciples, "Why are you so afraid? Do you still have no faith?" They were terrified and asked each other, "Who is this? Even the wind and the waves obey him!"

(Mark 4:39–41)

Satan's action upon the heart may be illustrated by the action of the wind upon the sea. The sea sometimes appears smooth; but it is always disposed to swell and rage, and to obey the impulse of every storm. Thus the heart may be sometimes quiet; but the wind of temptation will awaken and rouse it in a moment; for it is essential to our depraved nature to be unstable and yielding as the water; and when it is under the impression of the enemy, its violence can only be controlled by him who says to the raging sea, "Be still, and here shall thy proud waves be stayed." The branches of temptation are almost innumerable.[1 2]

Lord of life's storms, I pray your blessing upon anyone who feels vulnerable or frightened today; those who are tempted to give in or sin in some way. Come to their hearts, Lord Jesus.

1 From *Cardiphonia: or, The Utterance of the Heart in the Course of a Real Correspondence, Volume One.*

2 Who better than the Reverend John Newton to employ this illustration? His words carry the authentic ring of someone well-seasoned in nautical matters and experienced in spiritual warfare.

June 12th

THEREFORE LET US NOT PASS JUDGMENT ON ONE ANOTHER ANY LONGER, BUT RATHER DECIDE NEVER TO PUT A STUMBLING BLOCK OR HINDRANCE IN THE WAY OF A BROTHER...THE FAITH THAT YOU HAVE, KEEP BETWEEN YOURSELF AND GOD. BLESSED IS THE ONE WHO HAS NO REASON TO PASS JUDGMENT ON HIMSELF FOR WHAT HE APPROVES

(Romans 14:13, 22 ESV)

Though I still think my infant sprinkling to be a really valid baptism, so far as to render any repetition unnecessary, I dare not pronounce absolutely upon a point wherein so many great and good men have been and are divided. With respect to persons, I look upon neither circumcision nor uncircumcision to be anything, but a new creature. And if my heart does not greatly deceive me, those believers who differ from me in circumstantials are as dear to me as those who agree with me, provided they will join me in this one thing, that they are but circumstantials, and consequently not pretend to enforce them with the same warmth as if they were absolutely essentials... I feel great cause to cry to the Lord for a candid spirit. Though I am apt sometimes to think highly of my Catholicism, I cannot but confess to much bigotry and spiritual pride residing in me. Oh that my censures might be more directed to my own faults![1 2 3]

Thank you, Lord, for my brothers and sisters from other Christian traditions. I pray your blessing upon their witness today.

1 From *John Newton of Olney and St Mary Woolnoth. An Autobiography and Narrative.*

2 John Newton was at pains to minister alongside fellow believers from all denominations, and none. He was anxious to focus on the supremacy of the gospel, regarding secondary matters as issues that, taken out of perspective, could become hindrances to Christian unity.

3 We note once again, the characteristic humility with which John Newton approached ecumenical affairs.

June 13th

Do not merely listen to the word, and so deceive yourselves. Do what it says. Anyone who listens to the word but does not do what it says is like someone who looks at his face in a mirror and, after looking at himself, goes away and immediately forgets what he looks like. But whoever looks intently into the perfect law that gives freedom, and continues in it – not forgetting what they have heard but doing it – they will be blessed in what they do

(James 1:22–25)

A man may be able to call a broom by twenty names, in Latin, Spanish, Dutch, Greek, etc, but my maid, who knows the way to use it, but knows it only by one name, is not far behind him.[1]

Applied theology, Lord – walking the walk as well as talking the talk! So help me, God.

1 From *John Newton of Olney and St Mary Woolnoth. An Autobiography and Narrative.*

June 14th

Boast not thyself of to-morrow; for thou knowest not what a day may bring forth

(Proverbs 27:1 KJV)

Time, with an unwearied hand,
Pushes round the seasons past,
And in life's frail glass, the sand
Sinks apace, not long to last:
Many, well as you or I,
Who last year assembled thus;
In their silent graves now life,
Graves will open soon for us!

Daily sin, and care, and strife,
While the Lord prolongs our breath,
Make it but a dying life,
Or a kind of living death:
Wretched they, and most forlorn,
Who no better portion know;
Better ne'er to have been born,
Than to have our all below.

Happy souls who fear the Lord!
Time is not too swift for you;
When your Saviour gives the word,
Glad you'll bid the world adieu:
Then He'll wipe away your tears,
Near Himself appoint your place;
Swifter fly, ye rolling years,
Lord, we long to see Thy face.[1]

Time, Lord, that precious commodity! Thank you for the time you have given me this day. I give it back to you, in your service. Take my hours, take my days.

1 First published in *Olney Hymns* (1779).

June 15th

My heart is inditing a good matter: I speak of the things which I have made touching the king: my tongue is the pen of a ready writer

(Psalm 45:1 KJV)

To be sure, [John Newton] lived in another age than ours. To him the Christian ministry did not mean one long struggle to compass several lives in one, to hurry from service to service, from address to sermon, from round of visiting to committee, to institute, to club. It meant rather, in that far-off time, the dangerous possibility of living a life lamentably easy and self-pleasing. But for a Newton those liberties only made, day by day, week by week, the long occasion for a measured, while unresting, diligence, as teacher, as visitor, and as the always accessible private friend and counsellor for Christ. They made also frequent opportunity for richly fruitful labour with the pen, not least in a department now almost obsolete, the loving toil of careful, deliberate letter-writing to friends and inquirers of many types.[1 2]

Let it be my privilege, Lord of my life, to follow your leading and guidance moment by moment.

1 From *John Newton: Sailor, Preacher, Pastor, and Poet.*

2 John Newton placed an enormous emphasis upon the importance of pastoral visitation and what we might call informal counselling. Likewise, he was a prolific writer of letters, spending hour upon hour dispensing friendship and Christian counsel in this way.

June 16th

Vanity of vanities, says the Preacher,
vanity of vanities! All is vanity

(Ecclesiastes 1:2 ESV)

I might inscribe vanity of vanity on the history of every day. My life seems such a blank… each page filled with folly and impertinence. I have sinned, and the Lord is withdrawn. How I lost Him I cannot particularly say, but I know by sad experience He is gone, and now I only weep away my time. Yesterday was a cold, unfruitful Sabbath indeed. Made some faint essays at prayer. When shall these heavy, tedious intervals be over? Oh, when shall I be all eye, all ear, all heart, in serving and waiting upon God?[1] [2]

Gracious God, draw alongside those who feel downhearted. Come in grace and mercy to those who have sinned. Warm the hearts of those who feel you to be at a distance. Forgive and restore.

1 From *John Newton of Olney and St Mary Woolnoth. An Autobiography and Narrative.*

2 John Newton was a living example of someone whose pursuit of holiness made him increasingly aware of what we might call his *un*holiness. The closer he came to Christ, the more he despaired of his sinful nature.

June 17th

No good thing will he withhold from them that walk uprightly

(Psalm 84:11 KJV)

[John Newton] speaks of having lately committed to memory some of the most expressive and comprehensive passages of the Greek Testament, and reads Cicero De Officiis[1] and Rollin's Ancient History.[2] Thus conscientiously and sedulously did Mr. Newton prepare himself for that work to which, in spite of all the discouragements he met with, he evidently felt assured that God had called him. To preach the gospel of Christ, to honour to his utmost ability Him whom he had so dishonoured, was the height of his ambition; and though it is evident his preferences were, on the whole, for the Establishment,[3] whether it was here or there was after all a matter of inferior consideration, so long as this, his heart's desire, was accomplished.[4] [5]

God of grace and understanding, my prayers today are for those who feel their lives to be unfulfilled. I ask you to come to them in the midst of any frustration or impatience. Help them not to lose heart.

1 A treatise by Marcus Tullius Cicero (106 BC–43 BC), in which Cicero expounds his thoughts on the best way to live, behave, and observe moral obligations. Cicero was a Roman statesman and philosopher.

2 Charles Rollin (1661–1741), French historian and educator.

3 The Church of England.

4 From *John Newton of Olney and St Mary Woolnoth. An Autobiography and Narrative.*

5 As we shall note in more detail later in this book, John Newton devoted several years to the pursuit of an ordained ministry, which he felt to be his vocation. This was his heart's desire, but he encountered a number of painful rebuttals along the way.

JUNE 18TH

THE LORD SAID, SIMON, SIMON, BEHOLD, SATAN HATH DESIRED TO HAVE YOU, THAT HE MAY SIFT YOU AS WHEAT: BUT I HAVE PRAYED FOR THEE, THAT THY FAITH FAIL NOT

(Luke 22:31–32 KJV)

[Satan] tempts the conscience. By working upon the unbelief of our hearts, and darkening the glory of the gospel, he can hold down the soul to the number, weight, and aggravation of its sins, so that it shall not be able to look up to Jesus, nor draw any comfort from his blood, promises and grace. How many go burdened in this manner, seeking relief from duties, and perhaps spending their strength in things not commanded, though they hear, and perhaps acknowledge the gospel? Nor are the wisest and most established able to withstand his assaults, if the Lord withdraw, and give him leave to employ his power and subtlety unrestrained. The gospel affords sufficient ground for an abiding assurance of hope; nor should we rest unsatisfied without it. However, the possession and preservation of this privilege depends upon the Lord's presence with the soul, and his shielding us from Satan's attacks; for I am persuaded he is able to sift and shake the strongest believer upon earth.[1]

Almighty God, I pray that you would intervene on behalf of those who are enduring powerful temptations this day. Protect them, I ask, and keep them within the boundary of your care. Likewise, Lord, strengthen those who are under spiritual attack, especially if they feel their hearts condemned.

1 From *Cardiphonia: or, The Utterance of the Heart in the Course of a Real Correspondence, Volume One.*

June 19th

Now may the God of peace... equip you with everything good for doing his will, and may he work in us what is pleasing to him

(Hebrews 13:20–21)

[Satan] has likewise temptations suited to the will. Jesus makes his people willing in the day of his power; yet there is a contrary principle remaining within them, of which Satan knows how to avail himself. There are occasions in which he prevails to set self again upon the throne, as Dagon was raised after he had fallen before the ark.[1] How else should any who have tasted that the Lord is gracious, give way to a repining spirit, account his dispensation hard, or his precepts too strict, as to shrink from their observance through the fear of men, or a regard to their worldly interest.[2]

May my will be no longer mine. Turn my will to your will, Lord.

1 1 Samuel 5.

2 From *Cardiphonia: or, The Utterance of the Heart in the Course of a Real Correspondence, Volume One.*

June 20th

I am fearfully and wonderfully made

(Psalm 139:14)

That wonderful power which we call the imagination is, I suppose, rather the medium of the soul's perceptions during its present state of union with the body, than a spiritual faculty, strictly speaking; but it partakes largely of that depravity which sin has brought upon our whole frame, and affords Satan an avenue for assaulting us with the most terrifying, if not the most dangerous of his temptations. At the best, we have but an indifferent command over it. We cannot, by an act of our own will, exclude a thousand painful, wild, inconsistent, and hurtful ideas, which are ever ready to intrude themselves upon our minds: and a slight alteration in the animal system, in the motion of the blood or nervous spirits, is sufficient to withdraw it wholly from our dominion, and to leave us like a city without walls or gates, exposed to the incursion of our enemy. We are fearfully and wonderfully made; and, with all our boasted knowledge of other things, can form no conception of what is so vastly interesting to us, the mysterious connexion between soul and body, and the manner in which they are mutually affected by each other.[1] [2]

Creator God, the more I know about myself, the less I understand! The mysteries of imagination, the connections between body and soul, my holistic nature. I commit myself to your hands this day: my complexities, my powers, and my weaknesses. God of all I am, hold me with all that you are.

1 From *Cardiphonia: or, The Utterance of the Heart in the Course of a Real Correspondence, Volume One.*

2 John Newton reveals himself here to be a marvellous student of human nature, gifted with extraordinary insight, spiritual awareness, and a rare eloquence, which enabled him to articulate such thoughts of Christian philosophy.

June 21st

In front of the mercy seat

(Leviticus 16:14 ESV)

Cheer up, my soul, there is a mercy seat,
Sprinkled with blood, where Jesus answers prayer;
There humbly cast thyself beneath his feet,
For never needy sinner perished there.

Lord, I am come! Thy promise is my plea,
Without thy word I durst not venture nigh;
But thou hast called the burdened soul to thee,
A weary burdened soul, O Lord, am I!

Bowed down beneath a heavy load of sin,
By Satan's fierce temptations sorely pressed,
Beset without, and full of fears within,
Trembling and faint I come to thee for rest.

Be thou my refuge, Lord, my hiding-place,
I know no force can tear me from thy side;
Unmoved I then may all accusers face,
And answer every charge, with "Jesus died."

Yes! Thou didst weep, and bleed, and groan, and die!
Well thou hast known what fierce temptation means,
Such was my love! And now enthroned on high,
The same compassion in thy bosom reigns.

Lord, give me faith – he hears! What grace is this!
Dry up thy tears, my soul, and cease to grieve;
He shows me what he did, and who he is,
I must, I will, I can, I do believe.[1]

Lord, this is me, in front of the mercy seat, kneeling at the mercy seat of my heart.

1 From *Olney Hymns* (1779) and *The Hartford Selection of Hymns* (1799).

June 22nd

Elisha prayed, "Open his eyes, Lord, so that he may see"

(2 Kings 6:17)

"Except a man be born again, he cannot see the kingdom of God."[1] A man may live in a deep mine in Hungary, never having seen the light of the sun. He may have received accounts of prospects, and by the help of a candle may have examined a few engravings of them; but let him be brought out of the mine, and set on the mountain, what a difference appears![2]

How blind we are, Lord, without the revelation of your Holy Spirit! Unless you show us salvation, we are like the man in the cave. To that end, gracious Father, I pray for my friends, neighbours, and loves ones who have not yet seen the cross. On their behalf, I pray Elisha's prayer today. Have mercy.

1 John 3.

2 From *The Life of the Rev. John Newton.*

JUNE 23RD

AN ELDER MUST BE BLAMELESS... HE MUST BE HOSPITABLE... HE MUST HOLD FIRMLY TO THE TRUSTWORTHY MESSAGE AS IT HAS BEEN TAUGHT, SO THAT HE CAN ENCOURAGE OTHERS BY SOUND DOCTRINE

(Titus 1:6, 8–9)

Claudius Buchanan,[1] a young Scotsman, tired of a dependent life, had left his home under false pretences and drifted to London. There he was impressed by a sermon which he heard at St Mary Woolnoth, and wrote anonymously to the Rector about his spiritual state. Newton sought and found his correspondent. "I called on him," says Buchanan, in a letter to his mother, "and experienced such a happy hour as I ought not to forget. If he had been my father, he could not have expressed more solicitude for my welfare." And of another occasion he says: "He received me with open arms, and in his family worship remembered me in a very affecting manner, and prayed for the Divine direction in his counsels to me." The young man's heart and course were wholly changed, and a close and lasting intimacy sprang up between the two. By Newton's advice... Buchanan entered the ministry of the Church of England.[2 3]

Thank you, Lord, for clergy who set a good example, and who give of their time and energy to encourage and bless others.

1 Reverend Claudius Buchanan (1766–1815), who went on to serve as Vice Provost of the College of Calcutta in India.

2 From *John Newton: Sailor, Preacher, Pastor, and Poet.*

3 This account is by no means untypical of John Newton's commitment to selfless encouragement and spiritual counsel. Such actions were an integral part of his ministry and service.

June 24TH

They cast lots

(Acts 1:26)

I have determin'd this day to have a ticket in the ensuing Lottery, not I hope with a desire to amassing money merely, but if it should be, of increasing my capacity for usefulness – for food, raiment and conveniences my gracious God has given me enough, in as much as he has given me some measure of contentment. I know when the lot is cast into the lap, the disposal is in the Lord's hand, and I hope and pray that it may not succeed to me unless I shall be enabled to be useful proportionately. If I lose my money, I think it will give me no uneasiness; but if I gain a prize, I determine (trusting in the Lord to enable me by his grace, without which I am incapable of keeping any resolution) that I will dedicate a fourth part, be it more or less, to works of mercy, charity, and for the promoting his glory – I mean that when all charges, deductions, and discounts are first taken away, a fourth part of the nett sum gained shall be the Lord's.[1][2]

Lord, this is such an unusual reading! What can I pray today? Only this: remind me, often, that all I have is yours, and yours alone. You have first claim on all I possess, and all that I am. I re-present my time and talents to you afresh.

1 From *An Ancient Mariner* (an extract from John Newton's diary).

2 This seems an unusual account of gambling, which we might assume went against John Newton's principles of faith, and trusting in God for provision. However, it is what it is, and ours is not to speculate!

June 25th

They cried unto thee, and were delivered: they trusted in thee, and were not confounded

(Psalm 22:5 KJV)

Many things offer to amuse us. Some deserve, and require, a degree of our attention; but one thing is especially needful. What a mercy is it, that this one thing, which mountains of gold and silver cannot purchase, is to be had, without money, and without price! May the Lord engrave it deeply on your heart and mine! His name is Love; his word is power; he is our Saviour. As sure as the sun will rise tomorrow, so sure is his promise, that he will, in no wise, cast out them that come unto him.[1] If we have a desire for his blessings, he first gave it to us, and therefore will not disappoint us. [2]

A God who "will not disappoint us"! You are my God.

1 John 6:37.

2 From *Letters to a Wife (Volume Two): By the Author of Cardiphonia.*

June 26th

A little that a righteous man hath is better than the riches of many wicked

(Psalm 37:16 KJV)

The failure of Newton's lottery ticket set his mind thinking over the whole question of material security, and stirred his conscience. He came across a book by John Wesley which "related to different kinds of oaths and showed how much they were violated". Newton began to worry about the unofficial gratuities of his office and the oath he had taken: "I am led to question my own conformity to the oath I took on entering into office, by which I renounced all taking of fees or gratuities, which, however, according to custom I have done."[1] He mentioned his scruples to the Collector, who assured him that when the oath was administered it was "meant that these perquisites should be taken". Not quite happy about this, Newton… refused all gratuities offered in future.[2 3]

Thank you, Lord, for this testimony.

1 This is in reference to John Newton's employment in Liverpool, as a Tide Surveyor.

2 From *An Ancient Mariner*.

3 This principled decision cost John Newton a fair amount of regular income, and for a while presented him with some financial difficulties.

June 27th

THOSE WHO ARE WISE WILL SHINE LIKE THE BRIGHTNESS OF THE HEAVENS, AND THOSE WHO LEAD MANY TO RIGHTEOUSNESS, LIKE THE STARS FOR EVER AND EVER

(Daniel 12:3)

How glorious will be the scene when the thousands of missionaries sent forth… and all their fellow-workers, pastors, preachers, and teachers in the mission fields, together with the vast company of converts from the many races and tribes whither the heralds of the Cross have gone, the spiritual offspring of John Newton and his companions, shall meet these their true Fathers in God, and fall down together with them and pour their united praise before the throne of their adorable Redeemer and Lord. And in that great gathering there will hardly be one who, having been neither conspicuous for learning nor eloquence, having neither social advantages nor high position, has been used by God for purposes wider, more lasting, and more beneficent than those which came from the life of John Newton.[1 2]

Thank you, Lord, for soul-winners, and those who play any part in bringing others to Christ. Bless those whom you have gifted with ministries of outreach and evangelism.

1 From *John Newton: Sailor, Preacher, Pastor, and Poet.*

2 An extract from a sermon given by The Reverend Prebendary H. E. Fox, entitled "Some after-fruits of John Newton's teaching" (Henry Elliott Fox, Secretary of the Church Missionary Society).

June 28th

I made a covenant with my eyes

(Job 31:1)

If we desire not to be led into temptation, surely we are not to run into it. If we wish to be preserved from error we are to guard against a curious and reasoning spirit. If we would preserve peace of conscience, we must beware of trifling with the light and motions of the Holy Spirit; for without his assistance we cannot maintain faith in exercise. If we would not be ensnared by the men of the world, we are to keep at a proper distance from them. The less we have to do with them the better, excepting so far as the providence of God makes it our duty, in the discharge of our callings and relations, and taking opportunities of doing them good. And though we cannot wholly shut Satan out of our imaginations, we should be cautious that we do not willingly provide fuel for his flame; but entreat the Lord to set a watch upon our eyes and our ears, and to teach us to reject the first motions and the smallest appearances of evil.[1]

Thank you, Lord, for this important insight. I know you are always willing to grant me your protection in the battle, but these words remind me of the part I am expected to play in my own spiritual success and progress. So help me, God.

1 From *Cardiphonia: or, The Utterance of the Heart in the Course of a Real Correspondence, Volume One.*

June 29th

"I have the right to do anything," you say – but not everything is beneficial. "I have the right to do anything" – but not everything is constructive

(1 Corinthians 10:23)

I shall proceed to consider the Christian's temper respecting himself. He lives godly and soberly. By sobriety we mean more than that he is not a drunkard; his tempers towards God of course form him to a moderation in all temporal things. He is not scrupulous or superstitious; he understands the liberty of the gospel, that every creature of God is good if it be received with thanksgiving: he does not aim at being needlessly singular, nor practises self-devised austerities. The Christian is neither a Stoic nor a Cynic; yet he finds daily cause for watchfulness and restraint. Satan will not often tempt a believer to gross crimes: our greatest snares and sorest conflicts are usually found in things lawful in themselves, but hurtful to us by their abuse, engrossing too much of our time, or of our hearts, or somehow indisposing us for communion with the Lord. The Christian will be jealous of anything that might entangle his affections, damp his zeal, or straiten him in his opportunities of serving his Saviour.[1]

I give you thanks, Heavenly Father, for sending this word to me today: a gentle reminder to watch my step in the everyday. Grant me the enjoyment of the freedom that comes from living within your supervision.

1 From *Cardiphonia: or, The Utterance of the Heart in the Course of a Real Correspondence, Volume One.*

June 30th

Jesus said: "A man was going down from Jerusalem to Jericho, when he was attacked by robbers… a Samaritan, as he travelled, came where the man was… he took pity on him. He… bandaged his wounds, pouring on oil and wine"

(Luke 10:30, 33–34)

How kind the good Samaritan
To him who fell among the thieves!
Thus Jesus pities fallen men,
And heals the wounds the soul receives.

Men saw me in this helpless case,
And passed without compassion by;
Each neighbour turned away his face,
Unmoved by my mournful cry.

But He whose name had been my scorn
(As Jews Samaritans despise)
Came when He saw me thus forlorn,
With love and pity in His eyes.

Gently He raised me from the ground,
Pressed me to lean upon His arm;
And into every gaping wound,
He poured His own all-healing balm.

Thus saved from death, from want secured,
I wait till He again shall come,
When I shall be completely cured,
And take me to His heavenly home.

There through eternal boundless days
When nature's wheel no longer rolls;
How shall I love, adore, and praise,
This good Samaritan to souls![1]

"This good Samaritan to souls!" What a lovely description of Jesus!

1 From *Olnley Hymns*, but here from http://www.hymntime.com

July 1st

The Lord said to Moses, "When you return to Egypt, see that you perform before Pharaoh all the wonders I have given you the power to do. But I will harden his heart so that he will not let the people go"

(Exodus 4:21)

I recollect to have heard Mr. N. say… "When God is about to perform any great work, he generally permits some great opposition to it. Suppose Pharaoh had acquiesced in the departure of the children of Israel, or that they had met with no difficulties in the way, they would, indeed, have passed from Egypt to Canaan with ease; but they, as well as the church in future ages, would have been great losers. The wonder-working God would not have been seen in those extremities, which make his arm so visible. A smooth passage here would have made but a poor story."[1]

Lord of my good times and Lord of my bad times, I trust in you.

1 From *The Life of the Rev. John Newton*. Notes and observations of the Reverend Thomas Scott (1747–1821), then curate of Ravenstone and Underwood, close to John Newton's parish of Olney, Buckinghamshire, England. John Newton had been hugely influential in Thomas Scott's life and ministry, encouraging him to give up his life as a "career priest" in order to follow Christ as a true disciple.

July 2nd

Though the fig-tree does not bud and there are no grapes on the vines, though the olive crop fails and the fields produce no food, though there are no sheep in the sheepfold and no cattle in the stalls, yet I will rejoice in the Lord, I will be joyful in God my Saviour

(Habakkuk 3:17–18)

Is Jesus mine! I am now prepar'd
To meet with what I thought most hard;
Yes, let the winds of trouble blow,
And comforts melt away like snow;
No blasted trees, or failing crops,
Can hinder my eternal hopes;
Tho' creatures change, the Lord's the same,
Then let me triumph in his name.[1 2]

Lord, I can but repeat my prayer of yesterday.

1 From *Olney Hymns* (1779) and *Selection of Hymns from the Best Authors, Intended to be an Appendix to Dr. Watts' Psalms and Hymns.*

2 In some hymnals, "Is Jesus mine" reads as "Jesus is mine".

July 3rd

How good and pleasant it is when brothers dwell in unity!

(Psalm 133:1 ESV)

After referring to the long silence of the latter, [John Newton] continues: "You are, I suppose, pushing on to be a good man, and I wish you all reasonable success; but consider what good your money, and offices, and titles do you, if they will not suffer you to remember what you owe to yourself and to your friends? I tell you all your thousands (when you get them) will not purchase you such cordial well-wishers as two old-fashioned acquaintances (not to say a sister and a brother) who lie by neglected at Liverpool. Surely you could rise a quarter of an hour earlier once in six months to retrieve an opportunity of favouring me with a letter! However, to encourage you, I send you a free and absolute pardon for all that is past, and exempt you from the trouble of apologies of every kind, real or imaginary, provided that, before... this Christmas, you testify your repentance by amendment."[1] [2]

What a letter, Lord! Is there someone who would like to hear from me today? A letter I can write? A phone call I can make? Prompt me today, Holy Spirit. Bring that person to mind.

1 From *John Newton of Olney and St Mary Woolnoth. An Autobiography and Narrative.*

2 An extract from one of John Newton's letters to his brother-in-law, with whom there had evidently been some kind of breach in communication. This letter appears unusually harsh, and we can only assume John Newton's patience had been tested to the limit by the failure of his brother-in-law to maintain family contacts over a length of time.

July 4th

Whatever you have learned or received or heard from me, or seen in me – put it into practice. And the God of peace will be with you

(Philippians 4:9)

Set out on a Yorkshire circuit. A hearty reception from Mr. Venn[1] at Huddersfield. Heard him twice on Sunday, and communed, and heard him address some catechumens. In every exercise, in the whole of his converse and carriage, he seems eminent and exemplary. I stayed with him about a week. A happy time at Leeds. Met there Mr. Ingham[2] and Miss Medhurst.[3] At Yeadon[4] had a pleasant day with my dear friends. Dined with Mr. Scott.[5][6][7]

Father God, thank you for friends. I pray for mine today.

1 Reverend Henry Venn (1725–97), evangelical Church of England minister.

2 Reverend Benjamin Ingham (1712–72), Rector of Aberford, Yorkshire, and the husband of Lady Margaret Hastings.

3 A friend with whom John Newton corresponded regularly.

4 West Yorkshire.

5 Possibly Thomas Scott, whose conversion to authentic Christianity and a living faith was due in no small part to John Newton's influence. (See Footnote, July 1st.)

6 From *John Newton of Olney and St Mary Woolnoth. An Autobiography and Narrative.*

7 This excerpt is included as one of many available examples of John Newton's habit of visiting friends, ministers, and their churches, in all parts of the country. He was willing to travel great distances to further his intellectual and social interests. This was especially the case when he was growing in his Christian experience, and then, subsequently, exploring options for ordained ministry. Newton derived a great deal of satisfaction from listening to a number of preachers and making careful observations. This fed his insatiable desire to learn, and to imitate priests and church leaders whose example he sought to emulate.

July 5th

Rejoice with them that do rejoice, and weep with them that weep

(Romans 12:15 KJV)

A... branch of the Christian's temper respects his fellow-Christians. And here, methinks... I could enlarge with pleasure. We have in this degenerate day, among those who claim, and are allowed the name of Christian, too many of a narrow, selfish, mercenary spirit; but in the beginning it was not so. The gospel is designed to cure such a spirit, but gives no indulgence to it. A Christian has the mind of Christ, who went about doing good, who makes his sun to shine upon the good and the evil, and sendeth his rain on the just and the unjust. His Lord's example forms him to the habit of diffusive; he breathes a spirit of good will to mankind, and rejoices in every opportunity of being useful to the souls and bodies of others, without respect to parties or interests. He commiserates, and would if possible alleviate, the miseries of all around him; and if his actual services are restrained by want of ability, yet all share in his sympathy and prayers. Acting in the spirit of his Master, he frequently meets with a measure of the like treatment; but if his good is requited with evil, he labours to overcome evil with good.[1]

To be like Jesus!

1 From *Cardiphonia: or, The Utterance of the Heart in the Course of a Real Correspondence, Volume One.*

July 6th

Do to others as you would have them do to you

(Luke 6:31)

[The Christian] feels himself a sinner, and needs much forgiveness: this makes him ready to forgive. He is not haughty, captious, easily offended, or hard to be reconciled; for at the feet of Jesus he has learned meekness; and when he meets with unkindness or injustice, he considers, that though he has not deserved such things from men, they are instruments employed by his heavenly Father (from whom he has deserved to suffer much more), for his humiliation and chastisement; and is therefore more concerned for their sins than for his own sufferings, and prays, after the pattern of his Saviour, "Father, forgive them, for they know not what they do." He knows he is fallible; therefore cannot be positive. He knows he is frail; and therefore dares not be censorious. As a member of society, he is just, punctual in the discharge of every relative duty, faithful in his engagements and promises, rendering to all their dues, obedient to lawful responsibility, and acting to all men according to the golden rule of doing as he would be done by.[1]

Lord Jesus, you bear with me even with all my flaws and shortcomings. I have such a long way to go before I am like you! Please keep working within me, I pray.

1 From *Cardiphonia: or, The Utterance of the Heart in the Course of a Real Correspondence, Volume One.*

July 7th

Whether you turn to the right or to the left, your ears will hear a voice behind you, saying, "This is the way; walk in it"

(Isaiah 30:21)

Mr. Newton speaks of frequent correspondence with Mr. Haweis.[1] "He has prevailed upon me to engage in an important and difficult work – an Ecclesiastical History, to trace the gospel spirit, with its abuses and oppositions, through the several ages of the Church – a subject of my own pointing out; but I little expected to have it devolved on me, and I have desired to decline it, sensible how poorly I am furnished for the undertaking; but my friend will have it so, and the Lord can supply. I am collecting books for the purpose."

Newton received proposals from a Presbyterian congregation in Yorkshire, but clogged with some unfavourable conditions, so that he says, "I believe I shall not have pursued it, even if I had no other engagements in view."[2] [3]

My prayer is for guidance, Lord, and for discernment; whether to say "yes" or "no". I pray for anyone with an important decision to make, that you would speak to them and confirm whether they should accept or decline a specific proposal. May your will be done in our lives.

1 See Footnote 1, January 9th.

2 Both excerpts from *John Newton of Olney and St Mary Woolnoth. An Autobiography and Narrative.*

3 John Newton was a great believer in the importance of waiting upon the Lord for guidance, and would lay every matter before him in prayer. He was always anxious to be obedient in his service.

July 8th

They only heard the report: "The man who formerly persecuted us is now preaching the faith he once tried to destroy." And they praised God because of me

(Galatians 1:23–24)

One word concerning my views to the ministry… I have told you, this was my dear mother's hope concerning me; but her death, and the scenes of life in which I afterwards engaged, seemed to cut off the probability. The first desires of this sort in my own mind, arose many years ago, from a reflection on Gal.i, 23, 24. I could not but wish for such a public opportunity to testify the riches of divine grace. I thought I was, above most living, a fit person to proclaim that faithful saying, "That Jesus Christ came into the world to save the chief of sinners": My life has been full of remarkable turns, and I seemed selected to show what the Lord could do, I was in some hopes that perhaps, sooner or later, he might call me into his service.[1 2 3]

Lord, I pray today for those who sense any call to the ministry.

1 From *An Authentic Narrative of Some Remarkable and Interesting Particulars in the Life of — Communicated, in a Series of Letters, to the Reverend T. Haweis.*

2 As is emphasized elsewhere, this book is intended to be essentially *devotional* in nature. It does not, therefore, pretend to be especially chronological or biographical. These glimpses into Newton's pilgrimage and ministry are intended for the primary purpose of daily prayer and reflection, carrying the spirit of John Newton within each excerpt but not outlining every sequential aspect of his life and narrative.

3 Some pages, such as this one, will touch upon John Newton's call to the ministry, but only ever in the context of Footnote No. 2.

July 9th

When I preach the gospel, I cannot boast, since I am compelled to preach. Woe to me if I do not preach the gospel!

(1 Corinthians 9:16)

I was long distressed… about what was or was not a proper call to the ministry; it now seems to me an easy point to solve, but perhaps will not be so… till the Lord shall make it clear… in brief, I think it principally includes… A warm and earnest desire to be employed in this service. I apprehend, the man who is once moved by the Spirit of God to this work, will prefer it, if attainable, to thousands of gold and silver; so that, though he is at times intimidated by a sense of its importance and difficulty, compared with his own great insufficiency (for it is to be presumed a call of this sort, if indeed from God, will be accompanied with humility and self-abasement), yet he cannot give it up. I hold it a good rule to inquire in this point, whether the desire to preach is most fervent in our most lively and spiritual frames, and when we are most laid in the dust before the Lord? If so, it is a good sign. But if, as is sometimes the case, a person is very earnest to be a preacher to others, when he finds but little hungerings and thirstings after grace in his own soul, it is then to be feared his zeal springs from a selfish principle than from the Spirit of God.[1]

Lord of vocations, I pray for those who assess and scrutinize applications for ministry. Grant them wisdom, compassion, and grace as they deliberate.

1 From *Letters of John Newton.*

July 10th

Take note of this: everyone should be quick to listen, slow to speak

(James 1:19)

Mr. Jones, minister of St Saviour's, Southwark,[1] died. He was a man of great gifts, and great trials, and was eminently useful. The removal of this "dear and honoured friend" of Mr. Newton's greatly affected him, and quickened his desire to enter upon the ministry. He felt he could no longer be silent, and thought that he might make an effort in Liverpool. From this, however, Mrs. Newton dissuaded him; and in referring to the subject long afterwards he says: "I believe no arguments but hers could have restrained me, for almost two years, from taking a rash step; of which I should have perhaps repented, and which would have led me far wide of the honour and comfort I have since been favoured with."[2]

Thank you, Father God, for the good counsel of caring wives. Help those of us who are husbands to listen well and, in doing so, avoid costly mistakes. I pray especially for married couples who are considering life-changing decisions. Help them with your guidance.

1 Reverend Thomas Jones, non-conformist minister (London, England).

2 From *John Newton of Olney and St Mary Woolnoth. An Autobiography and Narrative.*

July 11th

Who dares despise the day of small things?

(Zechariah 4:10)

The conversation of some friends, led my thoughts to the [ministry]. The first mention made little impression on me, but in a small time it took firmer hold of my mind, and at length found a place in my prayers so far only, as to profess my readiness to enter on that service, if the Lord should at any time see fit to call, prepare and send me – in a little time this submission to be employed, improved into a wish and desire that I might, which still continues and increases. I have many times in this interval given myself to the Lord for his service – I hope without reserve or condition – and I referred myself to the time when I should be able to read a chapter in the Hebrew Bible with tolerable ease for a farther and close enquiry into this matter, in which I determined to join my own serious deliberations, the advice of my best and most judicious friends, and a course of prayer, and waiting upon the Lord.[1]

Help me, Lord, to note those little ideas and small thoughts that might just be your Spirit talking to me. Grant me sensitivity to those soul-whispers, lest I miss your direction and guidance. Teach me to guard against too quickly dismissing "divine nudges" simply because they are not loud or prominent.

1 From *Ministry on my mind*. This booklet, written by Marylynn Rouse and published by the John Newton Project, is perhaps the most detailed publication on the specific subject of John Newton's call to the ministry.

July 12th

We who are strong ought to bear with the failings of the weak and not to please ourselves

(Romans 15:1)

For the sake of the church, and the influence example may have upon his fellow Christians, the law of charity and prudence will often require a believer to abstain from some things, not because they are unlawful, but inexpedient. Thus the apostle [Paul], though strenuous for the right of his Christian liberty, would have availed himself of the use, so as to eat no meat, rather than offend a weak brother, rather than mislead him to act against the present light of his conscience. Upon this principle, if I could, without hurt to myself, attend some public amusements, as a concert or oratorio, and return from thence with a warm heart to my closet (the possibility of which in my own case I greatly question), yet I should think it my duty to forbear, lest some weaker than myself should be encouraged by me to make the like experiment, though in their own minds they might fear it was wrong, and have no other reason to think it lawful but because I did it.[1]

Help me today, gracious Spirit, to think before I act.

1 From *Cardiphonia: or, The Utterance of the Heart in the Course of a Real Correspondence, Volume One.*

July 13th

WHAT WE HAVE RECEIVED IS NOT THE SPIRIT OF THE WORLD, BUT THE SPIRIT WHO IS FROM GOD, SO THAT WE MAY UNDERSTAND WHAT GOD HAS FREELY GIVEN US

(1 Corinthians 2:12)

In our way of little life in the country, serious people often complain of the snares they meet with from worldly people, and yet they must mix with them to get a livelihood. I advise them, if they can, to do their business with the world as they do it in the rain. If their business calls them abroad, they will not leave it undone for fear of being a little wet; but then, when it is done, they presently seek shelter, and will not stand in the rain for pleasure. So providential and necessary calls of duty, that lead us into the world, will not hurt us, if we find the spirit of the world unpleasant, and are glad to retire from it, and keep out of it as much as our relative duties will permit. That which is our cross is not so likely to be our snare; but if that spirit, which we should always watch and pray against, infects and assimilates our minds to itself, then we are sure to suffer loss, and act below the dignity of our profession.[1]

Gracious Spirit, stay with me this day, wherever I need to be, and in whatever company I find myself. I pray too for Christians whose employment is within a secular environment. Protect them, I ask, as they seek to maintain their witness and standards.

1 From *Cardiphonia: or, The Utterance of the Heart in the Course of a Real Correspondence, Volume One.*

July 14th

TEACH US TO NUMBER OUR DAYS, THAT WE MAY GAIN A HEART OF WISDOM

(Psalm 90:12)

The value of time is… to be taken into account. It is a precious talent, and our Christian profession opens a wide field for the due improvement of it. Much of it has already been lost, and therefore we are exhorted to redeem it. I think many things which custom pleads for will be excluded from a suitableness to a Christian, for this one reason, that they are not consistent with the simplest notion of the redemption of time. It is generally said we need relaxation; I allow it in a sense; the Lord himself has provided it; and because our spirits are too weak to be always upon the wing in meditation and prayer, he has appointed to all men, from the king downwards, something to do in a secular way. The poor are to labour, the rich are not exempted from something equivalent. And when everything of this sort in each person's situation is properly attended to, I apprehend, if the heart be alive and in a right state, spiritual concernments will present themselves, as affording the noblest, sweetest, and most interesting relaxation from the cares and business of life; as, on the other hand, that business will be the best relaxation, and unbending of the mind from religious exercises; and between the two, perhaps there ought to be but little mere leisure-time. A life, in this sense, divided between God and the world, is desirable; when one part of it is spent in retirement, seeking after and conversing with him whom our souls love; and the other part of it employed in active service for the good of our family, friends, the church, and society, for his sake. Every hour which does not fall in with one or other of these views, I apprehend is lost time.[1]

All my days and all my hours shall be yours, Lord.

1 From *Cardiphonia: or, The Utterance of the Heart in the Course of a Real Correspondence, Volume One.*

July 15th

Cast all your anxiety on him because he cares for you

(1 Peter 5:7)

A letter from Mr. Haweis,[1] stating that... he had prevailed on Lord Dartmouth[2] to give me the presentation of Olney, in Bucks, where Mr. Moses Browne[3] has many years preached the gospel. He desired to know whether I would accept it... I sent him my acceptance, with many thanks to him and Lord Dartmouth. Thus I find the Lord fulfilling His promises, and giving me light to guide me through the perplexities of my own mind... Wonderful is the chain of Divine providence. My first acquaintance and renewed intimacy with Mr. Haweis were quite unsought by me. I would not be too sanguine, but I cast myself in this matter upon Him who careth for me... I received a kind letter from Lord Dartmouth, with the offer of the living at Olney, accompanied with a letter from Mr. Haweis, directing me to break off everything, and to repair to London for ordination.[4]

Heavenly Father, you work "behind the scenes" to influence people according to your will. Help me to trust that my prayers are being answered, even if I can't see what's happening in the background. I bring my plans, hopes, and dreams to you today, praying that you will bring them to fulfilment.

1 See Footnote 1, January 9th.
2 William Legge, 2nd Earl of Dartmouth, who was influential in recommending Newton to William Markham, Bishop of Chester.
3 Reverend Moses Browne (1704–87), a clergyman of the Church of England.
4 From *John Newton of Olney and St Mary Woolnoth. An Autobiography and Narrative.*

July 16th

Our Lord Jesus, that great Shepherd of the sheep

(Hebrews 13:20)

Great shepherd of thy people, hear,
Thy presence now display;
As thou hast given a place for prayer,
So give us hearts to pray.

Within these walls let holy peace
And love and concord dwell;
Here give the troubled conscience ease,
The wounded spirit heal.

May we in faith receive thy word,
In faith present our prayers,
And in the presence of our Lord
Unbosom all our cares.

The hearing ear, the seeing eye,
The contrite heart, bestow;
And shine upon us from on high,
That we in grace may grow.[1]

Receive this prayer, Lord Jesus, be it for a home or a church, a family or a congregation. So many needs are represented in this hymn, yet you know each and every one of them. Such is the beauty of prayer.

1 Originally from *Olney Hymns* (1779).

July 17th

"I know the plans I have for you," declares the Lord, "plans to prosper you and not to harm you, plans to give you hope and a future"

(Jeremiah 29:11)

Several weeks were spent in London[1]… "I met," [Newton] says, "with some difficulties, but all were overruled. My protracted stay gave me the opportunity of acquaintance with many whom perhaps I should otherwise never have known. I have cause for wonder, praise, and humiliation, when I think what favour the Lord gave me in the eyes of His people – some of rank and eminence… I was with the Bishop of Lincoln[2]… and he has fixed [the date] for my examination…

It [the examination] lasted about an hour, and was chiefly upon the principal heads of divinity. As I was resolved not to be charged hereafter with dissimulation, I was constrained to dissent from his Lordship upon some points, but he was not offended. He declared himself satisfied, and has promised to ordain me… Let us praise the Lord"…[3]

Mr. Newton was admitted to deacon's orders at Buckden.[4] "The Bishop," he says, "behaved throughout with the greatest candour and kindness. Having received my papers, I took leave of him the next day, and went to Olney to take a glance at the place and the people."

Thank you, Lord, for your faithfulness along life's journey. Thank you for your help in overcoming obstacles. Thank you for those people you introduce into my life along the way. Thank you for influencing other people on my behalf. Help me always to follow your leading, and to trust you with each step I take.

1 See July 15th.
2 Bishop John Green (1706–79).
3 From *John Newton of Olney and St Mary Woolnoth. An Autobiography and Narrative.*
4 Cambridgeshire, England, at that time within the Diocese of Lincoln.

July 18th

The Lord will watch over your coming and going both now and for evermore

(Psalm 121:8)

The Lord was very gracious to me at Liverpool. He enabled me to preach His truth before many thousands. I hope with some measure of faithfulness, I trust with some success, and in general with much greater acceptance than I could have expected.

When we came away I think the bulk of the people, of all ranks and parties, were very sorry to part with us. How much do I owe to the restraining and preserving grace of God, that when I appeared in a public character, and delivered offensive truths in a place where I had lived so long, and there appeared a readiness and disposition in some to disparage my character, nothing could be found or brought to light on which they could frame an accusation!…

We took our leave of Liverpool (where the Lord has shown us so many mercies during a residence of eight years)… Slept this night at Warrington… reached Northampton without the least inconvenience, by the favour of a kind providence… where we met with some friends, who conducted us safely to Olney.[1] [2]

What grace, Lord: whether I am travelling from Liverpool to Warrington, or to Northampton, or to Olney, or to anywhere else, your word promises me your abiding presence. Geography is no obstacle to your love. Boundaries and borders cannot restrain you. Thank you, Lord, for your loving concern wherever I might be. Be with those who travel today.

1 From *John Newton of Olney and St Mary Woolnoth. An Autobiography and Narrative.*

2 John Newton left his employment as a Tide Surveyor in Liverpool, in order to take up his appointment as a Church of England deacon in Olney. Throughout his time in Liverpool, prior to ordination, he was in some demand as a lay preacher in a number of churches (not exclusively Anglican).

JULY 19TH

YOU DID NOT CHOOSE ME, BUT I CHOSE YOU AND APPOINTED YOU SO THAT YOU MIGHT GO AND BEAR FRUIT

(John 15:16)

Opened my commission at Olney,[1] preaching in the morning from Psalm Ixxx.[1]; afternoon, 2 Cor. Ii.15, 16. Blessed be God for enabling me and honouring me thus far. I find a cordial reception amongst those who know the truth, but many are far otherwise minded. I desire to be faithful and honest, and patiently to pursue the path of duty through both good and ill report.[2]

Gracious God, be with all those who are about to be ordained or commissioned. You know what – and whom! – they will encounter; lovers of the truth, but also those who "are far otherwise minded". Bless them, Lord, and their families, as they take up their appointments.

1 John Newton's path to the ministry was a torturous one. He struggled for some time to define and clarify his calling, making it a matter of diligent prayer and heart-searching. He received a number of rebuttals from friends to whom he had turned for references, and was rejected by some denominations who doubted his conversion story or regarded him as inadequately educated on a formal level. He was, though, convinced of his calling, and even went so far as to write personally to some bishops asking for acceptance. His persistence in the face of misunderstanding and hurtful rejection is especially to be noted.

2 From *John Newton of Olney and St Mary Woolnoth. An Autobiography and Narrative.*

July 20th

In your thinking be mature

(1 Corinthians 14:20 ESV)

In childhood Newton had been shown the more austere teaching of Isaac Watts,[1] especially the Preservatives from the Sins and Follies of Youth.[2] It was later that he discovered the more cheerful, the more positive, Watts; the Watts who wrote Our God our help in ages past, and who advised Christians, "… let our joys be known. Religion never was designed to make our pleasures less."[3] During the years that Newton was at Liverpool… he was inclined to criticise and even to admonish the frivolous. He had an anxious concern lest they failed to realise the dangers to a mortal soul, dangers which his own violent experiences made so plain.[4]

Heavenly Father, help me to mellow as the years go by. Bless me with the ongoing benefits of maturity, hindsight, and reflection. Teach me, Lord, not to compromise, but to view things differently, sometimes, with a wisdom and a generosity of spirit I may not have possessed in my younger days.

---

1 Isaac Watts (1674–1748), English Congregationalist minister and hymn writer, credited with over 750 hymns.

2 A book by Isaac Watts, published in 1765.

3 From Watts' hymn, "Come Ye that Love the Lord".

4 From *An Ancient Mariner*.

July 21st

The steps of a good man are ordered by the Lord: and he delighteth in his way

(Psalm 37:23 KJV)

If we be sincere in intention we cannot make a mistake of any great importance. If a fever or a fall prevent a journey we must not call it a disappointment, but a leading. God deals not by angels but by providences. When we mean well and are not following God's will, He will hedge up our way. If we be in God's way, mountains will sink into plains.[1] [2]

Lord, my prayers today are for those who are seeking your will. Grant them faith to trust, even when the way is not clear.

1 From *John Newton: Sailor, Preacher, Pastor, and Poet.*

2 Throughout the many travails of his extraordinary life, not least his unflagging pursuit of his calling to ordination, John Newton not only believed these words, but lived them; by word and by deed.

July 22nd

PRAISE THE LORD, MY SOUL; ALL MY INMOST BEING, PRAISE HIS HOLY NAME. PRAISE THE LORD, MY SOUL, AND FORGET NOT ALL HIS BENEFITS – WHO FORGIVES ALL YOUR SINS AND HEALS ALL YOUR DISEASES

(Psalm 103:1–3)

Before our removal from Liverpool she [John Newton's wife, Mary] received a blow upon her left breast, which occasioned her some pain and anxiety for a little time, but which soon wore off. A small lump remained in the part affected, but I heard no more of it for many years. I believe that, latterly, she felt more than I was aware of; but her tenderness for me made her conceal it as long as possible, I have since wondered at her success, and how I could be kept so long ignorant of it… She applied, unknown to me, to a friend of mine, an eminent surgeon. Her design was, if he approved it, to submit to an operation, and so to adjust time and circumstances with him, that it might be performed in my absence, and before I could know it. But the surgeon told her that the malady was too far advanced, and the tumour, the size of which he compared to the half of a melon, was too large to warrant the hope of being extracted, without the most imminent danger of her life, and that he durst not attempt it.[1][2]

Heavenly Father, Great Physician, be with those who are coming to terms with the diagnosis of serious illness, and their loved ones. Draw close to them as they contemplate life-changing news. I pray for their healing, Lord, and for your peace to surround them in traumatic days.

1 From *The Life of the Rev. John Newton*.

2 John Newton's wife, his beloved Mary, whose loving presence at home had been the mainstay of his desire to return to England throughout his seafaring days, was diagnosed with cancer, and endured a lengthy illness.

July 23rd

For the righteous will never be moved... He is not afraid of bad news; his heart is firm, trusting in the Lord

(Psalm 112:6–7 ESV)

[The surgeon] could give [Mary Newton] but little advice, more than to keep herself as quiet, and her mind as easy as possible; and little more encouragement, than by saying that the pains to which she was exposed were generally rendered tolerable by the use of laudanum;[1] to which, however, she had a dislike, little short of an antipathy. I cannot easily describe the composure and resignation with which she gave me this recital, the next day after her interview with the surgeon; nor of the sensations of my mind when I heard it.[2]

Heavenly Father, my prayers today are for those who carry the heavy responsibility of breaking sad news to hospital patients and their loved ones. Likewise, Lord, I pray for members of the emergency services whose task can be to inform family members of the death of a relative. Bless them.

1 Opium, morphine, and codeine.

2 From *The Life of the Rev. John Newton*.

July 24th

Brothers and sisters, we do not want you to be uninformed about those who sleep in death, so that you do not grieve like the rest of mankind, who have no hope. For we believe that Jesus died and rose again, and so we believe that God will bring with Jesus those who have fallen asleep in him

(1 Thessalonians 4:13–14)

We seek a rest beyond the skies,
In everlasting day;
Through floods and flames the passage lies,
But Jesus guards the way:
The swelling flood, and raging flame,
Hear and obey His word;
Then let us triumph in His name,
Our Saviour is the Lord.[1] [2]

Thank you, Lord Jesus, for the great Christian hope of Heaven – unmerited and undeserved, yet offered by grace. Beyond the blue horizon!

1 From http://www.traditionalmusic.co.uk
2 Written in 1779.

July 25th

The jar of flour was not used up and the jug of oil did not run dry, in keeping with the word of the Lord spoken by Elijah

(1 Kings 17:16)

By the poor widow's oil and meal
Elijah was sustained;
Though small the stock it lasted well,
For God the store maintained.

It seemed as if from day to day,
They were to eat and die;
But still, though in a secret way,
He sent a fresh supply.

This to His poor He still will give
Just for the present hour;
But for tomorrow they must live
Upon His word and power.

No barn or storehouse they possess,
On which they can depend;
Yet have no cause to fear distress
For Jesus is their friend.

Then let not doubts your mind assail,
Remember, God has said
"The cruse and barrel shall not fail;
My people shall be fed."

Though in ourselves we have no stock,
The Lord is nigh to save;
His door flies open when we knock,
And 'tis but ask and have.[1][2]

You know my needs, Lord. You know my needs today. I lay them before the throne of grace, and leave them there.

1 From http://www.traditionalmusic.co.uk
2 Written in 1779.

July 26th

It is God who makes both us and you stand firm in Christ. He anointed us, set his seal of ownership on us, and put his Spirit in our hearts

(2 Corinthians 1:21–22)

From the account you give me of your sentiments, I cannot but wonder you find it so difficult to accede to the Athanasian Creed,[1] when it seems to me you believe and avow what that creed chiefly sets forth. The Doctrines of the Trinity, some explication of the terms being subjoined, is the Catholic Faith,[2] without the belief of which a man cannot be saved. This damnatory clause seems to me, proved by Mark xvi.15, "He that believeth shall be saved", &c. The object of faith must be truth. The doctrine of the Deity of Christ and of the Holy Spirit in union with the Father, so that they are not three Gods, but one God, is not merely a proposition expressed in words, to which our assent is required, but is absolutely necessary to be known; since without it no truth respecting salvation can be rightly understood, no one promise duly believed, no one duty spiritually performed. I take it for granted, that this doctrine must appear irrational and absurd in the eye of reason, if by reason we mean the reason of man in his fallen state, before it is corrected and enlightened by a heavenly Teacher.[3]

Trinitarian God, doctrine is not always easy to understand. You yourself are a great mystery! Help me, therefore, I pray, to live by faith and not by sight or intellect. Stamp the mysteries of belief upon my heart.

1 A statement of Christian belief focused on the doctrine of the Trinity.
2 Catholic as in all-embracing, as opposed to Roman Catholic.
3 From *Cardiphonia: or, The Utterance of the Heart in the Course of a Real Correspondence, Volume One.*

July 27th

No one can say, "Jesus is Lord," except by the Holy Spirit

(1 Corinthians 12:3)

No man can say Jesus is Lord, but by the Holy Ghost. I believe… that a man may be saved who never heard of the [Athanasian] creed, who never read any book but the New Testament, or perhaps a single Evangelist; but he must be taught of God the things that accompany salvation, or I do not think he can be saved. The mercies of God in Christ will not save any (as I apprehend), but according to the method revealed in his word, that is, those who are truly partakers of faith and holiness. For as the religion of the New Testament ascribes all power to God, and considers all goodness in us as the effect of his communication, we being by nature destitute of spiritual life or light; so those whom God himself is pleased to teach, will infallibly attain the knowledge of all that they are concerned to know.[1]

Lord, salvation is your most wonderful gift. There is nothing any of us can bring, or do, whereby we may attain eternal life. It is all of you. All is grace. I pray today for anyone who is thinking they need to earn their way into the kingdom; those who are relying on good works and endless deeds to merit your favour and approval. Speak to their hearts by your Spirit, that they may relax in your mercy. Empty us, Lord, in order to fill us.

1 From *Cardiphonia: or, The Utterance of the Heart in the Course of a Real Correspondence, Volume One.*

July 28th

I BESEECH YOU, BRETHREN, MARK THEM WHICH CAUSE DIVISIONS AND OFFENCES CONTRARY TO THE DOCTRINE WHICH YE HAVE LEARNED; AND AVOID THEM

(Romans 16:17 KJV)

When I think of an enclosure, some hedge, wall, bank, ditch, &c. is of course included in my idea; for who can conceive of an enclosure without a boundary? So, in a national church, there must be, I apprehend, something marked out, the approbation or refusal of which will determine who do or not belong to it. And for this purpose articles of some kind seem not improper. You think it would be better to have these articles in scriptural expressions. But if it be lawful to endeavour to exclude from our pulpits men who hold sentiments the most repugnant to the truth, I wish you to consider, whether this can be in any measure secured by articles in which the scripture doctrines are not explained and stated, as well as expressed.[1 2]

Lord of the church, I pray two things today: your protection from divisive and unsound doctrine, and your influence upon those who are in error.

1 From one of John Newton's letters, this one to "Reverend Mr S.—" John Newton tried desperately hard to find employment within different denominations, such was his conviction regarding a calling to ordination. He did, though, regard the Church of England as his preferred option, and it is that denomination to which he refers here.

2 From *Cardiphonia: or, The Utterance of the Heart in the Course of a Real Correspondence, Volume One.*

July 29th

Has not the Lord anointed you?

(1 Samuel 10:1)

I hope... the Lord will make you comfortable and useful in your present rank as a curate. Preferment is not necessary, either to our peace or usefulness. We may live and die contentedly, without the honours and emoluments which aspiring men thirst after, if he be pleased to honour us with a dispensation to preach his gospel, and to crown our endeavours with a blessing. He that winneth souls is wise; wise in the choice of the highest end he can propose to himself in this life; wise in the improvement of the only means by which this desirable end can be attained. Wherever we cast our eyes, the bulk of the people are ignorant, immoral, careless. They live without God in the world; they are neither awed by his authority, nor affected by his goodness, nor enabled to trust to his promises, nor disposed to aim at his glory. If, perhaps, they have a serious interval, or some comparative sobriety of character, they ground their hopes upon their own doings, endeavours, or purposes; and treat the inexpressible love of God revealed in Christ, and the gospel method of salvation by faith in his name, with neglect, often with contempt.[1]

Heavenly Father, guard and protect my heart and mind from thoughts of promotion or rank. Teach me to accept that which you have given me as a privilege, and shield me from thoughts of envy, I pray. Grant me the rich blessing of contentment in whichever work I am called to do.

1 From *Cardiphonia: or, The Utterance of the Heart in the Course of a Real Correspondence, Volume One.*

July 30th

What we preach is not ourselves, but Jesus Christ as Lord

(2 Corinthians 4:5)

When ministers themselves are convinced of sin, and feel the necessity of an Almighty Saviour, they presently account their former gain but loss, and determine, with the apostle, to know nothing but Jesus Christ, and him crucified. In proportion as they do this, they are sure to be wondered at, laughed at, and railed at, if the providence of God and the constitution of their country secure them from severer treatment. But they have this invaluable compensation, that they no longer speak without effect. In a greater or lesser degree a change takes place in their auditories: the blind receive their sight, the deaf hear, the lepers are cleansed: sinners are turned from darkness to light, and from the power of Satan to God; sinful practices are forsaken; and a new course of life in the converts, evidence that they are not following cunningly-devised fables, or taken up with uncertain notions; but that God has indeed quickened them by his Spirit, and given them an understanding to know him that is true. The preachers, likewise, while they attempt to teach others, are taught themselves; a blessing descends upon their studies and labours, upon their perusal of the scripture, upon their attention to what passes within them and around them.[1]

Lord of the church, once again I have the privilege of praying for my own minister. I ask you to bless him/her with renewed spiritual conviction, vigour, and vision.

1 From *Cardiphonia: or, The Utterance of the Heart in the Course of a Real Correspondence, Volume One.* John Newton is here referring to clergymen of his acquaintance for whom the ministry was an easy way of life, and more to do with philosophy than spiritual conviction. He urged such colleagues to refresh their spiritual lives, and to move away from preaching little more than classical homilies, to the true gospel.

July 31st

Am I a God at hand, saith the Lord, and not a God afar off?
(Jeremiah 23:23 KJV)

The events of every day contribute to throw light upon the word of God.[1]

Open my eyes, ears, and heart, Lord, to recognize you in the events of this day: in the people I meet, in my circumstances, and in that which I hear. What a blessed day this could become!

1 From *Cardiphonia: or, The Utterance of the Heart in the Course of a Real Correspondence, Volume One.*

August 1st

Be still, and know that I am God

(Psalm 46:10 KJV)

Quiet, Lord, my forward[1] heart,
Make me teachable and mild,
Upright, simple, free from art,
Make me as a weaned child:
From distrust and envy free,
Pleased with all that pleases Thee.

What Thou shalt today provide,
Let me as a child receive;
What tomorrow may betide,
Calmly to Thy wisdom leave:
'Tis enough that Thou wilt care,
Why should I the burden bear?

As a little child relies
On a care beyond his own;
Knows he's neither strong nor wise,
Fears to stir a step alone:
Let me thus with Thee abide,
As my Father, Guard, and Guide.

Thus preserved from Satan's wiles,
Safe from dangers, free from fears;
May I live upon Thy smiles,
Till the promised hour appears;
When the sons of God shall prove
All their Father's boundless love.[2][3]

Father, receive the prayers of all your children this day. Let not one of us be unheard.

1 Archaic, meaning awkward, difficult, not at rest or ease.
2 Written in 1779.
3 From http://www.traditionalmusic.co.uk

August 2nd

Let us hold fast the confession of our hope without wavering, for he who promised is faithful. And let us consider how to stir up one another to love and good works, not neglecting to meet together, as is the habit of some, but encouraging one another, and all the more as you see the Day drawing near

(Hebrews 10:23–25 ESV)

Soon after his settlement at Olney, Mr. Newton received from many of his friends strong expressions of sympathy in this happy issue of his long-cherished hopes.[1] Amongst those we find the following beautiful letter from Mr. [George] Whitefield…

Rev. and dear Sir, With great pleasure I this day received your kind letter. The contents gladdened my heart. Blessed be God, not only for calling you to the saving knowledge of Himself, but sending you forth also to proclaim the Redeemer's unsearchable riches amongst poor sinners. "God," says Dr. Goodwin,[2] "has but one son, and he made me a minister of him." Gladly shall I come whenever bodily strength will allow to join my testimony with yours in Olney pulpit, that God is love. As yet I have not recovered from the fatigues of my American expedition. My shattered bark is scarce worth docking any more. But I would fain wear, and not rust out. Oh! My dear Mr. Newton, indeed and indeed I am ashamed that I have done and suffered so little for Him that hath done and suffered so much for ill and hell-deserving me. "Less than the least of all" must be my motto still. Cease not, I entreat you, to pray for me. I am sure my good old friend, Mr. Hull, will join with you. As enabled, you shall both, with all your connections and dear flock, be constantly remembered by, my dear, dear sir, Yours, etc., in a never-failing Emmanuel, G. Whitefield.[3]

Lord, help me to remember the importance of encouragement. Prompt me to overcome any procrastination when it comes to sending an encouraging message. Likewise, speak to me in any such ways today.

1 See Footnote 1, July 19th.

2 Dr. Thomas Goodwin (1600–80), English Puritan, theologian, and preacher. Chaplain to Oliver Cromwell.

3 From *John Newton of Olney and St Mary Woolnoth. An Autobiography and Narrative.*

August 3rd

Who knows but that you have come to your royal position for such a time as this?

(Esther 4:14)

Mr. Newton commenced his ministry at a very important period in the religious history of our country. The apostolic labours of Whitefield and Wesley and their coadjutors had aroused the nation from its spiritual slumber, and all classes were led to inquiry. There was not… a more interested spectator of this work than Mr. Newton… and though circumstances prevented his taking any very prominent part in it, it engaged all his sympathies. When he entered the Church these feelings suffered no abatement; and though he did not feel himself called upon to be so "irregular"[1] as Venn[2] and Berridge[3] and Haweis,[4] and some others of his friends, he yet steadily promoted the same work; and before many years had passed he occupied a conspicuous and most influential position in the Evangelical party.[5]

Right place, right time. So help me, God, on both counts.

1 As opposed to a minister settled in one specific parish or district.

2 Henry Venn (1796–1873). Anglican clergyman and Protestant missions strategist. Honorary Secretary of the Church Missionary Society.

3 John Berridge (1716–93), Anglican evangelical and hymnist.

4 Referred to previously in these pages.

5 From *John Newton of Olney and St Mary Woolnoth. An Autobiography and Narrative.*

August 4th

The Lord appeared unto him, and said... dwell in the land which I shall tell thee of

(Genesis 26:2 KJV)

Mr. Newton's first impressions of Olney are given in the following words...

I have reason to be satisfied with my situation, if the Lord should fix me here. I have some very cordial friends already, both in town and country. There are some adversaries, but I think not many. Mr. Browne* endured the main brunt of the opposition, and they were almost weary before he left them. The situation of the place is very pleasant at this time of year; but I suppose we shall find it cold and damp in winter. This will call for large fires, an expensive article,** but which seems in a manner necessary to my well-being. However, I, above most, have reason to depend on those words, "The Lord will provide."

* The Rev. Moses Browne was appointed vicar by Lord Dartmouth, but having a large and expensive family, he accepted the chaplaincy of Morden College, Blackheath, and thus Olney became vacant. Mr. Browne was somewhat distinguished as a poet, but what is of more consequence, he was a good man, an earnest preacher of the gospel, and had been the instrument of much good work at Olney.

** Mr. Newton's income was £60 a year.[1]

Gracious Father, be with those who are moving from one location to another in your service. Bless them and their loved ones, perhaps especially their children, at times of upheaval and change.

1 From *John Newton of Olney and St Mary Woolnoth. An Autobiography and Narrative.*

August 5th

Zeal for your house will consume me

(John 2:17)

Deeply impressed with the responsibility of his present engagements, Mr. Newton at once betook himself to their fulfilment with a zeal that never grew weary, and with a skill in devising various means of usefulness which true devotion to a cause will always suggest.[1]

Heavenly Father, I pray for ministers whose workload requires zeal and endless energy. Grant them, I pray, the wisdom to know when to work and when to stop. Protect them from "burn out".

1 From *John Newton of Olney and St Mary Woolnoth. An Autobiography and Narrative.*

August 6th

He sendeth the springs into the valleys, which run among the hills

(Psalm 104:10 KJV)

Crystal streamlet! Gently flowing,
O'er the pebble-cover'd bed;
Where the water lily growing
Rears its bloom adorned head.

Lightly dance the waters on,
Glistening in the sunny beam;
Murmuring a pleasing song;
Sweet thy music, gentle stream.

It tells of joy, and peace serene,
Happy homes and smiling faces;
And all fair domestic scene,
Haunt of gentlest loves and graces.

It tells of reason, lucid, free,
Passion, noble, pure, refin'd,
In bonds of social harmony
Interweaving all mankind.

And then it plays a higher part,
And tells of Him who bid thee flow;
Who form'd the flowers, with curious art,
That on thy grassy margin grow.[1][2]

Lord Jesus, help me to share in John Newton's gift of sensing your presence in that which surrounds me today: rivers, streams, grassy margins, and those everyday sights I might otherwise take for granted.

1 From *Temperance Hymn Book and Minstrel: a collection of hymns, songs and odes for temperance meetings and festivals*, but here from https://hymnary.org

2 While it is probably fair to say this unusual little hymn will never feature on any list of great classics, John Newton's composition serves, nevertheless, to draw our attention from the sights and sounds of this world to the things of God the Creator. For that reason alone, it is included here, as an aid to worship.

AUGUST 7TH

JONAH RAN AWAY FROM THE LORD AND HEADED FOR TARSHISH. HE WENT DOWN TO JOPPA, WHERE HE FOUND A SHIP BOUND FOR THAT PORT. AFTER PAYING THE FARE, HE WENT ABOARD AND SAILED FOR TARSHISH TO FLEE FROM THE LORD

(Jonah 1:3)

Scarcely was Mr. Newton settled at Olney, before some of his friends, perhaps not very wisely, suggested to him another and better position at Hampstead.[1] But he most judiciously declined even to entertain the thought of such a change. He writes thus on the subject to Mrs. Newton… "I observe what you hint about Hampstead; it would indeed be a situation in many respects desirable, and was I to be governed only by my affection for you, I could not wish but to see you placed in circumstances so much more agreeable than I can expect to procure at Olney. But let us take warning by the striking example of Mr. Browne,[2] and rather prefer the place where the Lord shall fix me to an over-hasty prospect of good things. I have convincing proof that the Lord has led us thus far; and without as clear an intimation of His will, I hope I shall not indulge the remotest wish for a removal. The people love me so well, express so warm a desire of the gospel's continuance among them, our assemblies are so crowded, and the Lord's presence (as I trust) so comfortable with us, that I should be bad and ungrateful, and even blind to my own comfort if I was not satisfied."[3]

Heavenly Father, guide my footsteps, I pray, especially when attractive options present themselves and clamour for my attention. Grant me discernment, especially when ships sailing for Tarshish tempt me!

1 An affluent area of London. Olney was considerably more rural and less sophisticated.

2 Moses Browne, referred to previously.

3 From *John Newton of Olney and St Mary Woolnoth. An Autobiography and Narrative.*

August 8th

Lord, I have heard of your fame;
I stand in awe of your deeds, Lord.
Repeat them in our day, in our time make them known;
in wrath remember mercy

(Habakkuk 3:2)

The Lord was pleased to visit our dear adopted daughter with a dreadful fever, which at first greatly affected her nerves, and afterwards became putrid. She… was brought very near to the grave indeed; for we once or twice thought her actually dead. But He, who in the midst of judgment remembers mercy, restored her.[1] [2]

Gracious Father, I pray for parents whose children are ill, as they watch over them and long for their recovery. How heart-breaking such days must be. Bless those children, Lord, and all healthcare professionals engaged in their treatment. Give strength to anxious mums and dads.

1 John and Mary Newton adopted his two orphaned nieces, Elizabeth and Eliza Catlett, children of one of his brothers-in-law and his wife.

2 From *The Life of the Rev. John Newton*.

August 9th

My joy is gone; grief is upon me; my heart is sick within me

(Jeremiah 8:18 ESV)

The attention and anxiety occasioned by this heavy dispensation… were by no means suited to promote that tranquillity of mind which my good friend wished my dear wife would endeavour to preserve. She was often much fatigued, and often much alarmed. Next to each other, this dear child had the nearest place, both in her heart and mine. The effects were soon apparent… her malady rapidly increased; her pains were almost incessant, and often intense, and she could seldom lie one hour in her bed in the same position. Oh! My heart, what didst thou then suffer![1]

Lord, yesterday I prayed for parents whose hearts are broken when their children are ill. Today, I add a prayer for husbands and wives who are forced to stand by while their loved ones suffer in pain. Draw close to them in their helplessness and sorrow.

1 From *The Life of the Rev. John Newton.*

August 10th

An overseer... must be hospitable

(Titus 1:7–8)

In... Olney, Newton found a good field for exercising his gift. The people of that country district were simple folk and ready to speak all their heart... [Newton's] fame became more widespread and people came from far and near to seek his counsel and help.[1] His friendly and hospitable home at Olney... was a place to which the troubled and tempted resorted. They found in him one who had been a worse sinner than themselves and who could enter into their experiences with tenderness and sympathy.[2]

Thank you, Lord, for those whose special gift is hospitality. Thank you for their generous willingness to open their homes. Bless them, and give to them as they give to others.

1 On one occasion, a Native American Indian Chief, from the Mohican tribe, visited John Newton at Olney. He had been converted under the ministry of George Whitefield, when Whitefield had visited North America.

2 From *Letters of John Newton*.

August 11th

YE ARE OUR EPISTLE WRITTEN IN OUR HEARTS, KNOWN AND READ OF ALL MEN

(2 Corinthians 3:2 KJV)

Those who could not come to see him sought his help by letter and it was this that brought the best out of Newton. Marcus Loane[1] describes his as "the letter writer par excellence of the Evangelical revival"[2] and says that "this was his distinctive contribution to that great movement." He was not unconscious of his gift and of his usefulness in this department and his diligence was prodigious. "It is the Lord's will," he says, "that I should do most by my letters." Newton's letters are the expression of his inmost being; he speaks of his correspondents as those to whom "when I can get leisure I send my heart by turns." But while they thus reflect the work of grace in his own life they are at the same time a mirror of the Evangelical thought and practice of his day. This is particularly helpful to us, for the spiritual life of the Church of Christ is not always at the same level of power and purity, and it is all too easy in such an age as our own to forget the true nature of vital Evangelical religion.[3]

Holy Spirit, I pray that your influence within my life may make a lasting impression upon those I meet, like ink on paper. Help me too, to "send my heart".

1 Sir Marcus Lawrence Loane (1911–2009), Anglican Primate of Australia.

2 For more on this, see https://www.christianity.com/church/church-history/timeline/1701-1800/evangelical-revival-in-england-11630228.html

3 From *Letters of John Newton*.

August 12th

Jesus replied, "Blessed are you, Simon son of Jonah, for this was not revealed to you by flesh and blood, but by my Father in heaven"

(Matthew 16:17)

The truths of scripture are not like mathematical theorems, which present exactly the same ideas to every person who understands the terms. The word of God is compared to a mirror, 2 Cor. iii.18; but it is a mirror in which the longer we look the more we see: the view will be growing upon us; and still we shall see but in part while on this side of eternity. When our Lord pronounced Peter blessed, declaring he had learnt that which flesh and blood could not have taught him, yet Peter was at that time much in the dark. The sufferings and death of Jesus, though the only and necessary means of his salvation, were an offence to him; but he lived to glory in what he once could not bear to hear of. Peter had received grace to love the Lord Jesus, to follow him, to venture all, and to forsake all for him; these first good dispositions were of God, and they led to further advances. So it is still.[1]

Loving God, assist me, I pray, to reveal supernatural information to the human heart; that which does not come naturally is shown to us by grace. Assist me, I pray, to live within that realm whereby my own heart is attuned to your influence and presence.

1 From *Cardiphonia: or, The Utterance of the Heart in the Course of a Real Correspondence, Volume One.*

AUGUST 13TH

THE FRIENDSHIP OF THE LORD IS FOR THOSE WHO FEAR HIM, AND HE MAKES KNOWN TO THEM HIS COVENANT

(Psalm 25:14 ESV)

By nature, self rules in the heart; when this idol is brought low, and we are truly willing to be the Lord's, and to apply to him for strength and direction, that we may serve him, the good work is begun; for it is a truth that holds universally and without exception, a man can receive nothing except it be given him from heaven. The Lord first finds us when we are thinking of something else, Isaiah lxv.1;[1] and then we begin to seek him in good earnest, and he has promised to be found of us. People may, by industry and natural abilities, make themselves masters of the external evidences of Christianity, and have much to say for and against different schemes and systems of sentiments; but all this while the heart remains untouched. True religion is not a science of the head, so much as an inward and heart-felt perception, which casts down imaginations, and every impulse that exalteth itself in the mind, and brings every thought into a sweet and willing subjection to Christ by faith.[2]

Thank you, seeking God, that you go out of your way to find the lost, and to bring them within the boundary of your love and grace. Thank you that you seek, find, and keep. This is my God.

1 "I revealed myself to those who did not ask for me; I was found by those who did not seek me. To a nation that did not call on my name, I said, 'Here am I, here am I'" (Isaiah 65:1).

2 From *Cardiphonia: or, The Utterance of the Heart in the Course of a Real Correspondence, Volume One.*

August 14th

Jesus answered and said unto them,
Ye do err, not knowing the scriptures, nor the power of God
(Matthew 22:29 KJV)

I am far from thinking the Socinians[1] all hypocrites, but I think they are all in a most dangerous error; nor do their principles exhibit to my view a whit more of the genuine fruits of Christianity than Deism[2] itself. You say, "If they be sincere, and fall not for want of diligence in searching, I cannot help thinking that God will not condemn them for an inevitable defect in their understandings." Indeed… I have such a low opinion of man in his depraved state, that I believe no one has real sincerity in religious matters till God bestows it: and when he makes a person sincere in his desires after truth, he will assuredly guide him to the possession of it in due time, as our Lord speaks, John vi.44, 45. To suppose that any persons can sincerely seek the way of salvation, and yet miss it through an inevitable defect of their misunderstandings, would contradict the plain promises of the gospel, such as Matt. vii.7, 8, John vii.16,17; but to suppose that nothing is necessary to be known, which some persons who profess sincerity cannot receive, would be in effect to make the scripture a nose of wax, and open a wide door for scepticism.[3]

A very specific prayer today, Lord: I ask that you would focus your light of grace and truth upon those who feel trapped within pseudo-Christian cults where truths are warped and twisted. Bless those, Lord, who work to counsel and support such people.

---

1 See Footnote 1, February 5th.
2 Belief in the existence of a supreme being; a creator who does not intervene in the universe.
3 From *Cardiphonia: or, The Utterance of the Heart in the Course of a Real Correspondence, Volume One.*

August 15th

NOT MANY OF YOU SHOULD BECOME TEACHERS, MY BROTHERS, FOR YOU KNOW THAT WE WHO TEACH WILL BE JUDGED WITH GREATER STRICTNESS

(James 3:1 ESV)

In a letter addressed to Mrs. Newton, her husband thus writes of Mr. Cecil:[1] "I heard him at St Antholin's.[2] He is a good speaker and a good preacher for a young man – for young men, not having had time to be duly acquainted with the depths of the hearts and the depths of Satan, cannot ordinarily be expected to speak with so much feeling and experience as they who have been in many conflicts and exercises. I love young preachers, for they are sprightly, warm, and earnest. I love old preachers, for they are solid, savoury, and experimental. So I love them all, and am glad to hear all as an occasion offers. But I own I like the old wine best.[3]

Thank you, Heavenly Father, for preachers young and old! Bless them, Lord. Inspire their efforts.

1 Richard Cecil (1748–1810), evangelical Anglican priest.

2 St Antholin, Budge Row, or St Antholin, Watling Street, was a church in the City of London. Of medieval origin, it was rebuilt to the designs of Sir Christopher Wren, following its destruction in the Great Fire of London in 1666. The seventeenth-century building was demolished in 1874. (https://en.wikipedia.org/wiki/St_Antholin,_Budge_Row)

3 From *John Newton of Olney and St Mary Woolnoth. An Autobiography and Narrative.*

August 16th

My grace is sufficient for you

(2 Corinthians 12:9)

The God who heareth prayer mercifully afforded relief, and gave such a blessing to the means employed that [Mrs. Newton's] pains ceased. And though I believe she never had an hour of perfect ease, she felt little of the distressing pains incident to her malady, from that time to the end of her life... excepting at three or four short intervals, which, taken together, hardly amounted to two hours; and these returns of anguish, I thought, were permitted, to show me how much I was indebted to the goodness of God for exempting her feelings, and my sympathy, from what would have been terrible indeed.[1]

Lord, for those in pain, I ask your comfort. For those caring for those in pain, I ask your strengthening grace.

1 From *The Life of the Rev. John Newton*.

August 17th

I was hungry and you gave me food

(Matthew 25:35 ESV)

In the close of summer [Mrs. Newton] was able to go to Southampton, and returned tolerably well. She was twice at church in the first week after she came home. She then went no more abroad, except in a coach for a little air and exercise: but she was cheerful, tolerably easy, slept as well as most people who are in perfect health, and could receive and converse with her kind friends who visited her. It was not long after, that she began to have a distaste for food, which continued and increased: so that, perhaps, her death was, at last, rather owing to weakness, from want of nourishment, than to her primary disorder. Her dislike was, first, to butcher's meat, of which she could bear neither the sight nor the smell. Poultry and fish, in their turns, became equally distasteful. She retained some relish for small birds, awhile after she had given up the rest; but it was at a season when they were difficult to be obtained. I hope I shall always feel my obligations to the kind friends who spared no pains to procure some for her, when they were not to be had in the markets. At that time I set more value upon a dozen of larks than upon the finest ox in Smithfield.[1] But her appetite failed to these also, when they became more plentiful.[2]

Thank you, Heavenly Father, for friends who rally round with kindness and support at a time of need and distress; those who will call with a casserole, or go the second mile in practical ways. They are worth their weight in gold.

1 Smithfield Market (also referred to as Smithfield Meat Market), London.

2 From *The Life of the Rev. John Newton*.

August 18th

Jesus was led by the Spirit into the wilderness to be tempted by the devil. After fasting forty days and forty nights, he was hungry. The tempter came to him and said, "If you are the Son of God, tell these stones to become bread." Jesus answered, "It is written: 'Man shall not live on bread alone, but on every word that comes from the mouth of God.'" Then the devil took him to the holy city and set him on the highest point of the temple. "If you are the Son of God," he said, "throw yourself down. For it is written: 'He will command his angels concerning you, and they will lift you up in their hands, so that you will not strike your foot against a stone.'" Jesus answered him, "It is also written: 'Do not put the Lord your God to the test.'" Again, the devil took him to a very high mountain and showed him all the kingdoms of the world and their splendour. "All this I will give you," he said, "if you will bow down and worship me." Jesus said to him, "Away from me, Satan! For it is written: 'Worship the Lord your God, and serve him only.'" Then the devil left him, and angels came and attended him

(Matthew 4:1–11)

I have always taken the account of our Lord's temptation literally. It corresponds to those of His people:

To despondency;
To presumption;
To ambition.[1]

Thank you, Lord, for this little insight: food for thought. Help me to think it through and apply it to my own life.

1 From *John Newton: Sailor, Preacher, Pastor, and Poet.*

AUGUST 19TH

EVEN IN LAUGHTER THE HEART MAY ACHE

(Proverbs 14:13 ESV)

The... death of Mr. Foote[1] ought to affect me. The papers abound with accounts of his gaiety a few hours before he was snatched into eternity. How awful, to spend a life in disseminating folly and wickedness, and then to be summoned without time or heart to ask for mercy! Thou wilt have mercy on whom Thou wilt; Thou art sovereign. I equalled him in inclination, however I fell short of him in his ability and opportunity for mischief. But I was spared, and he hardened.[2]

How often, Lord, might it be the case that those who laugh and joke on the surface are hurting on the inside, and wearing something of a perpetual mask? Laughter has its place, and good humour is invaluable, but I pray for anyone today who is relying on playing the joker as a social crutch. Cause them to think about serious issues of life and eternity.

1 Samuel Foote (1720–77), a popular and famous British satirist, dramatist, actor, writer, and theatre manager. He lost a leg in an accident, but turned this to comedic effect, often appearing on stage wearing a cork leg. His propensity towards dressing up on stage as a woman led to accusations of transvestitism.

2 From *John Newton of Olney and St Mary Woolnoth. An Autobiography and Narrative.*

August 20th

Whatever you do, do it all for the glory of God

(1 Corinthians 10:31)

It was in a letter… that Mr. Newton… expresses himself on the subject of theatrical entertainments… "If there is any practice in this land sinful, attendance in the play-house is properly and eminently so. The theatres are fountains and means of vice; I had almost said in the same manner and degree as the ordinances of the gospel are the means of grace; and I can hardly think there is a Christian upon earth who would dare to be seen there, if the nature and effects of the theatre were properly set before him. Dr. Witherspoon,[1] of Scotland, has written an excellent piece upon the Stage, or, rather, against it, which I wish every person who makes the best pretence to fear God had an opportunity of perusing."[2]

Times have changed, Lord! Nevertheless, please imprint today's Bible text upon my mind and heart, and let that be the yardstick for my choices when it comes to entertainment, and my use of leisure time.

1 John Knox Witherspoon (1723–94), Scottish-American Presbyterian minister and a Founding Father of the United States. He had a reputation for "Scottish common sense".

2 From *John Newton of Olney and St Mary Woolnoth. An Autobiography and Narrative.*

August 21st

EVEN THE DARKNESS IS NOT DARK TO YOU;
THE NIGHT IS BRIGHT AS THE DAY, FOR DARKNESS IS AS LIGHT WITH YOU

(Psalm 139:12 ESV)

Past three o'clock, and a cloudy morning. So says the watchman. I hope my dearest is now in a sweet sleep. When I have done writing, I shall proceed to the coach, which sets off exactly at four. Pray do not fear my being robbed, or hurt, in the dark. For I expect a guard will go with me, one to whom the darkness and the light are both alike. I went through a very long dark lane… with my dear Mr. Th—, but no one disturbed me, for the Lord was our preserver. You may be sure that my heart is continually with you. I seldom pass many minutes, without darting a thought upwards, in your behalf.[1] [2]

Loving God, you are with me when life can seem dark. You are with me when the light of your love appears to burn only dimly. Be with, I pray, those who are walking along life's darkest paths today; may they realize your guardianship and presence.

1 From *Letters to a Wife (Volume Two): By the Author of Cardiphonia*. This large collection of letters, written by John Newton to his beloved Mary, was published by Newton after her death. Written over the course of his marriage, they represent an astonishing storehouse and treasury of love, affection, and spiritual union. Theirs was a tremendous marriage, and Newton's highly articulate correspondence amply illustrates his depth of feeling for his true soulmate, covering as they do a wide range of subjects and emotions.

2 John Newton's ministry took him away from home from time to time, sometimes in the course of pastoral visitation and sometimes as part of his preaching routines.

August 22nd

Thus speaketh the Lord God of Israel, saying,
Write thee all the words that I have spoken unto thee in a book

(Jeremiah 30:2 KJV)

Breakfast with Mr. Scott. Heard him read a narrative of his conversion (The Force of Truth)[1] which he has drawn up for publication. It is striking and judicious, and will I hope by Divine blessing be very useful. I think I can see that he has got before me already. Lord, if I have been useful to him, do Thou, I beseech Thee make him now useful to me.[2]

Lord, I thank you for books and magazines that spread your word – biographies that inspire and stories that encourage. My prayers today are for writers and publishers. I ask you to bless their ministry.

1 See Footnote, July 1st.
2 From *John Newton of Olney and St Mary Woolnoth. An Autobiography and Narrative.*

August 23rd

THE PERSON WITHOUT THE SPIRIT DOES NOT ACCEPT THE THINGS THAT COME FROM THE SPIRIT OF GOD BUT CONSIDERS THEM FOOLISHNESS, AND CANNOT UNDERSTAND THEM BECAUSE THEY ARE DISCERNED ONLY THROUGH THE SPIRIT

(1 Corinthians 2:14)

There are some sentiments which I believe essential to the very state and character of a true Christian - and these make him a Christian, not merely by being his acknowledged sentiments, but by a certain peculiar manner in which he possesses them. There is a certain important change takes place in the heart, by the operation of the Spirit of God, before the soundest and most orthodox sentiments can have their proper influence upon us. This work, or change, the scripture describes by various names, each of which is designed to teach us the marvellous effects it produces, and the almighty power by which it is produced. It is sometimes called a new birth, John iii.3; sometimes a new creature or a new creation, as 2 Cor.v.17; sometimes the causing light to shine out of darkness, 2 Cor.iv.6; sometimes the opening the eyes of the blind, Acts xxvi.18; sometimes the raising the dead to life, Ephes. 11.5. Till a person has experienced this change, he will be at a loss to form a right conception of it; but it means not being proselyted to an opinion, but receiving a principle of divine life and light in the soul. And till this is received, the things of God, the truths of the gospel, cannot be rightly discerned or understood, by the utmost powers of fallen man, who, with all his wisdom, reason, and talents, is still but what the apostle calls the natural man, till the power of God visits his heart.[1]

Thank you, Lord, for this list of ways in which you reach the hearts of human beings, albeit only a glimpse of your creative and relentless love. You take the initiative and you make everything possible for salvation. I pray once again for those nearest and dearest to me who are not yet aware of such saving grace.

1 From *Cardiphonia: or, The Utterance of the Heart in the Course of a Real Correspondence, Volume One.*

August 24th

When he, the Spirit of truth, comes,
he will guide you into all the truth

(John 16:13)

[The work of God] is sometimes wrought suddenly, as in the case of Lydia, Acts xvi. 14; at other times very gradually. A person who before was a stranger even to the form of godliness, or at best content with a mere form – finds new thoughts arising in his mind, feels some concern about his sins, some desire to please God, some suspicions that all is not right. He examines his views of religion, hopes the best of them, and yet cannot rest satisfied in them. Today, perhaps, he thinks himself fixed; tomorrow he will be all uncertainty. He inquires of others, weighs, measures, considers, meets with sentiments which he had not attended to, thinks them plausible; but is presently shocked with objections, or supposed consequences, which he finds himself unable to remove. As he goes on in his inquiry, his difficulties increase. New doubts arise in his mind; even the scriptures perplex him, and appear to assert contrary things. He would sound the depths of truth by the plummet of his reason; but he finds his line is too short. Yet even now the man is under a guidance which will at length lead him right.[1] [2]

Heavenly Father, I pray for anyone who is searching for you today, and especially for anyone whose spiritual progress appears to be slow or frustrating – confusing, even. Keep them within the sphere of your light and guidance, and move them gradually towards understanding.

1 From *Cardiphonia: or, The Utterance of the Heart in the Course of a Real Correspondence, Volume One.*

2 Here, once again, we note evidence of John Newton's pastoral concern for those whose spiritual pilgrimage was not always satisfying, or easy to understand. He was always keen to encourage, or to offer a word of sympathy and understanding. Such concern was typical of Newton's ministry of correspondence.

August 25th

That night the king could not sleep; so he ordered the book of the chronicles, the record of his reign, to be brought in and read to him. It was found recorded there that Mordecai had exposed Bigthana and Teresh, two of the king's officers who guarded the doorway, who had conspired to assassinate King Xerxes. "What honour and recognition has Mordecai received for this?" the king asked

(Esther 6:1–3)

Great events sometimes spring from small causes. There is no proportion between causes and their issue. The sleepless night of Ahasuerus[1] was the preservation of the Jews.[2] [3]

Heavenly Father, help me to be sensitive towards apparently insignificant or unimportant events and happenings, lest I miss their significance and lose a blessing. Grant me that tenderness of heart whereby I can sense you at work even in that which initially appears mundane.

1 Or Artaxerxes II or Xerxes.
2 From *John Newton: Sailor, Preacher, Pastor, and Poet.*
3 As recorded in Esther 6–7.

August 26th

If by grace, then is it no more of works:
otherwise grace is no more grace

(Romans 11:6 KJV)

The gospel… is a salvation appointed for those who are ready to perish, and is not designed to put them in a way to save themselves by their own works. It speaks to us as condemned already, and calls upon us to believe in a crucified Saviour, that we may receive redemption through his blood, even the forgiveness of our sins. And the Spirit of God, by the gospel, first convinces us of unbelief, and misery; and then by revealing the things of Jesus to our minds, enables us, as helpless sinners, to come to Christ, to receive him, to behold him, or, in other words, to believe in him; and expect pardon, life, and grace from him; renouncing every hope and aim in which we were once rested, and "accounting all things loss and dung for the excellency of knowledge of Christ".[1]

Saving God, I pray that you will reach out in mercy to those who are trying to reach you via good works. Reveal your grace to them, so that they might realize that your love cannot be earned, but simply received.

1 From *Cardiphonia: or, The Utterance of the Heart in the Course of a Real Correspondence, Volume One.*

AUGUST 27TH

LOVE NEVER FAILS

(1 Corinthians 13:8)

An incident... cured Newton of any tendency to censoriousness. One of his friends... visited a woman in prison who was under sentence of transportation. He spoke of her crime and of eternal punishment; but found her quite indifferent. It surprised him that a woman so obviously in danger of Hell should care so little; and he changed his tactics and spoke of God's love and redemption. At once the woman was interested, then moved, and at last comforted. This story made a great impression on Newton. It did not lead him to abandon the orthodox notion of Hell... From this time onwards he disapproved of the many books which tried to make men good by frightening them with threats of punishment to come. He said, "Love and fear are like the sun and moon, seldom seen together."[1]

Help me, Lord, to square this circle!

1 From *An Ancient Mariner.*

August 28th

A man leaves his father and mother and is united to his wife

(Genesis 2:24)

If Newton's beliefs were few and plain, they included one that is difficult to understand. He felt that his love of [his wife] Mary was idolatry. "Notwithstanding all my encomiums upon Love," he told her, "I hold it very dangerous or indeed destructive unless regulated and governed by a sense of religion and a forethought for Eternity." A diary entry recalls… "thou knowest O Lord how much and how long we have been each other's Idols, thou mightiest justly have separated us by death or plunged us into affliction." Even Mary accepted this idea. She wrote, "I delight, admire, and love to hang upon every sentence, and every action of my dearest John; and yet how wanting, and how cold, am I to the gracious Author of all our mercies, to whom we owe each other, our happy affection, and all the satisfaction that flows from it!"[1]

Heavenly Father, guiding Spirit, teach me, I pray, to enjoy holy order in every area of my life. Teach me to grant you priority in all I do, and am.

1 From *An Ancient Mariner*.

August 29th

Fulfil ye my joy, that ye be likeminded, having the same love, being of one accord, of one mind

(Philippians 2:2 KJV)

The principle of true love to the brethren, is the love of God, that love which produceth obedience, I John, v.2. "By this we know that we love the children of God, when we love God, and keep his commandments." When people are free to form their connections and friendships, the ground of their communion is in a sameness of inclination. The love spoken of is spiritual. The children of God, who therefore stand in the relation of brethren to each other, though they have too many unhappy differences in points of smaller importance, agree in the supreme love they bear to their heavenly Father, and to Jesus their Saviour; of course they agree in disliking and avoiding sin, which is contrary to the will and command of the God whom they love and worship. Upon these accounts they love one another, they are like-minded; and they live in a world where the bulk of mankind are against them, have no regard to their Beloved, and live in the sinful practices which his grace has taught them to hate. Their situation, therefore, increases their affection to each other. They are washed by the same blood, supplied by the same grace, opposed by the same enemies, and have the same heaven in view: therefore they love one another with a pure heart fervently.[1] [2]

Today, Lord, I thank you for my friends at church. We may not always see eye-to-eye, and we may not agree on everything. Nevertheless, these are my Christian comrades, and I ask your blessing on each and every one of them.

1 From *Letters of John Newton*.

2 An extract from a letter John Newton wrote to a fellow clergyman. Newton was in great demand mongst his peers for spiritual counsel, sometimes especially with regard to church matters.

August 30th

THOU SHALT PROVIDE OUT OF ALL THE PEOPLE ABLE MEN, SUCH AS FEAR GOD, MEN OF TRUTH, HATING COVETOUSNESS; AND PLACE SUCH OVER THEM, TO BE RULERS OF THOUSANDS, AND RULERS OF HUNDREDS, RULERS OF FIFTIES, AND RULERS OF TENS

(Exodus 18:21 KJV)

In [Newton's] days some public affairs which would now be settled by the cabinet[1] were dealt with by the Privy Council.[2] In 1788 a meeting of the Privy Council, attended only by King George III,[3] five noblemen and Mr. Pitt (the Prime Minister),[4] called for a report on the Slave Trade. John Newton… gave evidence against the trade. When it was his turn to enter the council chamber, Mr. Pitt came out, took his arm and led him in, introducing him to the council. Newton gave evidence also to the House of Commons.[5]

Almighty God, my prayers this day are for the government. I pray too for those who visit Parliament in order to give evidence, or to make representation on behalf of a particular cause. Bless the cause of right.

1 The Cabinet of the United Kingdom, the decision-making body of the government. The modern cabinet is composed of the Prime Minister and twenty-one cabinet ministers.
2 A formal body of advisors to the Sovereign of the United Kingdom.
3 1738–1820
4 William Pitt the Younger (1759–1806).
5 From *John Newton and the Slave Trade.*

AUGUST 31ST

GIVE THANKS IN ALL CIRCUMSTANCES

(1 Thessalonians 5:18)

Under this trying discipline [his wife's illness] I learned more sensibly than ever to pity those whose sufferings, of a similar kind, are aggravated by poverty. Our distress was not small, yet we had everything within reach, that could in any degree conduce to her refreshment or relief; and we had faithful and affectionate servants, who were always willingly engaged to their power, yea... attending and assisting her by night and by day. What must be the feelings of those who, when afflicted with grievous diseases, pine away, unpitied, unnoticed, without help, and, in a great measure, destitute of common necessaries? This reflection, among others, contributed to quiet my mind, and to convince me that I still had much more cause for thankfulness than for complaint.[1]

Lord, forgive me when I find this instruction difficult to follow. Forgive me if I sometimes think it unreasonable, when times are tough. In your mercy, teach me the art of gratitude. Be close to those who are struggling today.

1 From *The Life of the Rev. John Newton.*

SEPTEMBER 1ST

MY RIGHT HAND HATH SPANNED THE HEAVENS

(Isaiah 48:13 KJV)

God sometimes changes His hand. An angel is sent to call Joseph into Egypt. Why was not this means used to call him at first to Bethlehem? All the world is to be disturbed to bring this about. The right hand of God is His leading hand, and the left that of permission. I would bring this subject down to all the common incidents of life. A knock at the door or a turning of a corner may be events which lead to important consequences. There is no such thing as accident.[1]

Lord of all, I place this day in your hands; where I go, what I do, all that I might encounter, and the people I meet. If there is "no such thing as accident", then it follows that what happens to me today is under your supervision. I place my trust in that assumption, and I thank you for your interest in the details.

1 From *John Newton: Sailor, Preacher, Pastor, and Poet.*

September 2nd

Do not put your trust in princes, in human beings, who cannot save. When their spirit departs, they return to the ground; on that very day their plans come to nothing. Blessed are those whose help is the God of Jacob, whose hope is in the Lord their God

(Psalm 146:3–5)

It is a great thing to be strong in the grace that is in Christ Jesus! But it is a hard lesson: it is not easy to understand it in theory; but when the Lord has taught us so far, it is still more difficult to reduce our knowledge to practice. But this is one end he has in view, in permitting us to pass through such a variety of inward and outward exercises, that we may cease from trusting in ourselves, or in any creature, or frame, or experiences, and be brought to a state of submission and dependence upon him alone. I was once visited something in the same way, seized with a fit of the apoplectic kind,[1] which held me near an hour, and left a disorder in my head, which quite broke the scheme of life I was then in, and was one of the means the Lord appointed to bring me into the ministry; but I soon perfectly recovered.[2]

How easy it is, Lord – how natural – to trust in oneself! Yet, how unreliable that self is – prone to illness, doubt, and weakness. Thank you for this much better option, of placing my all in your hands. Teach me, I pray, the benefits of submission and dependence!

1 In 1754, John Newton suffered a convulsive (epileptic?) fit and was forced to relinquish his seafaring life, although he did not, at that time, repudiate his support for the slave trade. This experience led to his employment at the docks in Liverpool and, subsequently, to his call to ordained ministry.

2 From *Cardiphonia: or, The Utterance of the Heart in the Course of a Real Correspondence, Volume One.*

September 3rd

Let your light shine before others,
that they may see your good deeds
and glorify your Father in heaven

(Matthew 5:16)

It seems to us impossible to read… of [John Newton's] labours, characterised by so much that was earnest and conscientious and Christian – of his happy contentment and trust in God – of his large catholic spirit – of his kindly and ever-wakeful sympathy – of the many valuable friends who seemed to be irresistibly attracted by his genial and devout temper – and not admire the man, and bless God on his behalf.[1]

Thank you, Lord, for those people you have introduced into my life, who have made a lasting impression. May I be one such person to the people I meet.

1 From *John Newton of Olney and St Mary Woolnoth. An Autobiography and Narrative.*

September 4th

Thou shalt remember the Lord thy God: for it is he that giveth thee power to get wealth

(Deuteronomy 8:18 KJV)

One thing might awaken our surprise, and even lead to the thought of impudence on the part of Mr. Newton, were we not in possession of the key to its solution… The vicarage at Olney was seldom without guests, but many came from far to seek his counsel, or to enjoy the benefits of his society and ministry; and it may well be asked, how could he thus keep open house upon the scanty income he was receiving? The simple explanation is this – Mr. Thornton,[1] as soon as he became acquainted with Mr. Newton, evidently formed a high estimate of his character. He was fully aware of the peculiarity of his circumstances, and of the expense his position was likely to involve; and so, in the exercise of his singular liberality, which so often flowed in unusual channels, he annually contributed a large sum to supply the wants of his friend. "Be hospitable," he says, "and keep an open house for such as are worthy of entertainment – help the poor and needy: I will statedly allow you £200 a year, and readily and whenever you have occasion to draw for more."[2]

Lord God, you have blessed some people with great wealth. Help them to use it wisely, and touch their hearts with a spirit of generosity. Thank you for benefactors whose kindness hugely benefits Christian work. And as for me, Lord, take my gold and silver, such as I have. I offer it back to you.

1 John Thornton (1720–90) was an investor and philanthropist who donated heavily to a number of Christian causes. He was a devout Anglican, but gave generously to ministries of all evangelical denominations. Thornton sponsored John Newton at Olney, and then again when Newton moved to St Mary Woolnoth, Lombard Street, London.

2 From *John Newton of Olney and St Mary Woolnoth. An Autobiography and Narrative.*

September 5th

He went out to the field one evening to meditate

(Genesis 24:63)

[I] proposed to spend this day in prayer, with fasting. I have not observed a day in this manner since I came to Olney. I am sensible of the advantage of occasions of more solemn retirement. As the weather was fine, I chose to wander in the woods and fields. I hope the Lord was, in a measure, with me, and gave me some sincere desires and breathings.[1] [2]

Gracious God, you deign to meet us wherever we are: at the kitchen sink, in church, in a field, out walking. This is my God.

1 From *John Newton of Olney and St Mary Woolnoth. An Autobiography and Narrative.*

2 John Newton was often in the habit of praying in the open air, while walking in fields in the countryside. It might be thought he preferred this means of communion with God to more formal approaches. The fact that he appears not to have walked and prayed in this way for some time indicates that he was busily engaged in parish matters in Olney, and that this venture was a welcome return to a familiar habit.

September 6th

Jesus said, "Let the little children come to me, and do not hinder them, for the kingdom of heaven belongs to such as these"

(Matthew 19:14)

There was... in Olney a mansion commonly called the Great House, the property of Lord Dartmouth.[1] Being unoccupied, and Mr. Newton thinking its spacious rooms might be available for some of his religious services, he obtained the use of it, the first instance for the meetings of the children. It became henceforth the scene of many very happy Christian gatherings. Here he began to meet the children on Thursday afternoons; "not so much," he says, "to teach them a catechism (though I shall attend to that likewise) as to talk, preach, and reason with them, and explain the Scriptures to them in their own little way." The number so increased that ultimately it was necessary to remove them to the chancel. Here more than two hundred would sometimes be gathered. Mr. Newton also commenced in the Great House an evening meeting for prayer and exhortation, which proved a service of great interest and usefulness.[2]

A prayer today, Heavenly Father, for Sunday schools, Sunday school teachers, and all forms of children's work – clubs, groups, and special events. How lovely it would be, Lord, to see such a work as this repeated in these days!

1 See Footnote 2, July 15th. (The Great House, Olney, was demolished sometime towards the end of the 1800s.)

2 From *John Newton of Olney and St Mary Woolnoth. An Autobiography and Narrative.*

SEPTEMBER 7TH

HE WHO IS IN YOU IS GREATER THAN HE WHO IS IN THE WORLD

(1 John 4:4 ESV)

The enemy assaults me more by sap than storm; and I am ready to think I suffer more by languor than some of my friends do by the sharper conflicts to which they are called.[1]

Only a small reading today, Lord, but one that is large in spiritual truth and importance. Stand by your people, I pray, whatever the nature of the opposition or attack they face. Be with us each in our personal conflicts.

1 From *Cardiphonia: or, The Utterance of the Heart in the Course of a Real Correspondence, Volume One.*

September 8th

The eyes of the Lord are on the righteous, and his ears are open to their prayer

(1 Peter 3:12 ESV)

Congregations [at Olney] large and serious. Almost every week I hear of some either awakened or seriously impressed. We have now a fixed little company who come to my house on Sabbath evening after tea. We spend an hour or more in prayer and singing, and part between six and seven…

All my plantations flourish. The prayer-meeting is well attended, and in general, I hope, proves a time of refreshment; so that some of the younger and more lively sort are encouraged to attempt another on Sunday mornings at six o'clock, to pray for their poor minister and for a blessing on the ordinances.[1]

Great reports from Olney, Lord! Rooted in prayer! Thank you, Lord, that you hear and answer prayer. You did in Olney, all those years ago, and you do so today.

1 From *John Newton of Olney and St Mary Woolnoth. An Autobiography and Narrative.*

September 9th

I will thank you in the great congregation

(Psalm 35:18 ESV)

The accommodation in the church at Olney was insufficient for the large numbers who now regularly attended Mr. Newton's ministry, and, to meet this want, he was anxious to erect a gallery. This object was effected, and it was opened… but there seemed no more room in the body of the church than before…

"The people are as lively and attentive as ever. All our meetings are well attended, and some new additions, which I have good hopes of… I have been engaged about six hours in speaking at church and at home, yet find myself in good ease, little or nothing fatigued; but, if there was occasion, I could readily go and preach again."[1] [2]

More of the same, please, Lord! More of the same!

1 From *John Newton of Olney and St Mary Woolnoth. An Autobiography and Narrative.*

2 John Newton's preaching attracted great crowds, as did his natural personality and his pastoral interest in people. Perhaps the strength of Newton's appeal as a minister lay in his empathy towards sinners. He knew himself very well, and was aware of his weaknesses and flaws. This awareness translated itself into a ministry and an influence based upon mercy and kindness, which others were quick to sense; and likewise, his unerring willingness to go to great lengths on behalf of others.

September 10th

The Lord, The Lord God, merciful and gracious, longsuffering, and abundant in goodness and truth

(Exodus 34:6 KJV)

One of my great complaints is that my time flies away and nothing done. This is much owing to my having lost the habit of early rising. This not only breaks in upon my study, but cuts me short of sacred exercises. What wonder I am lean when I often miss my regular meals!… I seek, I want, I mourn all too faintly, but I trust my desire to Jesus and holiness. I want more communion with Him, more conformity to Him. Oh, when shall it be?[1]

Thank you, Lord Jesus, that my relationship with you hinges on your grace and mercy, in that you are faithful towards me even if and when I am fickle towards you. Time and again, Lord, you retrieve my fellowship with you. You are a faithful friend.

1 From *John Newton of Olney and St Mary Woolnoth. An Autobiography and Narrative.*

September 11th

I am my beloved's and my beloved is mine

(Song of Solomon 6:3)

I remember when there were not only hills, but oceans between us. Then the Lord brought us together in safety. It seems to me now, almost as if we had been separated for the time of an African voyage.[1] But I wait with patience, your summons to meet you… I would rather see you than all the world accounts magnificent. I had rather hear you speak than hear all Handel's music. I would rather call you, Mine, than possess waggon loads of gold. Some persons would deem this the language of folly, but it is the language of love, and of truth.[2]

Thank you, Lord of love, for those who love me. They are my greatest human treasure.

1 Throughout his times at sea, and in particular when he was enduring dreadful treatment and the pains of homesickness, Newton's longing to see his beloved Mary again was sometimes the only lifeline he had. The hope of reunion was all that kept him alive at times.

2 From *Letters to a Wife (Volume Two): By the Author of Cardiphonia.*

September 12th

Let marriage be held in honour

(Hebrews 13:4 ESV)

It grows late. The maids are gone to bed, and I shall soon retire to mine. It is rather lonely at present; but I thank God, I am a stranger to the remotest wish, that it were lawful for me to have any companion, but yourself. Since the Lord gave me the desire of my heart, in my dearest dearest Mary, the rest of the sex are no more to me, than the tulips in the garden. Oh, what a mercy it is, that I can say this! I speak it not to my own profit, but to the profit of the Lord. I have a vile heart, capable of every evil; and, in myself, am as prone to change as a weather-cock. But, with respect to you, he has been pleased to keep me fixed, as the north pole, without one minute's visitation… and I humbly trust that he will keep me to the end of my life.[1]

My prayers today, Lord, are on the subject of marriage:
Thank you for marriages that are happy and successful, and have endured.
Bless them.
Help those whose marriages are in trouble. Have mercy.
Guide those who are contemplating marriage.
Help those whose marriages have broken down, and are now divorced.

1 From *Letters to a Wife (Volume Two): By the Author of Cardiphonia.*

SEPTEMBER 13TH

THE PATH OF THE RIGHTEOUS IS LIKE THE MORNING SUN,
SHINING EVER BRIGHTER TILL THE FULL LIGHT OF DAY

(Proverbs 4:18)

I hope the Lord has contracted my desires and aims almost to the point of study, the knowledge of his truth. All other acquisitions are transient, and comparatively vain. And yet, alas! I am a slow scholar; nor can I see in what respect I get forward, unless that every day I am more confirmed in the conviction of my own emptiness and inability to all spiritual good. And so, notwithstanding this, I am still enabled to stand my ground, I would hope, since no effect can be without an adequate cause, that I have made some advance, though in a manner imperceptible to myself, towards a more simple dependence upon Jesus as my all in all. It is given me to thirst and to taste, if it is not given me to drink abundantly; and I would be thankful for the desire. I see and approve the wisdom, grace, suitableness, and sufficiency of the gospel salvation; and since it is for sinners, and I am a sinner, and the promises are open, I do not hesitate to call it mine.[1]

Heavenly Father, how slow and halting my spiritual progress can seem: one step forward and two steps back at times! Nevertheless, I pray that you will continue to shine your light of grace upon my pathway, according to your faithfulness. May it be so today.

1 From *Cardiphonia: or, The Utterance of the Heart in the Course of a Real Correspondence, Volume One.*

September 14th

Those who know your name trust in you,
for you, Lord, have never forsaken those who seek you

(Psalm 9:10)

I am a weary, laden soul; Jesus has invited me to come. I seldom have an uneasy doubt, at least not of any continuance, respecting my pardon, acceptance, and interest in all the blessings of the New Testament. And, amidst a thousand infirmities and evils under which I groan, I have the testimony of my conscience when under the trial of his word, that my desire is sincerely towards him, that I choose no other portion, that I allowedly serve no other master… Undoubtedly I derive from the gospel a peace at bottom which is worth more than a thousand worlds.[1]

I bring my doubts to you today, Lord; likewise, any "infirmities and evils under which I groan". I simply place everything at the foot of your cross. Thank you for the privilege of being free to do so.

1 From *Cardiphonia: or, The Utterance of the Heart in the Course of a Real Correspondence, Volume One.*

September 15th

Devote your heart and soul to seeking the Lord your God

(1 Chronicles 22:19)

In the evening had a full house [at Olney]. I have lately sent tickets to those who I hope are serious, to exclude some who only come to look about them. Upon these occasions I have reckoned about seventy persons of both sexes, of whom I have good hope the Lord has touched their hearts. Oh that I had a greater thirst for souls... Have appointed a meeting for conversation at my own house on Monday evening for the few men who belong to our little society.[1]

What a fascinating idea, Lord – tickets to come to church! Thank you, though, for Newton's wisdom in giving the advantage to those who were seeking after truth, as opposed to just wasting their time in idle curiosity. I pray, Lord, for any who are seeking today, and whose search is genuine. Help your church always to be ready to place every advantage at their disposal.

1 From *John Newton of Olney and St Mary Woolnoth. An Autobiography and Narrative.*

SEPTEMBER 16TH

IF, AFTER THEY HAVE ESCAPED THE DEFILEMENTS OF THE WORLD THROUGH THE KNOWLEDGE OF OUR LORD AND SAVIOUR JESUS CHRIST, THEY ARE AGAIN ENTANGLED IN THEM AND OVERCOME, THE LAST STATE HAS BECOME WORSE FOR THEM THAN THE FIRST. FOR IT WOULD HAVE BEEN BETTER FOR THEM NEVER TO HAVE KNOWN THE WAY OF RIGHTEOUSNESS THAN AFTER KNOWING IT TO TURN BACK FROM THE HOLY COMMANDMENT DELIVERED TO THEM. WHAT THE TRUE PROVERB SAYS HAS HAPPENED TO THEM: "THE DOG RETURNS TO ITS OWN VOMIT, AND THE SOW, AFTER WASHING HERSELF, RETURNS TO WALLOW IN THE MIRE"

(2 Peter 2:20–22 ESV)

Apostasy, in all its branches, takes its rise from atheism. "I have set the Lord always before me," etc. We are surprised at the fall of a famous professor; but, in the sight of God, he was gone before; it is only we that have now first discovered it. "He that despiseth small things shall fall by little and little."[1] [2]

Lord, have mercy on those who abandon their faith. In such mercy, bring them back again, however long they remain away from a sense of belief and belonging. I pray especially for any known to me personally who have wandered away from a living relationship with Christ.

1 Ecclesiasticus 19:1 in *Revised version with Apocrypha*, 1895.

2 From *The Life of the Rev. John Newton.*

September 17th

Ears that hear and eyes that see – the Lord has made them both

(Proverbs 20:12)

Man is not taught anything to purpose till God becomes his teacher, and then the glare of the world is put out, and the value of the soul rises in full view. A man's present sentiments may not be accurate; but we make too much of sentiments. We pass a field with a few blades, we call it a field of wheat; but here is no wheat; no, not in perfection, but wheat is sown, and full ears may be expected.[1]

Help me, Lord, today, to see things as you see them; grant me your perspective on that which concerns me this day, so that, as I walk with you as my teacher, the sentiments of this world become less and less important, and I develop a kingdom perspective.

1 From *The Life of the Rev. John Newton*.

September 18th

Thou, even thou only, knowest the hearts of all the children of men

(1 Kings 8:39 KJV)

When I am in private, I am usually dull and stupid to a strange degree, or the prey to a wild and ungoverned imagination that I may truly say, when I would do good, horrid evil is present with me. Ah! how different is this from sensible comfort! And if I was to compare myself to others, to make their experience my standard, and was not helped to retreat to the sure word of God as my refuge, how hard should I find it to maintain a hope that I had either part or lot in the matter! What I call my good times are, when I can find my attraction in some little measure fixed to what I am about, which indeed is not always nor frequently any case in prayer, and still seldomer in reading the scripture. My judgment embraces these means as blessed privileges, and Satan has not prevailed to drive me from them; but in the performances, I too often find them tasks, feel a reluctance when the seasons return, and am glad when they are finished. Oh what a mystery is the heart of man![1] [2]

Lord, where would we be without your governance and kind control? Left to our own devices! What curious creatures we are! Please offer us fixed points of stability and belief, which influence our conduct. Hold on to us each, I pray.

1 From *Cardiphonia: or, The Utterance of the Heart in the Course of a Real Correspondence, Volume One.*

2 We can but admire the staggering humility that was part of John Newton's charm and attractiveness. Here he is, an ordained minister in the Church of England and increasingly seasoned in spiritual matters, yet still very much (increasingly) aware of his tendency towards the base nature. He never affected false piety or any kind of spirituality that wasn't genuine.

September 19th

Jesus was in the stern, sleeping on a cushion. The disciples woke him and said to him, "Teacher, don't you care if we drown?" He got up, rebuked the wind and said to the waves, "Quiet! Be still!" Then the wind died down and it was completely calm. He said to his disciples, "Why are you so afraid? Do you still have no faith?"

(Mark 4:38–40)

The ship was safe when Christ was in her, though he was really asleep… The times look dark and stormy, and call for much circumspection and prayer; but let us not forget that we have an infallible pilot, and that the power, and wisdom, and honour of God, are embarked with us. At Venice they have a fine vessel, called the Bucentaur,[1] in which, on a certain day of the year, the Doge[2] and nobles embark, and go a little way to sea, to repeat the foolish ceremony of a marriage between the Republic and the Adriatic… when they say, a gold ring is gravely thrown overboard. Upon this occasion, I have been told, when the honour and government of Venice are shipped on board the Bucentaur, the pilot is obliged by his office to take an oath safely back again.[3]

Stay with me, Lord Jesus, on my life's voyage. With you in the vessel, I cannot fail. Stay with me too, when I sail from this life to the next.

1 The state barge of the doges of Venice.
2 Governor of Venice.
3 From *Cardiphonia: or, The Utterance of the Heart in the Course of a Real Correspondence, Volume One.*

September 20th

Will you not revive us again,
that your people may rejoice in you?

(Psalm 85:6 ESV)

A revival is wanted… and I trust some of us are longing for it. We are praying and singing for one… Let us take courage; though it may seem marvellous in our eyes, it is not in the Lord's. He changed the desert into a fruitful field, and bid dry bones live. And if he prepare our hearts to pray, he will surely incline his ear to hear.[1]

Reviving God, we may not understand your ways in revival, or your timings, yet I pray today for your winds of refreshment to breeze through the church. Begin with my church, Lord. Begin with me.

1 From *Cardiphonia: or, The Utterance of the Heart in the Course of a Real Correspondence, Volume One.*

September 21st

There is a way that appears to be right,
but in the end it leads to death
(Proverbs 16:25)

Texts of scripture, brought powerfully to the heart, are very desirable and pleasant, if their testimony is to humble us, to give us a more feeling sense of the preciousness of Christ, or of the doctrines of grace; if they make sin more hateful, enliven our regard to the means, or increase our confidence in the power and faithfulness of God. But if they are understood as intimating our path of duty in particular circumstances, or confirming us in purposes we may have already formed, not otherwise clearly warranted by the general strain of the word, or by the leadings of Providence, they are for the most part ensnaring, and always to be suspected. Nor does their coming into the mind at the time of prayer give them more authority in this regard. When the mind is intent upon any subject, the imagination is often watchful to catch at any thing which may seem to countenance the favourite pursuit. It is too common to ask counsel of the Lord when we have already secretly determined for ourselves.[1] [2]

O Lord, grant me discernment when I pray. Grant me courage to admit the difference between your leadings and my preferences. Help me, Lord, to avoid even inadvertent disobedience.

1 From *Cardiphonia: or, The Utterance of the Heart in the Course of a Real Correspondence, Volume One.*

2 John Newton was an advocate of waiting upon the Lord in order to clarify and establish the guidance of the Holy Spirit in one's life. He applied this to his own decisions, rather than trusting feelings or even Bible verses that came to his mind.

September 22nd

If anyone does not provide for his relatives, and especially for members of his household, he has denied the faith

(1 Timothy 5:8 ESV)

Though the love of money is a great evil, money itself, obtained in a fair and honourable way, is desirable upon many accounts, though not for its own sake. Meat, clothes, fire, and books, cannot easily be had without it; therefore, if these be necessary, money which procures them must be necessary likewise... They who set the least value upon money, have in some respects the most need of it. A generous mind will feed a thousand pangs in strait circumstances, which some unfeeling souls would not be sensible of. You could perhaps endure hardships alone, yet it might pinch you to the very bone to see the person you love exposed to them.[1]

Give me a heart of compassion. Give me a heart of wisdom. Teach me wise and compassionate generosity.

1 From *Cardiphonia: or, The Utterance of the Heart in the Course of a Real Correspondence, Volume One.*

September 23rd

Why tempt ye God?

(Acts 15:10 KJV)

Is it not written, "The Lord will provide"? It is: but it is written again, "Thou shalt not tempt the Lord thy God." Hastily to plunge ourselves into difficulties, upon a persuasion that he will find some way to extricate us, seems to me a species of tempting him.[1]

Teach my heart and mind, Holy Spirit, the difference between faith and recklessness. May I never shy away from audacious confidence in your love. By the same token, though, may I never take risks that weren't commissioned in the courts of Heaven.

From *Cardiphonia: or, The Utterance of the Heart in the Course of a Real Correspondence, Volume One.*

September 24th

Each one of you says, "I follow Paul," or "I follow Apollos," or "I follow Cephas," or "I follow Christ." Is Christ divided? Was Paul crucified for you? Or were you baptized in the name of Paul?

(1 Corinthians 1:12–13 ESV)

Omitted our prayer-meeting and attended Mr. Bradbury,[1] who preached a very good sermon… I am glad of such opportunities at times, to discountenance bigotry and party spirit, and to set our dissenting brethren an example, which I think ought to be our practice towards all who love the Lord Jesus Christ and preach His gospel without respect to form or denominations.[2][3]

Father, some styles are too staid for my liking; some expressions of worship too lively! It doesn't matter. I thank you for my own church fellowship, but I thank you too for brothers and sisters who do things differently. I ask you to bless each Christian denomination in my town and district.

1 Reverend Thomas Bradbury (1677–1759), English congregational minister.

2 From *John Newton of Olney and St Mary Woolnoth. An Autobiography and Narrative.*

3 John Newton was well known for deliberately mixing and ministering within ecumenical circles. He was no supporter of denominational bias if it resulted in segregation, preferring Christian fellowship with all believers where there was an agreement of doctrine, if not style.

SEPTEMBER 25TH

BE SHEPHERDS OF GOD'S FLOCK THAT IS UNDER YOUR CARE, WATCHING OVER THEM – NOT BECAUSE YOU MUST, BUT BECAUSE YOU ARE WILLING, AS GOD WANTS YOU TO BE

(1 Peter 5:2)

"Another excursion today with Christian friends. Had a very pleasant walk to Turvey.[1] Added two gracious women there to my stock of Christian acquaintances. Had much conversation there and by the way, with which I hope were all refreshed."[2]

Thus did Mr. Newton cultivate and promote the fellowship of the saints, and this piously [sic] endeavour to search out and to build up their most holy faith the scattered members of Christ's flock. It mattered little to this truly good and earnest man how humble or how poor they might be, so long as they were among the number of true believers.[3]

Heavenly Father, help me today to build people up.

1 A village approximately four miles from Onley.
2 An extract from John Newton's diary notes.
3 From *John Newton of Olney and St Mary Woolnoth. An Autobiography and Narrative.*

September 26th

We wait in hope for the Lord; he is our help and our shield. In him our hearts rejoice, for we trust in his holy name. May your unfailing love be with us, Lord, even as we put our hope in you

(Psalm 33:20–22)

My inward frame I know not how to describe. In general I seem unable to get near the Lord, and yet by grace am restrained from wandering very far away. Coldness in prayer, and darkness, and formality in reading the word are almost my continual burden. I want to be more lively, feeling, and affectionate in spiritual things, but I feel the dead weight of unbelief and indwelling sin keeping me low. I think my desire is towards the Lord. My hope, my trust is in Jesus; other refuge I neither have nor desire.[1]
[2]

My prayers this day, Lord, are for those who are struggling in the ways John Newton describes here: some kind of apathy or distress within. I pray for you to help them, to lift their spirits, and, perhaps most of all, to keep them close to your heart.

1 From *John Newton of Olney and St Mary Woolnoth. An Autobiography and Narrative.*

2 John Newton was an intensely sensitive man, and someone who was very much in tune with his own feelings. To that end, he was acutely aware of his need to maintain a strong and steady faith in Christ, over and above the vagaries of changing emotions.

September 27th

I long to see you

(Romans 1:11)

I hope it will be better with me, when you return. I am not uncomfortable, but I am a little unsettled. I can do more business, in two days, when you are at home, than in three, when you are abroad. For though I sit many an hour in my study, without seeing you, yet to know, that you are in, or about the house, and that I can see you when I please, gives a sort of composure to my mind; so that I must not say, your company is a hindrance to me upon the whole. Though occasionally, my attention to you, may make me leave something undone, which I ought to have done. In that, whether with you, or without you, I am a poor creature, and see much to be ashamed of every day, and in every circumstance… However, I have great reason to bless God, that I ever saw you.[1]

Loving God, I pray for those who are separated from their loved ones. Whatever the reasons for such separations, I pray for your comfort and support when enforced absences are difficult.

1 From *Letters to a Wife (Volume Two): By the Author of Cardiphonia.*

September 28th

A time to embrace and a time to refrain from embracing

(Ecclesiastes 3:5)

How often we have deserved to be separated! Yet we are spared to each other. May our lives praise him, and may we be freed from idolatry! To love each other, and dearly too, is no sin; nay, it is our duty. But he will not suffer a creature, to usurp his place in the heart. The time of our ignorance, he mercifully winked at; but now he has shown us what is right, it behoves us to be on our guard. Oh! That he may so display the power of his grace, that the bonds, and shackles, which detain our souls might be broken! I now can judge, by my own feelings, how much you must have suffered, during my long long day in London, especially, sick and confined as you were, and anxious for the events of my journey. I never pitied you as I ought, till now. For though I likewise longed every day, and every hour, to see you, I had many things to divert my attention, and alleviate the feelings of absence.[1] [2]

Heavenly Father, John Newton's thoughts appear to be somewhat harsh and severe! However, I ask you to grant me that same spirit of single-mindedness, whereby you are Lord of all and first in my heart.

1 From *Letters to a Wife (Volume Two): By the Author of Cardiphonia.*

2 John Newton sometimes left Olney in order to travel to London, either to visit friends or to listen to other preachers. He was always anxious for good Christian company, and keen to learn from fellow ministers. On this occasion, he was obliged to leave Mary at home, even though she was increasingly unwell.

SEPTEMBER 29TH

WE DO NOT LOSE HEART. THOUGH OUTWARDLY WE ARE WASTING AWAY, YET INWARDLY WE ARE BEING RENEWED DAY BY DAY

(2 Corinthians 4:16)

I feel your headache at this distance. Your frequent indispositions are not pleasant, but I trust they are mercies, for which we have reason to be thankful. Our comforts and crosses are all from the same hand. We have chastisement, only because we need it. I aim to leave you in the Lord's hands. Should we not forget ourselves, if he did not seasonably remind us, what, and where, we are? In the case of some of your dear friends, for whom you grieve, you may see, how, in all probability, it would have been with you, if his eye of Love had not been fixed upon you from your birth. He prepared his dispensations, to withdraw you gradually from that life of vanity and dissipation, to which otherwise you might have been enslaved all your days. And he has been gently dealing with your heart, for several years past, leading you, if slowly, yet, I hope, surely, nearer to himself. How much of his ways, how many of his people, has he shown you! And he has given you a heart to love them, and reconcile you to things to which you were once as little inclined, to those whom you now pity.[1]

What a remarkable perspective, Lord! To note your good purposes even in the midst of illness, and to trust through difficult times. Strengthen my faith, I pray, so that I too may think like this. I pray for your blessing upon those whose confidence in your love is under strain, that they would not lose heart.

1 From *Letters to a Wife (Volume Two): By the Author of Cardiphonia.*

September 30th

In quietness and trust is your strength

(Isaiah 30:15)

I was abroad[1] when your letter came, but employ the first post to thank you for your confidence. My prayers (when I can pray) you may be sure of: as to advice, I see not that the case requires much. Only be a quiet child, and be patiently at the Lord's feet. He is the best friend and manager in these matters, for he has a key to open every heart.[2][3]

Lord, how difficult it can be to wait! Patience does not come naturally, and can all-too-easily destroy faith. I pray for anyone who is waiting; grant them quietness and trust even when it seems you are not responding to their prayers. Grant them, too, the support and counsel of kind and understanding friends.

1 Away from home, not necessarily overseas.
2 An extract from *Letters to the Rev. Mr R—*.
3 From *Cardiphonia: or, The Utterance of the Heart in the Course of a Real Correspondence, Volume One*.

October 1st

The fruit of the Spirit is… patience

(Galatians 5:22 ESV)

Mr. Self does not like suspense, but would willingly come to the point at once: but Mr. Faith (when he gets liberty to hold up his head) will own, that in order to make our temporal mercies wear well, and to give us a clearer sense of the hand that bestows them, a waiting and a praying time are very seasonable. Worldly people expect their schemes to run upon all-fours, as we say, and the objects of their wishes to drop into their mouths without difficulty; and if they succeed, they of course burn incense to their own drag,[1] and say, This was my doing: but believers meet with rubs and disappointments, which convince them, that if they obtain any thing, it is the Lord must do it for them.[2] [3]

What can I say, Lord, except to repeat my prayer of yesterday? I lay this before you once again.

1 This meaning is unclear.

2 An extract from *Letters to the Rev. Mr R—*.

3 From *Cardiphonia: or, The Utterance of the Heart in the Course of a Real Correspondence, Volume One*.

October 2nd

Devote yourself to the... reading of Scripture

(1 Timothy 4:13)

I have many books that I cannot sit down to read. They are indeed good and sound, but like halfpence there goes a great quantity to a little amount. There are silver books, and a very few golden books. But I have one book worth more than all, called the Bible, and that is a book of bank-notes.[1]

Thank you, Lord, for books – the "silver" ones and the "golden" ones. Thank you most of all, though, for my Bible.

1 From *John Newton: Sailor, Preacher, Pastor, and Poet.*

October 3rd

Jesus came to a village where a woman named Martha opened her home to him. She had a sister called Mary, who sat at the Lord's feet listening to what he said. But Martha was distracted by all the preparations that had to be made. She came to him and asked, "Lord, don't you care that my sister has left me to do the work by myself? Tell her to help me!" "Martha, Martha," the Lord answered, "you are worried and upset about many things, but few things are needed – or indeed only one. Mary has chosen what is better, and it will not be taken away from her"

(Luke 10:38–42)

Martha her love and joy expressed
By care to entertain her guest;
While Mary sat to hear her Lord,
And could not bear to lose a word.

The principle in both the same,
Produced in each a different aim;
The one to feast the Lord was led,
The other waited to be fed.

But Mary chose the better part,
Her Saviour's words refreshed her heart;
While busy Martha angry grew,
And lost her time and temper too.

With warmth she to her sister spoke,
But brought upon herself rebuke;
One thing is needful, and but one,
Why do thy thoughts on many run?

How oft are we like Martha vexed,
Encumbered, hurried, and perplexed!
While trifles so engross our thought,
The one thing needful is forgot.[1]

There are lessons in these lines, Lord!

1 Originally from *Olney Hymns* (1779).

October 4th

A happy heart makes the face cheerful

(Proverbs 15:13)

Scott said that Christ never laughed.[1] This is true perhaps, but levity is an expression of cheerfulness, not of joy. The perfectly happy man is not light. Jesus smiled perhaps. But if He never smiled it is no wonder, for He was especially "a man of sorrows and acquainted with grief". His example therefore is no proof that there is sin in levity (cheerfulness?). If we felt as our understanding directs, we should always be miserable (grave?). What is the world but an hospital and a bedlam? Half the world is wounded and half mad. There is no time for a sinner, a pardoned sinner, living amongst miserable sinners, to spend at pastimes. There is nothing in the New Testament from beginning to end recommending levity.[2]

Lord Jesus, I find it difficult to believe that you never laughed, as you were truly and properly God, yet also, truly and properly man. Whether I am right or wrong in that respect, help me to remember John Newton's thoughts today, bearing in mind my witness and Christian influence on others.

1 Reverend Thomas Scott (1747–1821), preacher and author, Rector of Aston Stanford, Buckinghamshire, England. See also Footnote, July 1st.

2 From *John Newton: Sailor, Preacher, Pastor, and Poet.*

October 5th

For he maketh sore, and bindeth up:
he woundeth, and his hands make whole

(Job 5:18 KJV)

Mr. [Newton] was afflicted with a tumour, or wen,[1] which had formed on his thigh; and, on account of growing more large and troublesome, he resolved to undergo the experiment of extirpation.[2] This obliged him to go to London for the operation, which was successfully performed... by the late Mr. Warner,[3] of Guy's Hospital. I remember hearing him speak several years afterwards of this trying occasion; but the trial did not seem to have affected him as a painful operation, so much as a critical opportunity in which he might fail in demonstrating the patience of a Christian under pain. "I felt," said he, "that being enabled to bear a very sharp operation, with tolerable calmness and confidence, was a greater favour granted to me than the deliverance from my malady."[4]

Lord, have mercy on those who are waiting for surgery. Be with them and their loved ones in their moments of anxiety. Guide the hands of the surgeons involved, I pray.

1 From the Old English *wenn*, cognate with Dutch *wen* ("goiter").
2 From the Latin *ex(s) tirptus*, plucked up by the stem.
3 Joseph Warner (1717–1801).
4 From *The Life of the Rev. John Newton*.

October 6th

I am the Lord thy God, which brought thee out of the land of Egypt: open thy mouth wide, and I will fill it

(Psalm 81:10 KJV)

We have this [diary] entry: "For several weeks past the Sabbath has found me unprepared of subjects for preaching; yet I believe, provided my time was properly filled up in other services, this would be no disadvantage to speak freely and simply, without previous plan, upon any suitable passage of Scripture that should occur."[1]

Heavenly Father, I pray for my minister today. No doubt s/he has had a busy week, possibly without as much time to study and prepare as would be ideal. Undertake for that, I pray, and compensate him/her with an extra portion of Holy Spirit inspiration.

1 From *John Newton of Olney and St Mary Woolnoth. An Autobiography and Narrative.*

October 7th

The Spirit of the Lord God is upon me; because the Lord hath anointed me to preach

(Isaiah 61:1 KJV)

At a later period Mr. Newton writes: "In the morning I had not a single subject in view. Lord, I am empty indeed, but, oh, the happiness of feeling some dependence upon Thee, and of receiving out of Thy fullness in measure and in season as services and occasions occur. Surely this is the more excellent way, and better than hoarding up upon paper, or in the memory, notions of truth, which are apt to breed the chorus of self-admiration and self-dependence. I conceive a ripeness in ministerial abilities to consist such in a gracious power of trusting in Thee for a readiness to bring out things new and old that shall be suitable to the subject and the auditory."[1]

Lord, there is of course a fine line between not preparing a sermon because of pressures upon time, and not preparing a sermon because of bad diary planning, but, for all that, I pray your fresh anointing upon preachers in churches up and down the country. May what they preach carry your inspiration, blessing, and power.

1 From *John Newton of Olney and St Mary Woolnoth. An Autobiography and Narrative.*

October 8th

Think of yourself with sober judgment

(Romans 12:3)

In a letter to Mrs. Newton... [John Newton] says: "Yesterday was a busy time... I am sufficiently indulgent to Mr. Self. Do not fear any pinching or overworking him. I need a spur more than a bridle. You often think I do too much. I much oftener see cause to confess myself – comparatively, at least – a slothful and unprofitable servant. In the concern of immortal souls, with eternity in view, and so much depending upon the present moment, what assiduity or importunity can be proportioned to the case? I ought to be always on the wing, whether by word or pen, and much more careful and diligent than I am to redeem the time."[1]

Grant me, Lord, in your presence, the important grace of honest introspection. Guard my heart from condemnation, but help me in all things to come to that "sober judgment".

1 From *John Newton of Olney and St Mary Woolnoth. An Autobiography and Narrative.*

October 9th

Moses said to him, "If your Presence does not go with us, do not send us up from here"

(Exodus 33:15)

Mr. Newton had now resided at Olney rather more than fifteen years.[1] On several occasions there had been some prospect of a change; but hitherto it had been the will of God that he should remain where he was. Now, however, Divine providence seemed very clearly to intimate that the time was come for his removal... We have the following entry in [his] diary: "The post has thrown me into a hurry of spirit by the kind offer of my dear friend (the offer by Mr. Thornton[2] of the presentation to the parish of St Mary Woolnoth, in London). I look up to Thee, my God, for Thy blessing on the acceptance of it. Thou knowest my heart. I know it not myself. But surely I love this people, and have often wished and prayed to live and die here. If other thoughts of late have sometimes had place, they have rather been transient and involuntary than allowed. Yet I think I see mercy in this new appointment. The trial will be great, but at my time of life a settlement might seem desirable. O my Lord, let me not be deceived in thinking it is Thy call. If Thy presence go not with us still I would pray, Carry us not up hence."[3]

Lord, my prayers today are with all clergy who are facing new appointments, and for their families who will move with them. May your Holy Spirit guide those who decide such matters. Help them to be sensitive to your voice, so that the right people are moved to the right places at the right time. Bless these days of transition.

1 John Newton lived in Olney from 1764 to 1779 as curate-in-charge of the church of St Peter and St Paul.

2 See Footnote 1, September 4th.

3 From *John Newton of Olney and St Mary Woolnoth. An Autobiography and Narrative.*

October 10th

Speaking the truth in love

(Ephesians 4:15)

The following is Mr. Thornton's characteristic letter on this occasion:

"Dear Sir, – I read in the papers today of the death of Dr. Plumptree;[1] and as I know of no one who will so fill his place as the curate of Olney, I should be glad to know if I may fill up the presentation of St Mary Woolnoth in that name, and have all ready for your translation when you purpose being resident at London and Mr. Foster[2] takes care of your church. With respect to Mrs. Newton and our friends at Orchard Side, I am, dear Sir, Your much devoted Friend, etc., John Thornton."[3]

Thank you, Lord, for those who, like Mr. Thornton, speak directly and without guile. Give me that clear-headedness today.

1 Or Plumptre. Dr Charles Plumptree (1712–79), Archdeacon of Ely and Rector of St Mary Woolnoth.

2 Reverend Henry Foster (1745–1844). Newton appealed to Foster to become his curate at Olney, but he declined. Foster did, though, fill in for Newton at Olney whenever Newton was absent from his parish.

3 From *John Newton of Olney and St Mary Woolnoth. An Autobiography and Narrative.*

OCTOBER 11TH

IT IS BETTER TO TRUST IN THE LORD THAN TO PUT CONFIDENCE IN MAN

(Psalm 118:8 KJV)

I was with you in spirit this evening… and prayed that the Lord would give you a blessing… To love, and trust, the Lord Jesus, is the great lesson we have to learn. We are slow scholars, but he can teach us effectually. Without him, the very best of this life is insipid, and his presence can make the worst, supportable. I often think, and hope you do not forget, how graciously he supported, and answered you, in your late distress. There was a something, that could, and did, bear you up, under pain and anguish, and refresh your spirit, when your bodily strength was almost worn out. This is an instance of what he can do; and should be a bond of gratitude upon both our souls.[1]

Thank you, Lord Jesus, that, when we reach the end of our own resources, you are there. Thank you that your strength compensates for our weaknesses. Thank you for sustaining grace. You are my God.

1 From *Letters to a Wife (Volume Two): By the Author of Cardiphonia.*

OCTOBER 12TH

WHATSOEVER THE LORD PLEASED, THAT DID HE IN HEAVEN, AND IN EARTH, IN THE SEAS, AND ALL DEEP PLACES

(Psalm 135:6 KJV)

Our Lord God has an absolute right to dispose of us, and of ours, as He sees fit. And as He is Sovereign, so He is wise and good. It is a great mercy to be enabled to yield to his will; for everything, and every heart, must either bend, or break, before it.[1]

You are Almighty God. You are my God. I worship you.

1 From *Letters to a Wife (Volume Two): By the Author of Cardiphonia.*

October 13th

As a father has compassion on his children, so the Lord has compassion on those who fear him; for he knows how we are formed, he remembers that we are dust

(Psalm 103:13–14)

I hope, in the midst of all your engagements, you find a little time to read his good word, and to wait at his mercy seat. It is good for us to draw nigh to him. It is an honour that he permits us to pray; and we shall surely find he is a God hearing prayer. Endeavour to be diligent in the means; yet watch and strive against a legal spirit, which is always aiming to represent him as a hard master, watching as it were to take advantage of us. But it is far otherwise. His name is Love; he looks upon us with compassion: he knows our frame, and remembers that we are but dust: and when our infirmities prevail, he does not bid us despond, but reminds us that we have an Advocate with the Father, who is able to pity, to pardon, and to save to the uttermost.[1] [2]

To the uttermost he saves! This is my God! Father of mercies!

1 From *Cardiphonia: or, The Utterance of the Heart in the Course of a Real Correspondence, Volume One*.

2 This extract from one of John Newton's letters demonstrates his strong belief in promoting the compassionate love of God as a means of wooing people back to the Father. Whereas many preachers relied more on threats of hellfire and damnation, Newton much preferred to preach mercy and grace. This was his predominant style.

October 14th

Be strong in the grace that is in Christ Jesus

(2 Timothy 2:1)

Think of the names and relations [God] bears. Does he not call himself a Saviour, a Shepherd, a Friend, and a Husband? Has he not made known to us his love, his blood, his righteousness, his promises, his power, and his grace, and all for our encouragement? Away, then, with all doubting, unbelieving thoughts: they will not only distress your hearts, but weaken your hands. Take it for granted, upon the warrant of his word, that you are his, and he is yours; that he has loved you with an everlasting love, and therefore in loving-kindness has drawn you to himself; that he will surely accomplish that which he has begun, and that nothing which can be named or thought of shall ever be able to separate you from him. This permission will give you strength for the battle; this is the shield which will quench the fiery darts of Satan; this is the helmet which the enemy cannot pierce. Whereas, if we go forth doubting and fearing, and are afraid to trust any further than we can feel, we are weak as water, and easily overcome. Be strong, therefore, not in yourself, but in the grace that is in Christ Jesus.[1]

I pray today, Lord Jesus, that you would impart strength to any who are weak.
I pray today, Lord Jesus, that you would impart faith to any who are doubting.
I pray today, Lord Jesus, that you would impart belief to any who are tempted towards unbelief.

1 From *Cardiphonia: or, The Utterance of the Heart in the Course of a Real Correspondence, Volume One.*

October 15th

I am astonished that you are so quickly deserting the one who called you to live in the grace of Christ and are turning to a different gospel – which is really no gospel at all

(Galatians 1:6–7)

Christians are often not aware how soon they may decline in their religious affection. The Israelites when singing on the seashore, would little have credited anyone who told them that they soon would be murmuring. Declension begins, says one, "at the closest door". Satan waits his opportunity. He will not come while impressions are fresh. The heart will cool if the means of grace are not habitually used. The declining professor grows formal in prayer and reading the Scriptures. It is often with us as with the Galatians – we are soon removed from Him who called us.

Laxness in the use of means
Itching ears in hearing the truth,
Listening to seducers – these are signs of decline.[1]

Lord, in your mercy, come to those who have fallen away, those who have abandoned your church and its teachings. Draw them back to your great heart of love. Likewise, Lord, draw close to those who still belong to your church, but whose spiritual declension set in years ago; warm them with a fresh touch of power, I pray.

1 From *John Newton: Sailor, Preacher, Pastor, and Poet.*

October 16th

He said to me, "My grace is sufficient for you, for my power is made perfect in weakness." Therefore I will boast all the more gladly of my weaknesses, so that the power of Christ may rest upon me"

(2 Corinthians 12:9 ESV)

I went yesterday into the pulpit very dry and heartless. I seemed to have fixed upon a text, but when I came to the pinch, it was so shut up that I could not preach from it. I had hardly a minute to choose, and therefore was forced to snatch all that which came first upon my mind, which proved 2 Tim. i.12.[1] Thus I set off at a vesture, having no resource but in the Lord's mercy and faithfulness; and, indeed, what other can we wish for? Presently my subject opened; and I know not when I have been favoured with more liberty. Why do I tell you this? Only as an instance of his goodness, to encourage you to put your strength in him, and not to be afraid, even when you feel your own weakness and insufficiency most sensibly. We are never more safe, never have more reason to expect the Lord's help, than when we are most sensible that we can do nothing without him. This was the lesson Paul learnt, to rejoice in his own poverty and emptiness, that the power of Christ might rest upon him. Could Paul have done anything, Jesus would not have had the honour of doing all.[2]

How contrary this sounds, Lord, to our ways of thinking – that weakness is strength! In a world where power speaks volumes, how counter-cultural this message seems. Help me, Lord, to realign my perspective so that it is more attuned to yours.

1 "I know whom I have believed, and am convinced that he is able to guard what I have entrusted to him until that day".

2 From *Cardiphonia: or, The Utterance of the Heart in the Course of a Real Correspondence, Volume One.*

October 17th

Blessed are the poor in spirit, for theirs is the kingdom of heaven

(Matthew 5:3)

This way of being saved entirely by grace, from first to last, is contrary to our natural wills; it mortifies self, leaving it nothing to boast of, and through the remains of an unbelieving, legal spirit, it often seems discouraging. When we think ourselves so utterly helpless and worthless, we are too ready to fear that the Lord will therefore reject us; whereas, in truth, such a poverty of spirit is the best mark we can have of an interest in his promises and care.[1][2]

Is it, Lord, that I fear rejection if I admit my weakness and helplessness? Do I secretly worry that I may not impress you, or be regarded as worthy in your sight, the more feeble I appear? If so, Lord, correct this thinking in me, and in anyone else who feels the same, so that we are not deprived of your blessing.

1 From *Cardiphonia: or, The Utterance of the Heart in the Course of a Real Correspondence, Volume One*.

2 Arguably, John Newton at his very best, dispensing wise spiritual counsel and logic based upon Bible truth, and doing so with scholarly insight and compassion: here we see, even in just this brief paragraph, the heart and intellect of a devoted pastor well aware of human flaws and tendencies.

OCTOBER 18TH

I AM WITH YOU AND WILL WATCH OVER YOU WHEREVER YOU GO

(Genesis 28:15)

[I] wrote to my dear friend [Mr. Thornton], signifying my thankful acceptance of his offer [to move to St Mary Woolnoth]. I trust I can do it in faith. My own sentiment is likewise confirmed by the judgment of my dear Mrs. Unwin[1] and Mr. Cowper,[2] who, though they feel interested in the case and concerned that we must be parted, are satisfied that this call is from God and that I ought to obey... My race at Olney is nearly finished. I am about to form a connection for life with one Mary Woolnoth, a reputed London saint in Lombard Street. I hope you will not blame me. I think you would not if you knew all the circumstances. I am not elated at what this world calls preferment. London is the last situation I should have chosen for myself. The throng and hurry of the busy world, and noise and party contentions of the religious world, are very disagreeable to me. I love woods and fields and streams and trees – to hear the birds sing and the sheep bleat. I thank the Lord for His goodness to me here. Here I have rejoiced to live – here I have often wished and prayed that I might die. I am sure no outward change can make me happier, but it becomes not a soldier to choose his own post.[3]

Gracious God, may those who are planning to move from one place to another, or from one job to another, know the truth and certainty of today's Bible verse. I pray for such people, Lord, and their families. I pray too for those they are leaving behind – loved ones, colleagues, and church congregations – for whom such times of parting can also be unsettling.

1 Mary Unwin, companion and helper of John Newton's great friend William Cowper. She was the widow of Reverend Morley Unwin, who died in a tragic accident when he fell from his horse. John Newton reached out to her with an enormous amount of practical help and support, including arranging accommodation for her.

2 See January 25th, February 13th, and various other references to William Cowper.

3 From *John Newton of Olney and St Mary Woolnoth. An Autobiography and Narrative.*

October 19th

They all wept as they embraced him

(Acts 20:37)

Mr. Wilkinson preached. I spoke a few words to the people after sermon, and told them I was going. There are many weepers. May Thy gracious hand, my Lord, wipe away their tears, and turn their mourning into joy. I trust it shall be so if Thou art pleased to favour my wishes and endeavours for Mr. Scott[1] to supply my place, which he is willing to do, if Thou art pleased to appoint him… My heart is sometimes pinched at the prospect before me, but in the main I am peaceful, and trust that the event will prove it is the Lord's appointment.[2]

How lovely, Lord, that John Newton's congregation at Olney were so reluctant to see him go! I pray for such a spirit of love and grace to be alive in all our churches, perhaps especially if there have been times of division in times past. Bless us in such ways, with harmony and goodwill in our hearts, towards one another.

1 Reverend Thomas Scott (1747–1821), preacher and author. He and John Newton established a correspondence and a friendship when Scott was a curate in Ravenstone, close to the neighbouring parish of Olney. Reverend Scott succeeded his friend in the curacy of Olney. (See Footnote for July 1st.)

2 From *John Newton of Olney and St Mary Woolnoth. An Autobiography and Narrative.*

October 20th

Be strong and courageous. Do not be afraid or terrified…
for the Lord your God goes with you;
he will never leave you nor forsake you

(Deuteronomy 31:6)

[God] has a sovereign right to do with us as he pleases, and if we consider what we are, surely we shall confess we have no reason to complain; and to those who seek him, his sovereignty is exercised in a way of grace. All shall work together for good; everything is needful that he sends; nothing can be needful that he withholds. Be content to bear the cross; others have borne it before you. You have need of patience; and if you ask, the Lord will give it; but there can be no settled peace till our will is in a measure subdued. Hide yourself under the shadow of his wings; rely upon his care and power; look upon him as a physician who has graciously undertaken to heal your soul of the worst of sicknesses, sin. Yield to his prescriptions, and fight against every thought that would represent it as desirable to be permitted to choose for yourself. When you cannot see your way, be satisfied that he is your leader. When your spirit is overwhelmed within you, he knows your path; he will not leave you to sink. He has appointed seasons of refreshment, and you shall find he does not forget you. If we seem to get no good by attempting to draw near him, we may be sure we shall get none by keeping away from him.[1]

Gracious God, bless those who need spiritual reassurance today. Bolster them as only you can, in mind, heart, body, and spirit.

1 From *Cardiphonia: or, The Utterance of the Heart in the Course of a Real Correspondence, Volume One.*

October 21st

Since there is jealousy and quarrelling among you, are you not worldly? Are you not acting like mere humans?

(1 Corinthians 3:3)

To my surprise and grief, I have found a strong opposition against Mr. Scott, so that he has given up the thought of coming. I have seen much of a wrong spirit in the business where I expected better things. Contempt has been cast upon one whom God has honoured, and my care for their prosperity has given offence and provoked anger. Lord, enable me to bear it as I ought, to pray for them, to continue to love, and to endeavour to save them. Let not my spirit be hurt, and pity and provide for the faithful few who would have rejoiced in such a minister.[1] [2]

Lord, forgive your church when it gets it wrong. Forgive your people when we act "like mere humans". Have mercy.

1 Scott accepted the curacy of Olney in 1781. However, he moved to London in 1785, to become a hospital chaplain at the Lock Hospital there.

2 From *John Newton of Olney and St Mary Woolnoth. An Autobiography and Narrative.*

OCTOBER 22ND

REMEMBER NOT THE FORMER THINGS, NOR CONSIDER THE THINGS OF OLD. BEHOLD, I AM DOING A NEW THING; NOW IT SPRINGS FORTH, DO YOU NOT PERCEIVE IT? I WILL MAKE A WAY IN THE WILDERNESS AND RIVERS IN THE DESERT

(Isaiah 43:18–19 ESV)

We have the following [diary] entry, the last made at Olney:

"This evening service is to terminate my connection with Olney. Tomorrow I return to London. My gracious Lord, bless the people from whom Thou removest me. Oh, give me a heart to praise Thee for the years of service I have known in this place, provision, protection, support, acceptance, and, I hope, usefulness. If we have had trials, comforts have more abounded. Prepare us a habitation, and oh, above all, prepare in our hearts a habitation for Thyself. Sanctify this removal, and fit us for our great change, our final removal from a world of sin and sorrow, that we may be with Thee for ever. Amen and Amen."[1]

Help those, Lord, who are on the cusp of change in their lives, whatever might be the reason for those changes: a new line of work, an alteration in circumstances, bereavement, perhaps. Enable us each to best honour the past by looking towards the future.

1 From *John Newton of Olney and St Mary Woolnoth. An Autobiography and Narrative.*

October 23rd

The eternal God is your refuge, and underneath are the everlasting arms

(Deuteronomy 33:27)

The young Christian is like a man walking on the ice. He carries a sense of his weight about with him. But put him on [London's] Westminster Bridge, and though he were as heavy as a waggon he would not fall. If I am born with one leg I should go limping to the grave. My diseased nature will never be so wholly cured in this life as to prevent me limping. The onward work in my soul will tell me what o'clock it is, like a dial, if the sun shines, but not if the sun be absent.[1]

Remind me, Lord, often, to cast all my cares on you, the full weight of them. Teach me not to tread like someone walking on ice, but to move forward in full confidence of your love and unending support.

1 From *John Newton: Sailor, Preacher, Pastor, and Poet.*

October 24th

Your works… they will not benefit you

(Isaiah 57:12)

Since you know that you are a sinner, and that he is the only Saviour, what should prevent your comfort? Had he bid you do some great thing, you would, at least, have attempted it. If a pilgrimage to some distant place was the appointed means of salvation, would you be content to sit at home and perish? How much rather then, should you keep close to the throne of grace, when he has only said, Ask, and you shall receive.[1]

Simply to the cross I cling.

1 From *Letters to a Wife (Volume Two)*: By the author of *Cardiphonia*.

October 25th

Speak truthfully to your neighbour

(Ephesians 4:25)

All sorts of persons found their way to the vestry of St Mary Woolnoth, but they did not always get the advice they anticipated. The introspective who came to talk of their spiritual trials were told to take a holiday and refresh their bodies with sea bathing or country air. Others, inclined to self-pity, found the picture of their misfortunes re-focussed to show the sharp outlines of materialism. One parishioner lamenting the loss of a house by fire was congratulated because he had treasure in heaven which fire could not destroy. Another rejoicing that she had a successful lottery ticket was told, "Madam, as for a friend under temptation, I will pray for you." A group of grumbling City Merchants was told, "There is a great and old established house, which does much business and causes no small disturbance in the world and in the church. The firm is Satan, Self & Co." Members of the Protestant Association, urging Newton to denounce Rome received the reply, "I have read of many wicked popes, but the worst pope I ever met with is Pope Self."[1 2 3]

I pray for Christian ministers and counsellors today, Lord, asking that you would grant them the grace of tactful honesty. Theirs is not an easy calling, handling people's lives, feelings, and sensitivities. Give them the right words to say: words that will heal and not hurt.

1 From time to time, Newton referred to "Mr. Self" or "Pope Self".

2 From *An Ancient Mariner.*

3 We see here that John Newton has continued his ministry of counselling, picking up in London where he had left off in Olney. His pastoral heart continued to beat, no doubt to the benefit of the great numbers who sought his advice.

October 26th

The wisdom of this world is foolishness in God's sight

(1 Corinthians 3:19)

Thus in the desert's dreary waste,
By magic pow'r produced in haste,
As old romances say,
Castles and groves, and music sweet,
The senses of the trav'ller sweet,
And stop him in his way:
But while he gazes with surprise,
The charm dissolves, the vision dies;
'Twas but enchanted ground:
Thus, if the Lord our spirit touch,
The world, which promis'd us so much,
A wilderness is found.[1 2]

Remind me once again today, Lord, of that which is important and eternal. Remind me once again today, Lord, to live within that light. Remind me once again, Lord, to hold the things of this world only lightly. Thank you.

1 Originally, from *Olney Hymns* (1779), but here as an extract from a letter Newton wrote to someone on the subject of the vanity of the world.

2 From *Letters of John Newton.*

October 27th

We know that in all things God works for the good of those who love him, who have been called according to his purpose

(Romans 8:28)

[The Lord] is not like a man that should fail or change, or be prevented by anything unforeseen from doing what he has said. And yet we find it easier to trust to worms than to the God of truth. Is it not so with you? And I can assure you it is often so with me. But here is the mercy, that his ways are above ours, as the heavens are higher than the earth. Though we are foolish and unbelieving, he remains faithful; he will not deny himself. I recommend to you especially that promise of God, which is so comprehensive that it takes in all our concernments; I mean, that all things shall work together for good.[1]

In every circumstance of life, you are my God.

1 From *Cardiphonia: or, The Utterance of the Heart in the Course of a Real Correspondence, Volume One.*

October 28th

Thy will be done

(Matthew 6:10 KJV)

How hard is it to believe, that not only things which are grievous to the flesh, but even those things which draw forth our corruptions, and discover to us what is in our hearts, and fill us with guilt and shame, should in the issue work for our good! Yet the Lord has said it. All your pains and trials, all that befalls you in your own person, or that affects you upon the account of others, shall in the end prove to your advantage. And your peace does not depend upon any change of circumstances which may appear desirable, but in having your will bowed to the Lord's will, and made willing to submit all to his disposal and management. Pray for this, and wait patiently for him, and he will do it.[1]

Help me, Lord, in those times when I struggle to submit to your will for my life, to at least want to submit, and then leave the rest to you.

1 From *Cardiphonia: or, The Utterance of the Heart in the Course of a Real Correspondence, Volume One.*

October 29th

He must increase, but I must decrease

(John 3:30 ESV)

Be not surprised to find yourself poor, helpless, and vile; all whom he favours and teaches will find themselves so. The more grace increases, the more we shall see to abase us in our own eyes; and this will make the Saviour and his salvation more precious to us. He takes his own wise methods to humble you, and to prove you, and I am sure he will do you good in the end.[1]

Lord, these are great kingdom truths – contrary to the ways of the world, where self-promotion is so often the standard and aim. Yet, in your economy, the more we see of our sin, the more, correspondingly, we see of your salvation in Christ. Help me to trust in this unusual gospel.

1 From *Cardiphonia: or, The Utterance of the Heart in the Course of a Real Correspondence, Volume One.*

October 30TH

He shall not much remember the days of his life; because God answereth him in the joy of his heart

(Ecclesiastes 5:20 KJV)

Mr. Newton left Olney, where he had spent so many happy and useful years of his ministerial life. In his own opinion and that of his most judicious friends he was following the leadings of Divine providence. Nevertheless, like all such changes, it was accompanied with many regrets. "Oh, my beloved leisure," exclaims Mr. Newton, when settled in London, "my sweet retirements, how I should regret your loss, if I were not checked by the thought that the post I am in must needs be the best upon the whole, because the Lord has assigned it for me!… I loved the people so that it was in my heart and in my prayers to live and die with them." Then he adds, as giving some of his reasons for living: "Our privileges were great; and the enjoyment of them for a long course of years without interruption made them seem to too many as a matter of course. Weeds sprang up, offences appeared. I hope it was in mercy to them, as well in mercy to me that the Lord removed me."[1]

God of our days, we all experience those days when we reflect, or reminisce. We all experience those quiet nights when we look back, and review our lives. Some memories, Lord, can be uncomfortable, painful, even, and the source of regret. Draw alongside us at such moments, with your tender reassurance of unending love.

1 From *John Newton of Olney and St Mary Woolnoth. An Autobiography and Narrative.*

October 31st

Let us draw near to God with a sincere heart and with the full assurance that faith brings, having our hearts sprinkled to cleanse us from a guilty conscience

(Hebrews 10:22)

May the Lord open your ears, and your heart, that you may receive profit where you are. Do not give place to unbelief. Jesus is both an able, and a willing Saviour. Pray for a tender conscience, and a dependant [sic] spirit. Watch against the motions of self, they are subtle and various. Let no engagements prevent you from reserving seasons of retirement, for prayer, and reading the scriptures. The best company, the best public ordinances, will not compensate for the neglect of these. At the same time, guard against a spirit of bondage; nor fetter your mind, by too many rules and resolves. It is our privilege to serve the Lord with cheerfulness; not considering him as a hard master, but as a tender Father, who knows, and pities our weakness; who is ready to pardon our mistakes, and to teach us to do better. He accepts us, freely and graciously, when we present ourselves before him, in the name of Jesus, his beloved Son.[1]

A "tender Father". This is my God.

1 From *Letters to a Wife (Volume Two): By the Author of Cardiphonia.*

November 1st

Show no partiality as you hold the faith in our Lord Jesus Christ

(James 2:1 ESV)

It is not choice, but necessity, that makes me sometimes live, as it were, from hand to mouth. While my head is full of new persons, and places, I cannot do otherwise. And I have reason to be thankful, that my hopes are seldom disappointed, upon much occasions: though I know not when I have been so straitened, and embarrassed, as I was the other night… I rather wonder, that this happens so seldom, than that it happens at all. How justly might the Lord take his word of truth, out of my unworthy mouth! Perhaps he saw it good for me, that Mr. Self should have his comb cut rather there,[1] than in another place; and I hope there is that in me, which is as willing to appear to a disadvantage (if it must be so)… though, to be sure, flesh and blood is pleased to be thought somebody, when among dear friends, or fine folks.[2]

God of compassion, how awkward, humiliating, even, it can be for those who have little choice but to live as "have nots" in a world of "haves". Grant me a heart of sympathy, Lord – empathy, maybe – that will always seek to put someone at their ease, regardless of status or wealth. God forbid that matters of riches or poverty should ever affect the way in which I regard and evaluate a fellow human being.

1 As in, to be humbled, or robbed of one's dignity; from the practice of cutting the comb on the head of poultry. This used to be carried out for reasons of hygiene, but would inevitably have the effect of making, say, a cockerel look less impressive and proud than it did prior to such surgery.

2 From *Letters to a Wife (Volume Two)*: By the Author of *Cardiphonia*.

November 2nd

We are ambassadors for Christ

(2 Corinthians 5:20 KJV)

An ambassador magnifies his office when he keeps close to his instructions. He may sometimes stand upon his "p's" and "q's," but not for himself, but for the honour of the court he represents.[1]

An ambassador for Christ! So help me, God.

1 From *John Newton: Sailor, Preacher, Pastor, and Poet.*

November 3rd

Christ himself gave… the pastors and teachers, to equip his people for works of service, so that the body of Christ may be built up

(Ephesians 4:11–12)

A new and very distinct scene of action and usefulness was set before [John Newton]. Placed in the centre of London, in an opulent neighbourhood, with connections daily increasing, he had now a course of service to pursue, in several respects different from his former at Olney. Being, however, well acquainted with the word of God, and the heart of man, he proposed to himself no new weapons of warfare, for pulling down the strongholds of sin and Satan around him. He perceived, indeed, most of his parishioners too intent upon their wealth and merchandise to pay much regard to their new minister; but, since they would not come to him, he was determined to go, as far as he could, to them; and therefore, soon after his institution, he sent a printed address to his parishioners: he afterwards sent them another address, on the usual prejudices that are taken up against the gospel. What effects these attempts had then upon them does not appear; certain it is, that these, and other acts of his ministry, will be recollected by them, when the objects of their present pursuits are forgotten or lamented.[1 2]

A simple and straightforward prayer today, Lord Jesus: bless ministers new to their parishes!

1 From *The Life of the Rev. John Newton*.

2 Olney was a country parish, whereas St Mary Woolnoth stood in the very heart of London. A greater contrast is hard to imagine. Yet, it is heart-warming to note here that Newton's confidences were entirely the same, in both parishes. He was not easily swayed by prevailing culture, but held fast to the truths of the Bible and remained true to his responsibilities, wherever he was and whomever he was amongst.

NOVEMBER 4TH

THE KINGDOM OF HEAVEN IS LIKE TREASURE HIDDEN IN A FIELD. WHEN A MAN FOUND IT, HE HID IT AGAIN, AND THEN IN HIS JOY WENT AND SOLD ALL HE HAD AND BOUGHT THAT FIELD

(Matthew 13:44)

I truly pity those who rise early and take late rest, and eat the bread of carefulness, with no higher prize and prospect in view than the obtaining of academical honour. Such pursuits will ere long appear (as they really are) vain as the sports of children. May the Lord impress them with a noble ambition of living to and for him. If these adventurers, who are labouring for pebbles under the semblance of goodly pearls, had a discovery of the pearl of great price, how quickly and gladly would they lay down their admired attainments, and become fools that they might be truly wise![1] [2]

Priorities, Lord! Set mine today, please.

1 From *Cardiphonia: or, The Utterance of the Heart in the Course of a Real Correspondence, Volume One.*
2 An extract from a letter Newton wrote to "Mr. C—" on the latter's admission to the ministry.

NOVEMBER 5TH

MY PEOPLE ARE DESTROYED FOR LACK OF KNOWLEDGE

(Hosea 4:6 ESV)

I am pleased with your fears lest you should not be understood in your preaching. Indeed, there is a danger of it. It is not easy for persons of quick parts duly to conceive how amazingly ignorant and slow of apprehension the bulk of our congregations generally are. When our own ideas are clear, and our expressions proper, we are ready to think we have sufficiently explained ourselves; and yet, perhaps nine out of ten (especially of those who are destitute of spiritual light) know little more of what we say than if we were talking Greek. A degree of this inconvenience is always inseparable from written discourses. They cast our thoughts into a style which, though familiar to ourselves, is too remote from common conversation to be comprehended by narrow capacities; which is one chief reason of the preference I give caeteris paribus,[1] to extempore preaching. When we read to the people, they think themselves less concerned in what is offered, than when we speak to them point-blank. It seems a good rule, which I have met with somewhere, and which perhaps I have mentioned to you, to fix our eyes upon some of the auditory whom we judge of the least capacity; if we can make him understand, we may hope to be understood by the rest.[2][3][4]

Lord, grant patience to the quick-witted!

1 From the Latin to English: "All things being equal".

2 From *Cardiphonia: or, The Utterance of the Heart in the Course of a Real Correspondence, Volume One.*

3 As Footnote No. 2, November 4th.

4 Newton was an extremely intelligent man: a learned theologian, well-read, and fluent in several languages. Yet, here we see heart-warming evidence of his overwhelming desire to share the gospel in the most competent way possible, even though this sometimes, patently, frustrated him.

November 6th

The king assigned them a daily amount of food and wine from the king's table. They were to be trained for three years, and after that they were to enter the king's service... But Daniel resolved not to defile himself with the royal food and wine, and he asked the chief official for permission not to defile himself this way. Now God had caused the official to show favour and compassion to Daniel, but the official told Daniel, "I am afraid of my lord the king, who has assigned your food and drink. Why should he see you looking worse than the other young men your age? The king would then have my head because of you." Daniel then said to the guard whom the chief official had appointed... "Please test your servants for ten days: give us nothing but vegetables to eat and water to drink. Then compare our appearance with that of the young men who eat the royal food, and treat your servants in accordance with what you see." So he agreed to this and tested them for ten days. At the end of the ten days they looked healthier and better nourished than any of the young men who ate the royal food

(Daniel 1:5, 8–15)

He who caused Daniel to thrive upon pulse, can make you strong and cheerful even in the Fens,[1] if he sees that best for you. All things obey him, and you need not fear but he will enable you for whatever service he has appointed you to perform.[2] [3]

Help those, Lord, whose appointments in ministry are difficult, or trying. Help those ministers whose efforts appear to bear little fruit, where people seem to show little or no interest in their message. Grant sustaining grace, I pray.

1 A marshy region in eastern England; a flat, damp, agricultural district. It is likely that, in Newton's day, the majority of Fens labourers were uneducated, or possibly even illiterate, hence his comment "even in the Fens".

2 See Footnote 2, November 4th.

3 From *Cardiphonia: or, The Utterance of the Heart in the Course of a Real Correspondence, Volume One.*

November 7th

Love bears all things... endures all things

(1 Corinthians 13:7 ESV)

Some of his friends thought, not without reason, that Mr. Newton's real influence at Olney had suffered by over-much familiarity on his part, and from an excess of charitable feeling by which his judgment was sometimes led astray; that this, in some instances, he lost that esteem and love to which he had really so good a title. It was, moreover, his own conviction, as expressed by him on a review of this period, that he had encouraged his people in a liberty in the exercise of their gifts which, in the end, he could not control, and which became a source of uneasiness to him. It may be well supposed that Mr. Newton's loss was deeply felt, not only by many of his people at Olney, but by those of his more immediate neighbours, who best knew and appreciated him. How pathetically does Mr. Cowper write on the subject: "The vicarage house became a melancholy object as soon as Mr. Newton left it. As I walked in the garden this evening I saw the smoke issue from the study chimney, and said to myself, 'that used to be a sign that Mr. Newton was there,' but it is so no longer. The walls of the house know nothing of the change that has taken place; the bolt of the chamber door sounds just as it used to do... but Mr. Newton's foot will never be heard upon that staircase again."[1]

My prayers today, Heavenly Father, are for all those separated from friends and loved ones, especially when the miles between them can make such separations seem all the more painful and poignant. Bless those whose contact with their nearest and dearest is somewhat hindered by geography and distance, especially when sights and sounds provoke memories.

1 From *John Newton of Olney and St Mary Woolnoth. An Autobiography and Narrative.*

November 8th

They were welcomed by the church and the apostles and elders

(Acts 15:4)

Writing to Mr. Newton soon after he left the neighbourhood, Mr. Bull[1] speaks of his removal as one of the greatest trials he ever met with: "I rode to Olney this week. I believe it is only the second time since you left it. The name of the place seems quite to have altered its signification, and the once dear Mr. Newton is (in a great measure) to me no more." And not long afterwards, "I have this week had again to lament your absence from Olney. On Wednesday night I preached there. I believe almost every one of your serious friends came to the meeting, and, indeed, I may say, I think that they seemed to love you in me."[2]

Lord, for churches lamenting the departure of a minister, I ask your mercy; likewise, for the new minister in situ, faced with a measure of sadness over the absence of his or her predecessor. These are complex issues that require delicate handling on all sides.

1 William Bull (1738–1814), English independent minister. John Newton often invited him to preach at the Great House in Olney (see September 6th). Bull and Newton were lifelong friends and frequently exchanged letters.

2 From *John Newton of Olney and St Mary Woolnoth. An Autobiography and Narrative.*

November 9th

We have this ministry, we do not lose heart

(2 Corinthians 4:1)

Mr. Newton... speaks of the state of religion in the Establishment... "There are," he says, "but two gospel ministers who have churches of their own, Mr. Romaine[1] and myself. But we have about ten clergymen, who, either as morning preachers or lecturers, preach either on the Lord's Day or at different times of the week in, perhaps, fifteen or sixteen churches. There is likewise the Lock,[2] and another chapel in Westminster;[3] the former served chiefly by Mr. Coetlogen,[4] the latter by Mr. Peckwell[5] – well attended."[6]

Lord, I ask you to help those denominations whose clergy personnel are stretched very thinly indeed, and who struggle to recruit ministers. Come with your Spirit, I pray, and call men and women into the ministry, so that the workload (and the privilege) can be more evenly distributed. Help those ministers whose workload is heavy.

1 Reverend William Romaine (1714–95), from Hartlepool: evangelical Church of England priest.
2 The Lock Hospital. (See Footnote 1, October 21st.)
3 Princes Street Chapel, Westminster, London.
4 Reverend Charles Edward de Coetlogon (or Coetlogen) (1746–1820).
5 Reverend Dr Henry Peckwell (1747–87), English clergyman with sympathies towards Methodism.
6 From *John Newton of Olney and St Mary Woolnoth. An Autobiography and Narrative.*

November 10th

Whoso removeth stones shall be hurt therewith

(Ecclesiastes 10:9 KJV)

Mr. Newton had a fall and dislocated his shoulder, the only time, he says, of his receiving any hurt, though he had travelled so many leagues by land and water. "I was standing at my own door, put my foot carelessly back against a stone, which tripped me up, and threw me over a short post… I consider it a chastisement, though of a gentle and merciful kind. A sinner need not spend much time in searching out the cause of an affliction; but that the afflictions of such a sinner as I should be so seldom, so moderate, so soon removed, depends upon reasons which I should never have known, but by the Word of God. Thus I am taught to spell His name, 'The Lord, the Lord God, long-suffering, abundant in mercy, forgiving iniquity, transgression, and sin,' and thus I read the reason why I not consumed."[1]

Accidents happen, Lord! I will, therefore, take this opportunity to pray for nurses and doctors working today, and tonight, in Accident and Emergency units. Theirs is a pressurized workplace, where important decisions need to be made carefully but quickly. Bless them. I pray especially for such units in parts of the world where resources are scarce.

1 From *John Newton of Olney and St Mary Woolnoth. An Autobiography and Narrative.*

November 11th

For everything there is a season, and a time for every matter under heaven: a time to be born, and a time to die

(Ecclesiastes 3:1–2 ESV)

I wrote yesterday to Mr. A—, and, in my evening walk, my thoughts, and prayers, turned much upon the afflicting stroke he has received.[1] Indeed, it has been seldom out of my mind… Besides my concern for his loss… I consider it as a loud speaking lesson to me, and to you. How often has she been raised up from the brink of the grave, in answer to prayer; and yet, now, suddenly and unexpectedly removed! We, likewise, have been long preserved, and often restored to each other. But a time will come, when every gourd will wither, every cistern be broken. Let us pray for a waiting, resigned, and dependent frame of spirit; for ability to commit ourselves, and our all, into the merciful hands of him who careth for us; and that, while we are spared, we may walk together, as help-meets, and fellow-heirs of eternal life. We shall not be parted a moment sooner, for living in daily expectations of our appointed change; but the thought may be a happy mean of composing our minds, and of preserving us from being too much engrossed, either by the sweets, or the bitters, of this transitory life.[2]

Thank you, Heavenly Father, for the precious gift of marriage. Thank you, too, for your comfort when the days of marriage are sealed by death. I pray today for anyone experiencing the loss of a loved one. Gracious Lord, be their strength in bereavement.

1 The loss of his wife.

2 From *Letters to a Wife (Volume Two): By the Author of Cardiphonia.*

November 12th

We are strangers before thee, and sojourners, as were all our fathers: our days on the earth are as a shadow

(1 Chronicles 29:15 KJV)

Many occasions of care, and perplexity, that are apt to waste our time, and wound our peace, would be avoided, could we duly consider how soon we shall have done with all these things. May you, may I, be more rooted and grounded in the truth, more humbled and comforted, more filled with that love, joy, and unspeakable peace, which the gospel reveals, and for which the promises of God warrant us to pray. Be not discouraged, because you have nothing of your own. The bucket is put into the well, empty, and because it is empty; the Lord has opened wells of salvation for us, and has promised, that we shall not seek his face in vain.[1]

The long view, Lord!

1 From *Letters to a Wife (Volume Two): By the Author of Cardiphonia.*

NOVEMBER 13TH

THE PEACE OF GOD, WHICH SURPASSES ALL UNDERSTANDING

(Philippians 4:7 ESV)

[Mary's] head became so affected, that I could do little more than sit and look at her. Our intercourse by words was nearly broken off. She could not easily bear the sound of the gentlest foot upon the carpet, nor of the softest voice… When I was preparing for church in the morning, she sent for me, and we took a final farewell, as to this world. She faintly uttered an endearing appellation, which was familiar to her, and gave me her hand, which I held, while I prayed by her bedside. We exchanged a few tears: but I was almost as unable to speak as she was. But I returned soon after, and said, "If your mind, as I trust, is in a state of peace, it will be a comfort to me if you can signify it by holding up your hand." She held it up, and waved it to and fro several times. That evening, her speech, her sight, and, I believe, her hearing, wholly failed. She continued perfectly composed, without taking notice of anything, or discovering any sign of pain or uneasiness.[1]

Gracious Father, I ask you to draw alongside those who hold the hands of the dying: loved ones and relatives, medical professionals, hospice staff, and so on. Heavenly Father, bestow a tender peace in those heart-breaking moments.

1 From *The Life of the Rev. John Newton.*

November 14th

He stood, and blessed all the congregation of Israel with a loud voice

(1 Kings 8:55 KJV)

I am not sure that the length and vehemence of your sermons, which you tell me astonish many people, may not be rather improper and imprudent, considering the weakness of your constitution; at least if this expression of yours be justly expounded by a report which has reached me, that the length of your sermons is frequently two hours, and the vehemence of your voice so great, that you may be heard beyond the church walls. Unwilling should I be to damp your zeal; but I feel unwilling likewise, that by excessive unnecessary exertions, you should wear away at once, and preclude your own usefulness. This concern is so much upon my mind… I am perhaps the more ready to credit the report, because I know the spirits of you nervous people are highly volatile. I consider you as mounted upon a fiery steed; and, provided you use due management and circumspection, you travel more pleasantly than we plodding folks upon our sober phlegmatic nags; but then, if instead of pulling the reins you plunge in the spurs, and add wings to the wind, I cannot but be in pain for the consequences.[1]

Lord, I don't quite know what to pray today in response to this! May I just invite your blessing on all who preach the gospel, whatever their preferred style and volume?

1 From *Cardiphonia: or, The Utterance of the Heart in the Course of a Real Correspondence, Volume One.*

November 15th

Seated in a window was a young man named Eutychus, who was sinking into a deep sleep as Paul talked on and on. When he was sound asleep, he fell to the ground from the third story and was picked up dead

(Acts 20:9)

As to long preaching. There is still in being an old-fashioned instrument called an hour-glass, which, in days of yore, before clocks and watches abounded, used to be the measure of many a good sermon, and I think it a tolerable stint. I cannot wind up my ends to my own satisfaction in a much shorter time, nor am I pleased with myself if I greatly exceed it. If an angel was to preach for two hours, unless his hearers were angels likewise, I believe the greater part of them would wish he had done. It is a shame it should be so; but so it is, partly through the weakness, and partly through the wickedness of the flesh, we can seldom stretch our attention to spiritual things for two hours together without cracking it, and hurting its spring; and when weariness begins, edification ends. Perhaps it is better to feed our people like chickens, a little and often, than to cram them like turkeys, till they cannot hold one gobbet more. Besides, overlong sermons break in upon family concerns, and often call off thoughts from the sermon to the pudding at home, which is in danger of being overboiled.[1]

Lord, I can but repeat yesterday's prayer!

1 From *Cardiphonia: or, The Utterance of the Heart in the Course of a Real Correspondence, Volume One.*

November 16th

The Lord went before them by day in a pillar of a cloud, to lead them the way; and by night in a pillar of fire, to give them light; to go by day and night

(Exodus 13:21 KJV)

I have one more report to trouble you with, because it troubles me; and therefore you must bear a part of my burden. Assure me it is false, and I will send you one of the handsomest letters I can devise by way of thanks. It is reported then (but I will not believe it till you say I must), that you stand upon your tiptoes, upon the point of being whirled out of our vortex, and hurried away comet like, into the regions of eccentricity; in plain English, that you have a hankering to be an itinerant… It is a serious subject, let me beg you to deliberate well, and to pray earnestly before you take this step. Be afraid of acting in your own spirit, or under a wrong impression; however honestly you mean, you may be mistaken. The Lord has given you a little charge; be faithful in it, and in his good time he will advance you to a greater; but let his providence evidently open the door for you, and be afraid of moving one step before the cloud and pillar.[1]

Lord, preserve me from self-will. Grant me patience to pray, and then to wait for your will to become clearer and clearer in my heart and mind. Preserve me from impatience too. By the same token, Lord, help me to clearly discern your voice, and not to mistake it for any other. Give me a listening heart.

1 From *Cardiphonia: or, The Utterance of the Heart in the Course of a Real Correspondence, Volume One.*

November 17th

Redeeming the time, because the days are evil

(Ephesians 5:16 KJV)

The theatre is the very last of all places to which I would allow a child of mine to go. Some men do not see the evil of these places, but let them ask themselves, "Is this doing all to the glory of God? Is it redeeming the time?" Tragedies are usually full of blasphemies. Comedies tend to defend and promote what is called gallantry. They not only dissipate, but they tend to impregnate the mind with evil. The matter is so plain to me that I wonder at Christians questioning it.[1]

Lord, I present my time to you, as yours: all my days, and all my hours.

1 From *John Newton: Sailor, Preacher, Pastor, and Poet.*

November 18th

As for the one who is weak in faith, welcome him, but not to quarrel over opinions

(Romans 14:1 ESV)

Calvinism should be diffused through our ministry as sugar is in tea; it should be tasted everywhere, though prominent nowhere.[1 2]

Grant me, Lord, balance in doctrine, reasonableness in disagreement, wisdom in handling truth, and the appreciation of differing points of view.

1 From *John Newton: Sailor, Preacher, Pastor, and Poet.*

2 Calvinism was/is noted for its somewhat rigid adherence to prescribed doctrine, with relatively little room for dissent or disagreement. John Newton would have been the first to acknowledge (and promote) the validity of some Calvinistic doctrines, but his temperament and nature would have made it difficult for him to follow strict theology whereby differences of opinion were not always welcome.

November 19th

A man with leprosy came and knelt before him and said, "Lord, if you are willing, you can make me clean." Jesus reached out his hand and touched the man. "I am willing," he said. "Be clean!"

(Matthew 8:2–3)

Oft as the leper's case I read,
My own described I feel;
Sin is a leprosy indeed,
Which none but Christ can heal.

Awhile I would have passed for well,
And strove my spots to hide;
Till it broke out incurable,
Too plain to be denied.

What anguish did my soul endure,
Till hope and patience ceased?
The more I strove myself to cure,
The more the plague increased.

While thus I lay distressed, I saw
The Saviour passing by;
To him, though filled with shame and awe,
I raised my mournful cry.

Lord, thou canst heal me if thou wilt,
For thou canst all things do;
O cleanse my leprous soul from guilt,
My filthy heart renew!

Come lepers, seize the present hour,
The Saviour's grace to prove;
He can relieve, for he is pow'r,
He will, for he is love.[1]

My sin. My need. My sickness. My confession. My helplessness. Your power. Your love. Your healing. Your mercy. Your pardon. This is my God.

1 Originally, from *Olney Hymns* (1779).

November 20th

My dear children, I write this to you so that yo
But if anybody does sin, we have an advocate with
Jesus Christ, the Righteous One

(1 John 2:1)

Sin is the sickness of the soul, in itself mortal and incurable, as to any power in . or earth but that of the Lord Jesus only. But he is the great, the infallible Physic. Have we the privilege to know his name? Have we been enabled to put ourselves into his hand? We have then no more to do but to attend his prescriptions, to be satisfied with his methods, and to wait his time. It is lawful to wish we were well; it is natural to groan, being burdened; but still he must and will take his own course with us; and however dissatisfied with ourselves, we ought still to be thankful that he has begun his work in us, and to believe that he will also make an end. Therefore, while we mourn, we should likewise rejoice; we should encourage ourselves to expect all that he has promised; and we should limit our expectations by his promises. We are sure, that when the Lord delivers us from the guilt and dominion of sin, he could with equal ease free us entirely from sin if he pleased. The doctrine of sinless perfection is not to be rejected, as though it were a thing simply impossible in itself, for nothing is too hard for the Lord, but because it is contrary to that method which he has chosen to proceed by. He has appointed that sanctification should be effected, and sin mortified, not at once completely, but by little and little; and doubtless he has wise reasons for it. Therefore, though we are to desire a growth in grace, we should at the same time acquiesce in his appointment, and not to be discouraged or despond, because we feel that conflict which his Word informs us will only terminate with our lives.[1]

What a mystery, Lord! What a struggle! All I can really ask, Lord, is that you help me "by little and little" to overcome my sin, and my sinful nature, until that day when both are swallowed up in death. Have mercy.

1 From *Cardiphonia: or, The Utterance of the Heart in the Course of a Real Correspondence, Volume One.*

November 21st

We know that the law is spiritual; but I am unspiritual, sold as a slave to sin. I do not understand what I do. For what I want to do I do not do, but what I hate I do. And if I do what I do not want to do, I agree that the law is good. As it is, it is no longer I myself who do it, but it is sin living in me. For I know that good itself does not dwell in me, that is, in my sinful nature. For I have the desire to do what is good, but I cannot carry it out. For I do not do the good I want to do, but the evil I do not want to do–this I keep on doing. Now if I do what I do not want to do, it is no longer I who do it, but it is sin living in me that does it. So I find this law at work: Although I want to do good, evil is right there with me

(Romans 7:14–21)

Some of the first prayers which the Spirit of God teaches us to put up, are for a clearer sense of the sinfulness of sin, and our vileness on account of it. Now, if the Lord is pleased to answer your prayers in this respect, though it will afford you cause enough for humiliation, yet it should be received likewise with thankfulness, as a token for good. Your heart is not worse than it was formerly, only your spiritual knowledge has increased; and this is no small part of the growth in grace which you are thirsting after, to be truly humbled, and emptied, and made little in your own eyes. Further, the examples of saints recorded in Scripture prove (and indeed of the saints in general), that the greater measure any person has of the grace of God in truth; the more conscientious and lively they have been; and the more they have been favoured with assurances of divine favour, so much the more deep and sensible their perception of indwelling sin and infirmity has always been; so it was with Job, Isaiah, Daniel, and Paul.[1]

Sinless and perfect, holy God, you deal with sinners graciously and mercifully. Assist me, I pray, to handle this paradox well; the more I strive to become like Jesus, the more I become aware of my sin. Help me not to be discouraged by that, but, rather, to receive this awareness as "a token for good" – a sign of your transforming work within my heart.

1 From *Cardiphonia: or, The Utterance of the Heart in the Course of a Real Correspondence, Volume One.*

November 22nd

Enlarge the place of your tent, stretch your tent curtains wide, do not hold back

(Isaiah 54:2)

Mr. Newton... thus speaks of his position in London: "If," he says, "the Lord had left me to choose my own situation, London would have been almost the last place I should have chosen. But since it was the Lord's choice for me, I am reconciled and satisfied. He has in this respect given me another heart; for now I am fixed here, I seem to prefer it. My sphere of service is extremely enlarged, and my sphere of usefulness likewise. And not being under any attachment to systems and parties I am so far suited to my situation."[1]

Lord, I pray for any churches planning to expand their influence: outposts, daughter churches, satellite missions, plants, and so on. I ask you to guide their deliberations by your Spirit, so that their plans are in accordance with your will. Bless too, those congregations seeking an ever-greater influence within their communities. May they too find their "sphere of usefulness" increasing, under your hand.

1 From *John Newton of Olney and St Mary Woolnoth. An Autobiography and Narrative.*

November 23rd

If it is possible, as far as it depends on you, live at peace with everyone

(Romans 12:18)

We know very well that Mr. Newton was exceedingly averse to controversy. There was no pugnacity in his disposition. If he erred it was in loving too well, and not always wisely. But because Mr. Newton was liberal and large-hearted, and because he often spoke of the comparative insignificance of the secondary matters of church government, there were those who impeached his probity by charging him with interested motives for continuing in the Church, and called in question the sincerity of his opinion regarding her ritual, discipline, and order.[1] [2]

O Lord! The difficult balance of being true to oneself, yet finding that not everyone is happy with that! Give me an easy mind today, I ask, one that is, ultimately, only interested in what you think of me. Make that my point of reference, over and above the clamour of an opinionated world.

1 From *John Newton of Olney and St Mary Woolnoth. An Autobiography and Narrative.*

2 Such suspicions and accusations were levelled at John Newton because of his refusal to abide only and uniquely by the teaching and the structure of the Church of England. He was a great believer in the fact that God's truth was by no means confined to one denomination, and he (unlike some of his colleagues and parishioners) maintained that dissenters were entitled to be regarded as Christian brothers and sisters. The secret of this charitable disposition lay in his great humility whereby he retained a teachable mind and personality.

November 24th

Have unity of mind

(1 Peter 3:8 ESV)

Mr. Newton escaped for a little time from "the noise, and smoke, and dust" of London, and enjoyed a pleasant session at Lymington and Southampton.[1] In the neighbourhood of Lymington he visited a Mr. Etty. "I was happy," he wrote, "at Prestlands with Mr. Etty. He told me that he was fifty-five years of age; that he has feared the Lord, and walked much in the way he does now for many years, but could never make an acquaintance to whom he could freely open his mind before I came to him." "I could tell you as much about Southampton, Mr. Taylor, and Mr. Kingsbury, etc., if I had time. I was very happy there. Preached in two churches on the Lord's days, and frequently in the evenings in Mr. Taylor's house. What with walking, talking, riding, sailing, and a little smoking, O Time, how pleasantly and how swiftly didst thou pass?"[2]

Thank you, Lord, for good friends who make conversation easy, and who can be trusted with confidences. Thank you for those who listen well. May I be such a confidant – trustworthy and attentive.

1 Both Hampshire, England.

2 From *John Newton of Olney and St Mary Woolnoth. An Autobiography and Narrative.*

November 25th

My grace is sufficient for thee:
for my strength is made perfect in weakness

(2 Corinthians 12:9 KJV)

I am as a pardoned rebel wearing a fetter. In preaching, the upper part of the score, which the people hear, runs off well. But there is an under part full of discord. If the people heard this, I should be ready to jump out of the pulpit.[1]

Touch my heart with charity, Holy Spirit, so that I may always remember to encourage and support my minister/preacher. Move me away from expecting perfection, whereas the reality is, my church leader is as human as anyone else. Rather, bearing this in mind, make me a builder, and not a demolisher.

1 From *John Newton: Sailor, Preacher, Pastor, and Poet.*

November 26th

BLESSED IS THE ONE WHO PERSEVERES UNDER TRIAL BECAUSE, HAVING STOOD THE TEST, THAT PERSON WILL RECEIVE THE CROWN OF LIFE THAT THE LORD HAS PROMISED

(James 1:12)

How are you to know experimentally either your own weakness, or the power, wisdom and grace of God, seasonably and sufficiently afforded, but by frequent and various trials? How are the graces of patience, resignation, meekness, and faith, to be discovered and increased, but by exercise? The Lord has chosen, called, and armed us for the fight; and shall we wish to be excused? Shall we not rather rejoice that we have the honour to appear in such a cause, under such a Captain, such a banner, and in such company? A complete suit of armour is provided, weapons not to be resisted, and precious balm to heal us if haply we receive a wound, and precious ointment to revive us when we are in danger of fainting. Further, we are assured of the victory beforehand; and O what a crown is prepared for every conqueror, which Jesus, the righteous Judge, the gracious Saviour, shall place upon every faithful head with his own hand! Then let us not be weary and faint, for in due season we shall reap.[1]

How easily, Lord, we flag and tire, and become discouraged, tempted to give up and abandon our course. Strengthen your people, Lord. Strengthen me, day by day. Enable me to bear trials if they serve to strengthen my faith. Impart righteous perseverance!

1 From *Cardiphonia: or, The Utterance of the Heart in the Course of a Real Correspondence, Volume One.*

NOVEMBER 27TH

TRULY I TELL YOU, IF YOU HAVE FAITH AS SMALL AS A MUSTARD SEED, YOU CAN SAY TO THIS MOUNTAIN, "MOVE FROM HERE TO THERE," AND IT WILL MOVE. NOTHING WILL BE IMPOSSIBLE FOR YOU

(Matthew 17:20)

The time is short; yet a little while, and the struggle of indwelling sin, and the contradiction of surrounding sinners, shall be known no more. You are blessed, because you hunger and thirst after righteousness; he whose name is Amen has said you shall be filled. To claim the promise, is to make it our own; yet it is becoming us to practise submission and patience, not in temporals only, but also in spirituals. We should be ashamed and grieved at our slow progress, so far as it is properly chargeable to our remissness and miscarriage; yet we must not expect to receive everything at once, but wait for a gradual increase; nor should we forget to be thankful for what we may account a little, in comparison of the much we suppose others have received. A little grace, a spark of true love to God, a grain of living faith, though small as a mustard seed, is worth a thousand worlds. One draught of the water of life gives interest in and earnest of the whole fountain. It becometh the Lord's people to be thankful; and to acknowledge his goodness in what we have received.[1]

Thank you, Lord Jesus, that in the strange economy of your kingdom, even the tiniest seed of faith is precious, and loaded with enormous potential. Open my eyes afresh to matters of faith, so that I do not miss opportunities to believe and, in doing so, see you at work in all kinds of ways.

1 From *Cardiphonia: or, The Utterance of the Heart in the Course of a Real Correspondence, Volume One.*

November 28th

Praise the Lord, my soul, and forget not all his benefits

(Psalm 103:2)

How great are our obligations, for uniting us at first, for restoring us so often; for raising you up from so many illnesses; for preserving our affection; for overruling our concerns; for providing us friends; and especially, for directing our hearts to seek his face. And still he is loading us with benefits. Though we have not been without our trials, yet, all things considered, who has passed more gently through life, thus far? And with whom, upon the face of the earth, could we be now content to change? But with nothing has my heart been more affected, in, and since, your late illness.[1 2]

Help those who are passing through trials of various kinds, Lord, not to forget your benefits in times past. May such reflections inspire confidence and strength. I pray especially for those known to me personally, who are passing through trying times. May today's Bible text encourage them in faith.

1 From *Letters to a Wife (Volume Two): By the Author of Cardiphonia.*

2 See Footnote 1, August 21st.

November 29th

One day is with the Lord as a thousand years,
and a thousand years as one day

(2 Peter 3:8 KJV)

If youth, and health, and life, could be prolonged for a thousand years, and every moment of that space be filled up, with the greatest satisfaction we can conceive; this seemingly long period must at last terminate; and, when once past, it would appear short, and inconsiderable, as the… years we have already spent together, do at present. But if we are united in the faith, and hope of the gospel, we shall never part. Even that separation, which must take place (so painful, at times, to think of), will not deserve the name of parting. It will be but like the one coming down first from London, and the other safely following in a few days… [The Lord] can support those who trust him, in the most trying circumstances. Let it, therefore, be our chief concern, to attain a good hope, that we are his, and he is ours, and then we may cheerfully commit the rest to him. He can forgive sin, impart grace, subdue corruption, silence unbelief, make us strong out of weakness, and do more than we can either ask or think.[1]

When we've been there ten thousand years,
Bright shining as the sun,
We've no less days to sing God's praise
Than when we'd first begun.

1 From *Letters to a Wife (Volume Two): By the Author of Cardiphonia.*

NOVEMBER 30TH

THY DAYS BE FULFILLED, AND THOU SHALT SLEEP WITH THY FATHERS

(2 Samuel 7:12 KJV)

She [Mrs. Newton] then began to breathe very hard: her breathing might be called groaning, for it was heard in every part of the house; but I believe it was entirely owing to the difficulty of expiration, for she lay quite still, with a placid countenance, as if in a gentle slumber. There was no start or struggle, nor a feature ruffled. I took my post by her bedside, and watched her nearly three hours, with a candle in my hand, till I saw her breathe her last… When I was sure she was gone, I took off her ring, according to her repeated injunction, and put it upon my own finger. I then kneeled down with the servants who were in the room, and returned the Lord my unfeigned thanks for her deliverance, and her peaceful dismission.[1 2]

What a privilege, Lord, and yet, how painfully difficult: to sit with the dying, even the Christian dying, whose hope is secure. Place your loving hands upon the shoulders of those who have that responsibility, Lord: wives and husbands, children, loved ones, church leaders and chaplains who are called to hospital bedsides, and the like. Grant them strength, wisdom, and faith.

1 From *The Life of the Rev. John Newton*.

2 See Footnote 2, July 8th.

December 1st

Brothers and sisters, we do not want you to be uninformed about those who sleep in death, so that you do not grieve like the rest of mankind, who have no hope. For we believe that Jesus died and rose again, and so we believe that God will bring with Jesus those who have fallen asleep in him

(1 Thessalonians 4:13–14)

How wonderful must be the moment after death! What a transition did she then experience! She was instantly freed from sin, and all its attendant sorrows, and, I trust, instantly admitted to join the heavenly choir. That moment was remarkable to me likewise. It removed from me the chief object which made another day or hour of life, as to my own personal concern, desirable. At the same time, it set me free from a weight of painful feelings and anxieties, under which nothing short of a Divine power could have so long supported me. I believe it was about two or three months before her death, when I was walking up and down the room, offering disjointed prayers, from a heart torn with distress, that a thought suddenly struck me, with unusual force, to this effect: The promises of God must be true; surely the Lord will help me, if I am willing to be helped! It occurred to me, that we are often led, from a vain complacency in what we call our sensibility, to indulge the unprofitable grief, which both our duty and our peace require us to resist, to the utmost of our power, I instantly said aloud, "Lord, I am helpless indeed in myself, but I hope I am willing, without reserve, that thou shouldest help me."[1]

Hope and comfort in the midst of grief. You are my God.

1 From *The Life of the Rev. John Newton*.

December 2nd

They will take nothing with them when they die

(Psalm 49:17)

I have her Bible by me, which I would not part with for half the manuscripts in the Vatican, in which almost every principal text, from the beginning to the end of the book, is marked in the margin with a pencil, by her own dear hand. The good word of God was her medicine and her food, while she was able to read it. She read Dr. Watts's Psalms and Hymns, and the Olney Hymns, in the same manner. There are few of them, in which one, two, or more verses, are not thus marked; and in many, which I suppose she read more frequently, every verse is marked.[1]

Gracious God, draw especially close to those who are sifting through and sorting possessions left behind by a deceased loved one. As memories come to the fore, Lord, comfort them in their great loss. Prompt and send others to help them with packing bags and boxes.

1 From *The Life of the Rev. John Newton*.

December 3rd

All the promises of God in him are yea, and in him Amen

(2 Corinthians 1:20 KJV)

While I was writing here yesterday I had a beautiful prospect of the Isle of Wight[1] and the sea from the hermitage window. I am looking through the same window now, and can see nothing of them. But I do not suppose the Isle of Wight is sunk because I cannot see it. I consider that this is a thick, rainy morning, and I expect when the weather clears up the island will be visible again. Thus it is with respect to many great truths, which you and I have seen with the eye of our minds. There may be returns of dark, misty hours when we can hardly perceive them, but these should not put us on questioning whether we ever saw them at all. Faith and obedience are like the road we travel, the frames and feelings of our spirits are like the weather. Though the weather may often change, the road is always safe, and they who travel upon it will renew their strength as they go on, and at length surely arrive at the end of their journey, and possess the promised land.[2]

A wonderful truth, Lord. Bring it to mind, I pray, when I look out of the window on dank and dismal days! Bring it to mind especially, I pray, when there are shadows in my heart and mind, even if it's lovely outside: keep me safe on the road, come rain or shine.

1 An English island just off the coast of Hampshire.

2 From *John Newton of Olney and St Mary Woolnoth. An Autobiography and Narrative.*

DECEMBER 4TH

WHEN HE CAME TO HIS SENSES, HE SAID, "HOW MANY OF MY FATHER'S HIRED SERVANTS HAVE FOOD TO SPARE, AND HERE I AM STARVING!"

(Luke 15:17)

Amongst his hearers at St Mary Woolnoth, there was found one Sunday an intelligent and well-educated young man, who was anxiously seeking the way of salvation. He had informed his mother of his state of mind, and she having heard of Mr. Newton had urged her son to seek his acquaintance.[1] The next day Mr. Newton received an anonymous letter from the same individual, detailing some remarkable circumstances in his history. He informed Mr. Newton that he was born in Scotland, and though well educated, and in comfortable circumstances, was seized with an irresistible desire to see the world, and entertained the romantic purpose of travelling over the Continent on foot. Quitting his home under a false pretext, he made his way southward, supporting himself by playing on his violin, till he came to Newcastle,[2] whence he sailed to London. There he was for some months in great destitution, but at length obtained a situation as clerk to an attorney. He states that he was not without impressions of religion during this period; but for three years he lived for the most part in the neglect of its great duties, till the conversation of a religious acquaintance… led him to serious thought.[3]

Heavenly Father, my prayers today reach out on behalf of those who are far from home spiritually, and walking the streets in despair: not necessarily homeless in a literal sense, but, nevertheless, lost and unhappy in their souls. May it be, Lord, that a "random" conversation takes place as it did with the man in the story – a word in season to reroute the wanderer and bring them back to the fold.

1 What a wonderful compliment to John Newton's reputation as a minister and counsellor, and the high regard in which he was obviously held.

2 Newcastle upon Tyne, north-east England. He would have sailed south from the River Tyne.

3 From *John Newton of Olney and St Mary Woolnoth. An Autobiography and Narrative.*

December 5th

Hearken now unto my voice, I will give thee counsel, and God shall be with thee: Be thou for the people to God-ward

(Exodus 18:19 KJV)

Continued from yesterday: "On the receipt of my mother's letter, I went the next Sunday evening to your church; and when you spoke I thought I heard the words of eternal life. I listened with avidity, and wished you had preached till midnight… Yet my sins do not affect me as I wish. All that I can speak of is a strong desire to be converted to my God. Oh sir, what shall I do to inherit eternal life? I see clearly that I cannot be happy to any degree, even in this life, until I make peace with God; but how shall I make that peace?"… Mr. Newton felt a deep interest in this anonymous communication; and unable otherwise to find out the writer, whom he was very anxious to benefit, he gave notice at St Mary's that if the person who had written to him anonymously on such a day were in the church, he should be happy to converse with him: "I called on him," says the young man… "and experienced such a happy hour as I ought not to forget. If he had been my father he could not have expressed more solicitude for my welfare. Mr. Newton encouraged me so much"… The person referred to in this statement was the afterwards well known Dr. Claudius Buchanan.[1] In the words of his biographer, Mr. Buchanan found in Mr. Newton an enlightened and experienced guide, a wise and faithful counsellor, and at length a steady and affectionate friend.[2]

Heavenly Father, help me never to underestimate the impact I may have on someone's life, even if I am unaware of it at the time. I pray that you would speak to me and then speak through me, leaving the results to you. Thank you for the encouraging story of this encounter.

1 Rev Claudius Buchanan DD FRSE (1766 –1815) was a Scottish theologian, an ordained minister of the Church of England, and an evangelical missionary for the Church Missionary Society. He served as Vice Provost of the College of Calcutta in India (https://en.wikipedia.org/wiki/Claudius_Buchanan).

2 From *John Newton of Olney and St Mary Woolnoth. An Autobiography and Narrative.*

December 6th

Cast your burden on the Lord, and he will sustain you
(Psalm 55:22 ESV)

After speaking of his great loss [Mr. Newton] continues, "My health and spirits are good; I eat and sleep well. I preach, write, and converse as usual. I hope in spirituals I have been rather a gainer by my loss than otherwise. I think, likewise, that in the time of my trial, and since, there has been an additional blessing going forth in the public ordinances. The church is more thronged than formerly, and there seems an attention and earnestness in the hearers which is very encouraging."[1 2]

Thank you, Heavenly Father, for sustaining grace.

1 From *John Newton of Olney and St Mary Woolnoth. An Autobiography and Narrative.*

2 As at Olney, John Newton was used by God at St Mary Woolnoth to grow his congregation and to influence any number of people for the gospel's sake.

DECEMBER 7TH

DO NOT CAST ME AWAY WHEN I AM OLD;
DO NOT FORSAKE ME WHEN MY STRENGTH IS GONE

(Psalm 71:9)

St. Mary Woolnoth was shut up for repairs, and Mr. Newton was absent from London for about four months. During this period he made several excursions… He left home for Cambridge, where he met with Mr. Simeon[1] and many other friends. He preached on two successive Sabbaths at Mr. Simeon's church. Then we find him at Yelling[2] and Merton.[3] "I find Mr. Berridge,"[4] he says, "very weak." Mr. Venn,[5] too, was growing feeble, and Mr. Newton observes of his old friends: "They may teach me what to expect. No matter: I am in the Lord's hands; I have had a favoured lot – a large share of all that is valuable in temporal wealth. My Lord, teach me to resign and forego with a good grace."[6]

Ah, Lord! An awareness of creeping old age! Help me to be gracious, I pray, if and when my faculties begin to fail. Preserve me from self-pity, but, by the same token, comfort me if my days become frustrating and I resent my limitations. I know you will hold on to me.

1 Reverend Charles Simeon (1759–1836), Holy Trinity Church, Cambridge.
2 Huntingdon, Cambridgeshire.
3 A London borough.
4 Reverend John Berridge (1716–93), Vicar of Everton, near Sandy, Bedfordshire, England.
5 Reverend John Venn (1759–1813).
6 From *John Newton of Olney and St Mary Woolnoth. An Autobiography and Narrative.*

December 8th

He will… sustain you in your old age

(Ruth 4:15)

His biographer, Mr. Cecil,[1] after Newton had turned eighty years of age, observing his increasing infirmities, said to him, "In the article of public preaching, ought it not be best to consider your work done before you evidently discover you can speak no longer?" "I cannot stop," he said, raising his voice. "What, shall the old blasphemer stop while he can speak?"[2]

Better, Lord, with your help, to wear out than to rust away!

1 Richard Cecil (1748–1810), Anglican priest and writer.

2 From *John Newton: Sailor, Preacher, Pastor, and Poet.*

December 9th

Freely you have received; freely give

(Matthew 10:8)

John Newton was remarkable for the men of light and leading he influenced and inspired by his own level-headed, large-hearted consecration to duty. There have been notable Johns since the apostolic fisherman John of the Galilean Sea, who served their God according to their gift and grace, as John Wycliff,[1] John Milton,[2] John Bunyan,[3] John Wesley,[4] John Thornton,[5] and others: so did the sailor-preacher, John Newton. Wilberforce,[6] in his tremendous fight for the slave, turned instinctively to the old slave-trader and master of slave-ships for guidance in a spiritual service… The outcome is writ large in history. Wilberforce and his peers struck the death-knell of slavery. Not only in the British Empire, but everywhere slavery was made impossible, though it had to be swept away in rivers of blood in the United States, and in every other State of the world calling itself Christian.[7]

Thank you, Heavenly Father, for those who have blessed and encouraged me along the way. As I think of such people now, I ask you to make up the blessing to them, so that as they have given to others, they may receive from you.

1 Or Wycliffe (1320s–84), priest, theologian, biblical translator. Wycliffe advocated translation of the Christian Scriptures into the vernacular, and in 1382 completed a translation directly from the Vulgate into Middle English: "Wycliffe's Bible".

2 John Milton (1608–74), poet and political activist, probably best known for his epic poem *Paradise Lost.*

3 See Footnote 3, January 11th.

4 See Footnote 1, January 2nd. See also *Through the Year with John Wesley* by Stephen J. Poxon, published by Lion Hudson/Monarch.

5 See Footnote 1, September 4th.

6 See Footnote 5, January 2nd.

7 From *John Newton: Sailor, Preacher, Pastor, and Poet.*

December 10th

Go and enjoy choice food and sweet drinks, and send some to those who have nothing prepared. This day is holy to our Lord. Do not grieve, for the joy of the Lord is your strength

(Nehemiah 8:10)

The joy of the Lord is the strength of his people; whereas unbelief makes our heads hang down, and our knees feeble, dispirits ourselves, and discourages others; and though it steals upon us under a semblance of humility, it is indeed the very essence of pride. By inward and outward exercises the Lord is promoting the best desire of your heart, and answering your daily prayers. Would you have assurance? The true solid assurance is to be obtained in no other way. When young Christians are greatly comforted with the Lord's love and presence, their doubts and fears are for that season at an end. But this is not assurance; so soon as the Lord hides his face, they are troubled, and ready to question the very foundation of hope. Assurance grows by repeated conflict, by our repeated experimental proof of the Lord's power and goodness to save; when we have been brought very low and helpless, sorely wounded and healed, cast down and raised again, have given up all hope, and been suddenly snatched from danger, and placed in safety; and when these things have been repeated to us and in us a thousand times over, we begin to learn to trust simply to the word and power of God, beyond and against appearances; and this trust, when habitual and strong, bears the name of assurance; for even assurance has degrees.[1][2]

Great teaching today, Lord – thank you! Time and again, you have reached out to me when assurance (reassurance) was needed – thank you for doing so. Have mercy on those who need just that today; those whose faith is challenged, or whose confidence is waning. Fill your people with fresh joy and strength.

---

1 From *Cardiphonia: or, The Utterance of the Heart in the Course of a Real Correspondence, Volume One.*

2 Primarily renowned as a pastor and counsellor, John Newton here shows his hand as an excellent teacher, once again demonstrating his intellectual ability to link theology with practical Christian living.

DECEMBER 11TH

IF YOU LOVE ME, KEEP MY COMMANDS

(John 14:15)

The love of the best Christians to an unseen Saviour is far short of what it ought to be. If your heart be like mine, and you examine your love to Christ by the warmth and frequency of your emotions towards him, you will often be in a sad suspense, whether or not you love him at all. The best mark to judge, and which he has given us for that purpose, is to inquire if his word and will have a prevailing, governing influence upon our lives and temper. If we love him, we do endeavour to keep his commandments; and it will hold the other way; if we have a desire to please him, we undoubtedly love him. Obedience is the best test; and when, amidst all our imperfections, we can humbly appeal concerning the sincerity of our views, this is a mercy for which we ought to be greatly thankful. He that has brought us to will, will likewise enable us to do according to his good pleasure. I doubt not but the Lord whom you love, and on whom you depend, will lead you in a sure way, and establish, and strengthen, and settle you in his love and grace.[1]

Lord Jesus, I do love you, deep in my heart. Help me today, in terms of obedience, to will, and to do.

1 From *Cardiphonia: or, The Utterance of the Heart in the Course of a Real Correspondence, Volume One.*

DECEMBER 12TH

OUR CITIZENSHIP IS IN HEAVEN. AND WE EAGERLY AWAIT A SAVIOUR FROM THERE, THE LORD JESUS CHRIST

(Philippians 3:20)

We were very happy in the company of — the only inconvenience was, that it renewed the pain it always gives me to part with them. Though the visit was full as long as I could possibly expect, it seemed very short. This must be the case while we are here; our pleasures are short, interrupted, and mixed with troubles: this is not, cannot be our rest. But it will not be always the case; we are travelling to a better world, where every evil and imperfection shall cease; then we shall be for ever with the Lord, and with each other. May the prospect of this blessed hope set before us revive our fainting spirits, and make us willing to endure hardships as good soldiers of Jesus Christ. Here we must often sow in tears, but there we shall reap in joy, and all tears shall be wiped from our eyes for ever.[1]

The great Christian hope! What a day of rejoicing that will be! Beyond the blue horizon!

1 From *Cardiphonia: or, The Utterance of the Heart in the Course of a Real Correspondence, Volume One.*

December 13th

WHEN YOU PRAY, GO INTO YOUR ROOM, CLOSE THE DOOR AND PRAY TO YOUR FATHER, WHO IS UNSEEN. THEN YOUR FATHER, WHO SEES WHAT IS DONE IN SECRET, WILL REWARD YOU

(Matthew 6:6)

How little does the world know of that intercourse which is carried on between heaven and earth! What petitions are daily presented, and what answers are received at the throne of grace! O the blessed privilege of prayer! O the wonderful love, care, attention, and power of our great Shepherd! His eye is always upon us; when our spirits are almost overwhelmed within us, he knoweth our path. His ear is always open to us; let who will overlook and disappoint us, he will not. When means and hope fail, when everything looks dark upon us, when we seem shut up on every side, when we are brought to the lowest ebb, still our help is in the name of the Lord who made heaven and earth. To him all things are possible; and before the exertion of his power, when he is pleased to arise and work, all hindrances give way and vanish like a mist before the sun. And he can so manifest himself to the soul, and cause his goodness to pass before it, that the hour of affliction shall be the golden hour of the greatest consolation.[1][2]

Sweet hours of prayer, calling me from a world of care! What a tremendous privilege! Thank you.

1 From *Cardiphonia: or, The Utterance of the Heart in the Course of a Real Correspondence, Volume One.*

2 Newton was a great exponent of personal prayer and an ongoing dialogue with his Heavenly Father, although he advocated prayer as conversation as well as formal, liturgical intercession and confession. One of his great joys was walking and praying in the fields and open countryside.

December 14th

The eternal God is your refuge, and underneath are the everlasting arms

(Deuteronomy 33:27)

After [Mary] was gone, my willingness to be helped and my desire that the Lord's goodness to me might be observed, for their encouragement, made me indifferent to some laws of established custom, the breach of which is often more noticed than the violation of God's commands. I was afraid of sitting at home, and indulging myself, by poring over my loss; and therefore I was seen in the street and visited some of my serious friends the very next day. I likewise preached three times while she lay dead in the house. Some of my brethren kindly offered their assistance; but as the Lord was pleased to give me strength, both of body and mind, I thought it my duty to stand up in my place, as formerly. And after she was deposited in the vault, I preached her funeral sermon, with little more sensible emotion than if it had been for another person. I have reason to hope that many of my hearers were comforted and animated, under their afflictions, by what they saw of the Lord's goodness to me, in my time of need. And I acknowledge that it was well worth standing a while in the fire, for such an opportunity of experiencing and exhibiting the power and faithfulness of his promises.[1]

Carrying on, Lord, after the death of a loved one. Carrying on, and hoping to maintain a good witness into the bargain. O, Lord, please help, strengthen and support those who are walking beneath the heavy burden of bereavement. Carry them, if necessary.

1 From *The Life of the Rev. John Newton.*

December 15th

Your strength will equal your days

(Deuteronomy 33:25)

When my wife died, the world seemed to die with her, I hope, to revive no more. I see little now but my ministry and my Christian profession, to make a continuance in life, for a single day, desirable; though I am willing to wait my appointed time. If the world cannot restore her to me (not that I have the remotest wish that her return was possible), it can do nothing for me. The Bank of England is too poor to compensate for such a loss as mine. But the Lord, the all sufficient God, speaks, and it is done. Let those who know him, and trust him be of good courage. He can give them strength according to their day; he can increase their strength, as their trials are increased, to any assignable degree. And what he can do, he has promised he will do. The power and faithfulness on which the successive changes of day and night depend, and which uphold the stars in their orbits, are equally encouraged to support his people, and to lead them safely and unhurt, if their path be so appointed, through floods and flames. Though I believe she has never yet been, and probably never will be, out of my waking thoughts for five minutes at a time; though I sleep in the bed in which she suffered and languished so long, I have not had one uncomfortable day, nor one restless night, since she left me. I have lost a right hand, but the Lord enables me to go on, cheerfully, without it.[1]

Bless the bereaved today, Lord, however long it is since they lost their loved one(s). Make them aware of your gentle strength as they try to adjust to life without their "right hand".

1 From *The Life of the Rev. John Newton.*

December 16th

The protection of wisdom is like the protection of money, and the advantage of knowledge is that wisdom preserves the life of him who has it

(Ecclesiastes 7:12 ESV)

Mr. Newton was entirely free from either the vanity or ambition which too often shows itself in some great and even good men; and so when the University of New Jersey[1] conferred on him at this time the degree of Doctor of Divinity,[2] while grateful for such an expression of respect, he refused to appropriate the title: "I have been hurt," he says in a letter… "by two or three letters direct to Dr. Newton. I beg you to inform my friends… as they come in your way, that after a little time if any letters come to me addressed to Dr. Newton I shall be obliged to send them back unopened. I know no such person, I never shall, I never will, by the grace of God… So far as this mark of their favour indicates a regard to the gospel truths which I possess, I am much pleased with it. But as to the title itself, I renounce it heartily. The dreary cost of Africa was the university to which the Lord was pleased to send me, and I dare not acknowledge a relation to any other."[3]

Thank you, Heavenly Father, for the "university of life". I may not always appreciate some of the lessons on offer, especially the tougher ones, but I thank you for the gift of hindsight. Keep me learning, I pray!

1 Now Princeton University.
2 In 1792.
3 From *John Newton of Olney and St Mary Woolnoth. An Autobiography and Narrative.*

DECEMBER 17TH

Let no debt remain outstanding,
except the continuing debt to love one another

(Romans 13:8)

So many were the claims made upon Mr. Newton, that nothing but the greatest economy of time would have enabled him to satisfy the growing demands of a correspondence that had become, to his fullest conviction, a means of very great blessing, and so, on his part, a matter of solemn duty. Indeed, on one occasion, at the close of his life,[1] upon a friend speaking to him of the profit and refreshment he derived from his letters, "Yes," he said, "the Lord saw that I should be most useful by them." And, be it remembered, Mr. Newton wrote letters long and "natter-full," and instructive or comforting in the highest degree… "I have about sixty unanswered letters, and while I am writing one I usually receive two; so that I am likely to die much in debt."[2]

May this be true of me, Lord; that even though, with your help, I love, I remain daily aware of my continuing debt. This should help me to avoid complacency in the matter, and might even make me a little more like Jesus.

1 The clear implication here is that John Newton was still engaged in his ministry of counselling via prolific correspondence, even in his latter days, or at least as long as he was physically able to be.

2 From *John Newton of Olney and St Mary Woolnoth. An Autobiography and Narrative.*

December 18th

Jesus… said to them, "Those who are well have no need of a physician, but those who are sick"

(Mark 2:17 ESV)

It has pleased God to favour me, with remarkable exemption from pain and sickness of body for many years past. But I have a sick soul labouring under a complication of disorders, each of them in their nature mortal and incurable by any physician but One. I had often heard of Him, but my prejudices prevented me from applying to Him till I was brought very low indeed. At length necessity compelling (it was a happy necessity), I went to Him, and He readily undertook my cure. It is now the business and pleasure of my life to procure Him more patients. I tell thousands in a year how much they need Him, how gracious and skilful He is, but I can prevail on very few to go. There is none like Him. He welcomes all who apply. No one miscarries under His hand, and He neither expects nor accepts any fees.[1]

The cure of souls. The Great Physician. You are my God.

1 From *John Newton of Olney and St Mary Woolnoth. An Autobiography and Narrative.*

December 19th

Let this mind be in you, which was also in Christ Jesus

(Philippians 2:5 KJV)

I hope the Lord will give me an humble sense of what I am, and that broken and contrite frame of heart in which he delights. This is to me the chief thing. I had rather have more of the mind that was in Christ, more of a meek, quiet, resigned, peaceful and loving disposition, than to enjoy the greatest measure of sensible comforts, if the consequence should be (as perhaps it would) spiritual pride, self-sufficiency, and a want of that tenderness to others which becomes one which has reason to style himself the chief of sinners. I know, indeed, that the proper tendency of sensible consolations is to humble; but I can see, that, through the depravity of human nature, they have not always that effect. And I have been sometimes disgusted with an apparent want of humility, an air of self-will and self-importance, in persons of whose sincerity I could not at all doubt. It has kept me from envying them those pleasant frames with which they have sometimes been favoured; for I believe Satan is never nearer us than at some times when we think ourselves nearer the Lord.[1] [2]

Lord Jesus, it seems too good to be true, that your mind should be in me; that you should be willing to activate this influence and impartation. I acknowledge my helplessness in this, and my need. Thank you for such a gracious transaction.

1 From *Cardiphonia: or, The Utterance of the Heart in the Course of a Real Correspondence, Volume One.*

2 Here we see, as indeed we have seen several times in these devotions, evidence of John Newton's great humility. His closeness to the Lord Jesus made him constantly aware of his Adamic nature and, likewise, his vulnerability to sin and temptation. Paradoxically, his spiritual strength lay in his awareness of his weakness.

December 20th

The Lord said to Moses, "I have heard the grumbling of the Israelites. Tell them, 'At twilight you will eat meat, and in the morning you will be filled with bread.'" That evening quail came and covered the camp, and in the morning there was a layer of dew around the camp. When the dew was gone, thin flakes like frost on the ground appeared on the desert floor. Moses said to them, "It is the bread the Lord has given you to eat. This is what the Lord has commanded: 'Everyone is to gather as much as they need.'" The Israelites did as they were told; some gathered much, some little. Everyone had gathered just as much as they needed. Then Moses said to them, "No one is to keep any of it until morning." However, some of them paid no attention to Moses; they kept part of it until morning, but it was full of maggots and began to smell

(Exodus 16:11–20)

What reason we have to charge our souls in David's words, "My soul, wait thou only upon God." A great stress should be laid upon that word only. We dare not entirely shut him out of our regards, but we are too apt to suffer something to share with him. This evil disposition is deeply fixed in our hearts; and the Lord orders all his dispensations towards us with a view to rooting it out; that, being wearied with repeated disappointments, we may at length be compelled to betake ourselves to him alone. Why else do we experience so many changes and crosses? Why are we so often in heaviness? We know that he delights in the pleasure and prosperity of his servants; that he does not willingly afflict or grieve his children; but there is a necessity on our parts, in order to teach us that we have no stability in ourselves, and that no creature can do us good but by his appointment. While the people of Israel depended upon him for food, they gathered up the manna every morning in the field; but when they would hoard it up in their homes, that they might have a stock within themselves, they had it without his blessing, and it proved good for nothing; it soon bred worms, and grew offensive. We may observe something like this occurs both in our temporal and spiritual concerns.[1]

Saviour, teach me day by day
Love's sweet lesson to obey;
Sweeter lesson cannot be,
Loving Him who first loved me.[2]

1 From *Cardiphonia: or, The Utterance of the Heart in the Course of a Real Correspondence, Volume One.*
2 From Jane Eliza Leeson's hymn "Saviour, Teach Me Day by Day", first published in 1842.

December 21st

I know whom I have believed, and am persuaded that he is able to keep that which I have committed unto him against that day

(2 Timothy 1:12 KJV)

About a month before Mr. N.'s death… he said, "It is a great thing to die; and, when flesh and heart fail, to have God for the strength of our heart, and our portion for ever: I know whom I have believed, and he is able to keep that which I have committed unto him against that day. Henceforth there is laid up for me a crown of righteousness, which the Lord, the righteous Judge, shall give me at that day." At another time he said, "More light, more love, more liberty. Hereafter I hope, when I shut my eyes on the things of time, I shall open them in a better world. What a thing it is to live under the shadow of the Almighty! I am going the way of all flesh." And when one replied, "The Lord is gracious," he answered, "If it were not so, how could I dare to stand before him?"

The Wednesday before he died, Mrs. G. asked him if his mind was comfortable; he replied, "I am satisfied with the Lord's will." Mr. N. seemed sensible to his last hour, but expressed nothing remarkable after these words. He departed on the 21st [of December], and was buried in the vault of his church the 31st of December, 1807.[1 2]

To die well, Lord: grant that gift, I pray, to those who will slip into eternity this day. Come with your peace to the dying, and whisper words of salvation, even at the last. Hold your cross before closing eyes.

1 From *The Life of the Rev. John Newton.*

2 For a fascinating article on the final resting place of John and Mary Newton, including details of its location, please visit https://historicengland.org.uk/listing/the-list/list-entry/1392852

December 22nd

In the case of a will

(Hebrews 9:16)

The following is a copy of the beginning of Mr. Newton's will, dated June 13, 1803:

"In the name of God, Amen. I, John Newton, of Coleman-street-building, in the parish of St Stephen, Coleman-street, in the city of London, clerk, being through mercy in good health and of sound and disposing mind, memory, and understanding, although in the seventy eighth year of my age, do, for the settling of my temporal concerns, and for the disposal of all the worldly estate which it hath pleased the Lord in his good providence to give me, make this my last will and testament as follows. I commit my soul to my gracious God and Saviour, who mercifully spared and preserved me, when I was an apostate, a blasphemer, and an infidel, and delivered me from that state of misery on the coast of Africa into which my obstinate wickedness had plunged me; and who has been pleased to admit me, though most unworthy, to preach his glorious gospel. I rely with humble confidence upon the atonement and mediation of the Lord Jesus Christ, God and man, which I have often proposed to others as the only foundation whereon a sinner can build his hope, trusting that he will guard and guide me through the uncertain remainder of my life, and that he will then admit me into his presence in his heavenly kingdom. I would have my body deposited in the vault under the parish church of Saint Mary Woolnoth… it is my desire that my funeral may be performed with as little expense as possible, consistent with decency."[1]

A witness even from beyond the grave! Thank you, Lord, for John Newton's life. Thank you for people who truly are trophies of grace. All is mercy.

1 From *The Life of the Rev. John Newton.*

December 23rd

There shall come in the last days scoffers

(2 Peter 3:3 KJV)

Reminding his hearers of the age in which Newton lived, the age of Wesley, of Pope,[1] of Voltaire,[2] and of Goethe,[3] Mr. Marston[4] said that Newton, like all the early Evangelicals, maintained an attitude towards the movements of the day which may be called one of august aloofness, yet which was far removed from either apathy or contemptuousness. Their minds were pre-engaged by the eternal and transcending verities of the Gospel, and to them they devoted their undivided energies.[5]

Carrying on, Lord, in the face of scepticism, agnosticism, and atheism, when faith is mocked and held up to ridicule. Help me to carry on, undaunted.

1 Alexander Pope (1688–1744), English poet.

2 François-Marie Arouet (1694–1778), known as Voltaire, French Enlightenment writer, known for his criticism of Christianity, and his advocacy of the separation of church and state.

3 Johann Wolfgang von Goethe (1749–1832), German writer noted for his scepticism in matters of faith.

4 Reverend J. H. R. Marston of Belgrave Chapel, London. (Sometimes referred to as Reverend H. J. R. Marston.)

5 From *John Newton: Sailor, Preacher, Pastor, and Poet.*

December 24th

This God is our God for ever and ever;
he will be our guide even to the end
(Psalm 48:14)

By a series of remarkable incidents, Newton had been taught to believe profoundly in the sovereignty and providence of God. Where many would talk of coincidences, he saw only the protecting and guiding hand of a Father. It is thus he writes: – "The way of man is not in himself, nor can he perceive what belongs to a single step. When I go to preach at St Mary Woolnoth, it seems the same whether I turn down Lothbury[1] or go through Old Jewry;[2] but the going through one street and not another may produce an effect of lasting consequences. A man cut down my hammock in sport, but had he cut in down half an hour later I had not been here... A man made a smoke on the seashore at the time a ship passed, which was thereby brought to, and afterwards brought me to England."[3][4]

No such thing as coincidence, Lord! Rather, your sovereign hand upon my life, even at times when I am unaware of your guidance. I pray for any today, Heavenly Father, who are unsure of which path to take in life. Guide them by your Spirit.

1 A short street in the City of London.
2 A one-way street in the City of London that was once part of a Jewish ghetto.
3 This passage is not entirely clear, except that we may deduce from it, Newton's belief in the sovereignty of a loving God watching over every circumstance of life.
4 From *John Newton: Sailor, Preacher, Pastor, and Poet.*

December 25th

Suddenly a great company of the heavenly host appeared with the angel, praising God and saying, "Glory to God in the highest heaven, and on earth peace to those on whom his favour rests"

(Luke 2:13–14)

When he came, the angels sung,
"Glory be to God on high;"
Lord, unloose my stamm'ring tongue,
Who should louder sing than I?

Did the Lord a man become,
That he might the law fulfil,
Bleed and suffer in my room,
And canst thou, my tongue, be still?

No, I must my praises bring,
Though they worthless are and weak;
For should I refuse to sing,
Sure the very stones would speak.

O my Saviour, Shield, and Sun,
Shepherd, Brother, Husband, Friend,
Ev'ry precious name in one,
I will love thee without end.[1]

Thank you, God, for your gift beyond words.

1 Found on https://www.poemhunter.com/poem/praise-for-the-incarnation/

December 26th

You, Bethlehem Ephrathah, though you are small among the clans of Judah, out of you will come for me one who will be ruler over Israel, whose origins are from of old, from ancient times

(Micah 5:2)

With respect to the application of some passages in the Old Testament to our Lord and Saviour, I hold it safest to keep close to the specimens the apostles have given us, and I would venture with caution if I go beyond their line; yet it is probable they have only given us a specimen, and that there are a great number of passages which have a direct reference to gospel truths, although we may run some hazard in making out the allusion. If St Paul had not gone before me, I should have hesitated to assert, that the prohibition, "Thou shalt not muzzle the ox that treadeth out the corn,"[1] was given not upon the account of oxen, but altogether for our sakes: nor should I, without his assistance, have found out that the history of Sarah and Hagar was a designed allegory, to set forth the difference between the law and gospel covenants. Therefore, when I hear ministers tracing some other allusions, I cannot be always sure that they push them too far; though perhaps they are not quite satisfactory in my judgment; for it may be that they have a further insight into the meaning of the places than myself.[2]

Thank you, Lord, for the glorious connections between Old and New Testaments. Thank you for teachers and ministers whom you have gifted with skills of exposition and insight. Thank you especially, at this time of year, for precious Old Testament prophecies foretelling the birth of Christ, my Saviour.

1 Deuteronomy 25:4 and 1 Timothy 5:18.

2 From *Cardiphonia: or, The Utterance of the Heart in the Course of a Real Correspondence, Volume One.*

December 27th

Rightly handling the word of truth

(2 Timothy 2:15 ESV)

I think scriptures may be sometimes used to advantage, by way of accommodation in popular discourse, and in something of a different sense from what they bear in the place where they stand, provided they are not alleged as proofs, but only to illustrate a truth already proved or acknowledged. Though Job's friends and Job himself were mistaken, there are many great truths in their speeches, which, as such, may, I think, stand as the foundation of a discourse. Nay, I either have, or have often intended to borrow a truth from the mouth even of Satan, "Hast thou not set a hedge about him?" such a confession, extorted from our grand adversary placing the safety of the Lord's people, under his providential care, in a very striking light.[1]

Lord, I owe it to my minister to prayer for him/her in the exercise of preaching and teaching. Grant him/her insight, so that today's Bible text may be ably demonstrated in their ministry. Help me too, Lord, to read my Bible well within the illumination of your light, lest I misunderstand or misapply certain verses.

1 From *Cardiphonia: or, The Utterance of the Heart in the Course of a Real Correspondence, Volume One.*

December 28th

Thus far the Lord has helped us

(1 Samuel 7:12)

Hitherto I feel no uneasiness about what is before me; but I am afraid my tranquillity does not wholly spring from trust in the Lord, and submission to his will, but that a part of it at least is derived from… assurance… that the operation would be neither difficult nor dangerous. I have not much of the hero in my constitution; if in great pains or sharp trials I should ever show a becoming fortitude, it must be given me from above. I desire to leave all with him, in whose hands my ways are, and who has promised me strength according to my day.[1][2]

The hopes and fears of all the years are met in thee tonight.[3]

1 From *Cardiphonia: or, The Utterance of the Heart in the Course of a Real Correspondence, Volume One.*

2 See October 5th. Although this extract relates to the surgery John Newton faced then, I have deliberately placed it here, as the year draws towards its conclusion, because for many people, this can be an anxious and uncertain time, as one year closes and another opens. Similar feelings of fear and reminiscence may arise, hence today's prayer.

3 See Footnote 2. From Phillips Brooks' carol "O Little Town of Bethlehem".

December 29th

THOU WILT KEEP HIM IN PERFECT PEACE, WHOSE MIND IS STAYED ON THEE: BECAUSE HE TRUSTETH IN THEE

(Isaiah 26:3 KJV)

Mr. Newton's heart was as large as it was loving. How many are the proofs of his catholicity…! Of narrowness, sectarianism, bigotry, he seemed utterly incapable, and he beautifully showed how a man may love the particular denomination to which he is by conviction attached, and yet possess a charity that can embrace all who without its pale are agreed in the great fundamentals of Christianity. In Mr. Newton's Christian character the essential elements of faith and love were strikingly manifest. His faith in the atoning work of Christ was simple and unwavering; and his gratitude for the mercy of God bestowed upon him, the "chief of sinners", was the ever-abiding feeling of his heart. But here we would especially speak of Mr. Newton's faith in the overruling providence of God. In all circumstances his soul stayed itself upon the Lord. Thus in the perils of the deep he possessed his soul in peace. When he had come to the settled conviction that it was the will of God he should be a minister he waited six long years, convinced that God would, in his own time, open the door of admission: and at length he gave up a comfortable income, and went to his curacy at Olney.[1]

Still my heart today, gracious God. Still me in your promises. Impart faith and trust, whereby I may experience peace in whatever this day holds for me. I pray, Lord, for any whose minds are troubled at present. May they too find you close at hand.

1 From *John Newton of Olney and St Mary Woolnoth. An Autobiography and Narrative.*

December 30th

Look to the Lord and his strength; seek his face always

(1 Chronicles 16:11)

Mr. Newton was eminently faithful to the trust which the Great Master had committed to him. Quietly and perseveringly he worked on in his own appointed sphere. It was not given to him to evangelise like Whitefield or Wesley, and, trumpet-tongued, to arouse the masses; but in another way he laboured to build up and edify the Church, and to influence perhaps a yet wider circle. To these ends he preached, wrote, talked, lived. And what was the great secret of Mr. Newton's power and steadfastness? Unquestionably it was his spirit of prayer. From the commencement of his religious history we find him cultivating this holy habit. It was ever his "vital breath".[1] Thus waiting on the Lord, he continually renewed his strength, and all that he attempted was made to prosper in his hand. Such was Mr. Newton's character, such the graces that distinguished him; and thus it was that he came to be a man revered and loved better and more widely than most of his fellows.[2]

Thank you, Lord, for the mystery of prayer. Thank you for the privilege of prayer. Thank you for your grace in listening to prayer. Thank you for answered prayer. Thank you, too, for prayer requests that are declined. I lift to you each and every prayer in this book; my year of prayer, day-by-day. Bless all those mentioned in these prayers, I ask.

1 "Prayer is the Christian's vital breath": from James Montgomery's hymn "Prayer is the Soul's Sincere Desire".

2 From *John Newton of Olney and St Mary Woolnoth. An Autobiography and Narrative.*

December 31st

Lord, you have been our dwelling-place throughout all generations. Before the mountains were born or you brought forth the whole world, from everlasting to everlasting you are God… May the favour of the Lord our God rest on us; establish the work of our hands for us – yes, establish the work of our hands

(Psalm 90:1–2, 17–18)

What… was the source of Mr. Newton's power in the pulpit? It might perhaps suffice to say that he was possessed in large measure of the two great elements of all such power. His whole soul was in sympathy both with the truth and with his hearers. He spoke that which he believed; and because he believed; and he spoke with the conviction that it was the great truth of God he was uttering. He appealed to sinners with the loving compassion of one who had been in like peril with themselves, and who longed that they might share in his happy deliverance; he was a restored prodigal, and they too might be reconciled to their Father. Again, in addressing his fellow travellers to the heavenly Canaan, he gathered lessons from the stores of his own rich and varied experiences, and this "showed them all the way" which his God and their God was leading them through the wilderness. It must further be remembered that striking illustrations, happy turns of thought, racy and telling expressions, often enriched Mr. Newton's extempore discourses. Then zeal, earnestness, and a winning affection breathed their spirit through all he said. And, finally, if there was often less of the direct preparation of thought and study than might have been desirable, there was ever the preparation of devout and earnest prayer, and that to an extent perhaps not very common.[1]

Thank you, gracious Father, for the amazing grace you shone into the astonishing life of John Newton. Even just this mere glimpse of it is humbling. I pray for such grace to stay with me, at this year's end. I pray for grace and mercy to overshadow my loved ones and friends, and all who claim any interest in my prayers and my witness. So help us, God.

1 From *John Newton of Olney and St Mary Woolnoth. An Autobiography and Narrative.*

Bibliography

An authentic narrative of some remarkable and interesting particulars in the life of John Newton, Communicated in a series of letters to the Reverend Mr. Haweis (London: J. Johnson, 1775)

Letters of John Newton (London: The Banner of Truth Trust, 1960)

The Life of the Rev. John Newton, Rector of St Mary Woolnoth, London (London: The Religious Tract Society)

The Works of the Rev. John Newton, Late Rector of the United Parishes of St. Mary Woolnoth, and St. Mary Woolchurch Haw, London; With Memoirs of the Author, and General Remarks on His Life, Connections, and Character (London: Hamilton, Adams, and Co, 1824)

Bull, Josiah, *John Newton of Olney and St Mary Woolnoth. An Autobiography and Narrative, Compiled Chiefly from His Diary and Other Unpublished Documents* (London: The Religious Tract Society, 1870)

Bull, Josiah, *Letters by The Rev. John Newton : of Olney and St. Mary Woolnoth: Including several never before published with biographical sketches and illustrative notes* (London: Religious Tract Society, 1869)

Callis, John (ed.), *John Newton: Sailor, Preacher, Pastor and Poet* (London: S. W. Partridge & Co, 1908)

Martin, Bernard, *An Ancient Mariner: A Biography of John Newton* (London: Wyvern Books, 1960)

Martin, Bernard, *John Newton and the Slave Trade* (London: Longmans, Green & Co Ltd, 1961)

Newton, John, *Cardiphonia, or The utterance of the heart in the course of a real correspondence* (London: J. Johnson, 1781)

Newton, John, *Letters to a Wife: By the Author of Cardiphonia* (London: J. Johnson, 1793)

Rouse, Marylynn, *365 Days with Newton* (Leominster: Day One Publications, 2006)

Rouse, Marylynn, *Ministry on My Mind* (Kettering: The John Newton Project, 2008)

Notes

NOTES

NOTES

Notes

Notes

Notes

Notes

THROUGH THE YEAR WITH

John Wesley

365 daily readings from John Wesley, the "father of Methodism"

"John Wesley was an explosive force in his own lifetime and beyond. The generosity of spirit of John Wesley, "the friend of all and the enemy of none" is here displayed again and again. As is the simplicity of his life, the depth of his faith, his determination to go on declaring the good news of the gospel until his last breath. This is a little gem of a book... day after day for an entire year, will lift the spirits of twenty-first century men and women and equip them to face the challenges of today's world."

– **Lord Leslie Griffiths**

Through the Year with John Wesley refreshes and presents key passages from the theological and reflective writings of the Reverend John Wesley, the renowned "father of Methodism".

A deeply spiritual man of high integrity and indomitable character, Wesley strove to present great Christian truths to the non-churchgoing masses of England throughout the 1700s, making a powerful impact upon the nation; the like of which has rarely been felt since.

Each day the reader is presented with passage that has been selected from Reverend John Wesley's thoughtful, passionate, and prolific writings. These passages have then been carefully married by Stephen Poxon to appropriate verses of Scripture and a daily prayer to bring to life Wesley's words.

Hardback ISBN 978 0 8572 1823 0 | Paperback ISBN 978 0 85721 888 9
eISBN 978 0 8572 1824 7

THROUGH THE YEAR WITH

William Booth

365 daily readings from William Booth, founder of The Salvation Army

"Some talk of changing the world. Others actually do it. If there is a voice for our day and our time, bringing social reform and spiritual passion together, it's William Booth."
– Major Danielle Strickland

William Booth – pawnbroker's assistant, firebrand preacher, advocate of women's rights, friend of the poor, confidant of statesmen, politicians and royalty, father of eight children, champion of the marginalised, and founder and first General of The Salvation Army. General Booth's courage, oratory, and passion changed Victorian Britain. He resolutely ignored his critics – including those who decried him as the Anti-Christ – and reached out to those who considered themselves well outside the concern of Almighty God. Prayer and practicality were his hallmarks: he ridiculed the idea of preaching to a beggar while that beggar was cold and hungry. William Booth worked tirelessly, campaigning, researching, negotiating, adapting music-hall songs – and writing. This book introduces us to his heart and convictions. Here we find the urgency, thought, and humanity which drove him on.

"A glorious treasure trove of daily readings from the pen of William Booth... a superb anthology of devotional gems."
– Jonathan Aitken

"William Booth was first of all a preacher and a student of the Bible. Stephen Poxon has quite brilliantly linked William's words to Scripture."
– Colonel Bramwell Booth

978-0-85721-614-4 | £12.99 | $19.99